To be or not to be . . .

- at ease with others, confident in yourself?
- comfortable with members of your own and the opposite sex?
- relaxed at both formal and informal occasions, socially and professionally?
- able to converse with people you've just met . . . and people you admire?
- aware of your own potential to enrich and enjoy your life?

Why do some people overcome their shyness, while others never do? "Those who were successful in overcoming shyness problems on their own did so because they knew that being shy was something *they themselves* had to do something about, and that they had everything from emotional well-being to career success to lose if they didn't try to change.

"People everywhere are awakening to the possibilities of self-renewal, and now is the time for you to unfold. Let this be *your* season to make a start!"

—Dr. Michel Girodo

Shy?

Dr. Michel Girodo

PUBLISHED BY POCKET BOOKS NEW YORK

Another *Original* publication of POCKET BOOKS

POCKET BOOKS, a Simon & Schuster division of
GULF & WESTERN CORPORATION
1230 Avenue of the Americas, New York, N.Y. 10020

ISBN: 0-671-43061-0

First Pocket Books printing May, 1978

10   9   8   7   6   5   4

POCKET and colophon are trademarks of Simon & Schuster.

Interior design by Sofia Grunfeld

Printed in the U.S.A.

TO PAUL

AUTHOR'S ACKNOWLEDGMENT

THIS BOOK REFLECTS A VARIETY OF PERSONAL EXPERI-
ences as a clinician, researcher, teacher, and participant in
social reality. Although the substantive content of the
book was the result of my work in the first three roles, its
tone and conviction are personal. In this connection I owe
a debt of gratitude to Martin Asher, senior editor at
Pocket Books. His faith in the possibility of bringing together these components spurred me on to greater efforts.
Karen Braziller's editorial pen provided continuity to what
was at first an intellectual mosaic, and she steered me and
the manuscript away from the worst excesses of academic
liberties.

I'm indebted to the hundreds of people who consented
to our probing questions and interviews. Susan Dotzenroth
gets most of my gratitude for sustaining my interest in the
psychology of shyness and for encouraging me along every step in the conception and writing of this book. Her
research with me on shyness, self-esteem, and psychological biases serves not only as the basis for this book, but
also makes, I believe, a distinct contribution in the area
of personality psychology.

Thanks also go to Madeleine Lalande, Diane Brazeau,
Suzanne Séguin, and Betty Currey for typing and secre-
tarial assistance.

I would also like to thank the following for giving me
permission to use their materials: The American Psychological Association, Inc.; Educational and Psychological Measurement; J.S. Lawson, W.L. Marshall, and P.
McGrath, from Queen's University, Canada; and D. Watson, University of Hawaii.

CONTENTS

Contents

Contents

Shy?

chapter 1

THE MANY FACES
OF SHYNESS

IT'S TOO BAD THAT SHYNESS ISN'T A MEDICAL PROBLEM. When you think that more then one hundred million people in North America suffer from one form of social anxiety and loneliness or another, you could be pretty sure that a vaccine to counteract it would have been developed long ago. But shyness is not taxable, crucial to our economy, or traceable to inherited or biological conditions. Its forms are too readily camouflaged by vanity. It can be disguised as being "reserved" or "modest" or being a "loner."

And, then again, not everyone is ready to admit to being shy. Who wants to say they have a "fear of people"? But if you ask gently and sympathetically, people will be honest with you. They'll tell you what it's like to be shy, and where, when, and with whom it happens, and then some interesting patterns begin to emerge.

For example, in the vast majority of cases, shyness is composed of three elements, and in any shy person one or more of these features can predominate.

1). *Undeveloped social skills*. How good are you at

starting a conversation with a stranger? With a person of
the opposite sex? Do you find it easy to keep a conversation going once it's been started? How about the skills for
bringing a social episode to a smooth and easy conclusion? Do you avoid social groups because you're unsure
of yourself in this regard?

2). *Social anxiety.* Most people, including those who
aren't typically shy, admit to some nervousness in talking
to someone of the opposite sex for the first time. For the
shy person, multiply this nervousness ten times and you
have anxiety and great social and emotional distress. The
symptoms of the non-shy and the shy are the same—increased heart rate, perspiration, some trembling, butter-
flies in the stomach, and tension—the only difference here
being that shy people experience these with greater intensity. But you have to look at what goes on inside one's
head to get a real understanding of what underlies this
fear. "Fear of negative evaluation"—that's our technical
term for it, meaning fear of embarrassment, fear that others may discover some social inadequacy and ridicule or
mock us, fear of not being liked, fear of being turned
down and rejected, fear of being seen as inadequate when
compared with others.

Take the example of this man, who recalls his first
social trauma and how he is still plagued by its memory
even today:

"I literally trembled, stuttered, and had moments
when my mind went blank. . . . The most important
obstacle, I found, was fear of rejection. . . . I was
haunted by the memory of visiting a teen dance show
in Newark, New Jersey, in 1966 (I was seventeen),
when the set director announced that it was ten seconds to show time and everyone should get ready to
dance. I summoned every ounce of courage I could
muster and went up to an average-looking girl and
asked her if I could be her partner. She broke out
into laughter, called to her friends who were nearby,
and loudly exclaimed something to the effect that
"this guy wants to dance with me?!" My heart sank
as I hurriedly left the studio. . . . The New Jersey incident still sends chills down my spine when I think
about it. . . ."

3). *Mental bias.* Shy people think negatively. They put themselves down when social affairs don't go the way they want. They rarely capitalize on opportunities for contacts, seldom put much effort into social challenges, and become easily discouraged and give up trying if the results aren't perfect. Because of this negative mental bias, they rob themselves of an essential ingredient that can make for eventual social success; this cornerstone of social adjustment is "hope." If you don't or can't hope that your social life can ever be better than what it is, then you give up trying to penetrate into social reality. If you avoid social situations, then you prevent yourself from developing new skills.

For some people, shyness is something that comes and goes, depending upon how unfamiliar the social context is. For others, shyness is something that they remember having outgrown. Yes, indeed, shyness does appear to be something that you can "outgrow." In a large cross-sectional survey of North American men and women, about forty percent stated that they were shy at one time, but are no longer so. Now that's interesting! What did these people do? How did they overcome their shyness? Was there some magical pill that they took twice a day for six months until all shyness reactions disappeared? One thing is for sure: these people did not simply sit at home and wait for the problem to disappear. Those who were successful in overcoming their shyness problems on their own did so because somewhere in the back of their mind they knew that: 1). the emotional upset and the social distress they experienced as a result of being shy was something *they themselves* had to do something about; 2). they were going to have to take social risks in relating with people, and that these risks involved a certain degree of apprehension and worry; 3). they had everything from emotional well-being to career success to lose if they didn't try to change.

The fortunate forty percent who were motivated enough to do something about their social distress, unease, lack of social skills, poor self-confidence, and social boredom were able to change on their own without the help of medication, psychotherapy, group encounter sessions, or nude marathon weekends. There are two common denominators for overcoming shyness reactions on your own. The first is to become more socially active and to risk the uncertainty and unpredictability of social encounters. The second is being able to see that your social successes are the result of *your own* efforts and realizing that you can give yourself credit only for successful social trials when you have risked something.

What about the sixty percent who are either too scared or unmotivated to try to overcome their shyness problems on their own? What happens to them? Well, some of them learn to live with their shyness and develop a small but safe and stable circle of friends, never wandering too far away from that which is socially familiar. Others remain shy, never learn to accept their shyness, and are perpetually troubled with feelings of social inadequacy. They are constantly anxious in social situations and worry about who they may encounter down the hall on their way to their coffee break.

Others get worse. Their shyness becomes an all pervasive preoccupation that slowly begins to creep into more and more social and non-social aspects of living. With time, they withdraw from even the most ritualized and briefest of social experiences, such as saying "hello" to a neighbor or co-worker, and they get more and more lonely and depressed. Sometimes the consequences of social withdrawal can be so severe that they leave the person with only his daydreams and fantasies to console him. This is not the kind of nourishment that is needed to maintain emotional well-being and adjustment, because in the end even the fantasies can turn sour and leave you empty. With no prospects for hope and only despair as a companion, some seek a final way out. We read about it in newspapers as a silent entry in the obituary column; others conjure up the most attention-getting plot which, when acted out, appears on the front page of the morning newspaper and assures them of instant recognition. In this form, the person often acts out against society and people in general—all in a symbolic attempt to destroy the social reality he had such difficulty penetrating. If he is angry enough at the world, he may turn into a sniper. With no anger present, he may jump off a bridge. If he is both angry and depressed, he may save the last round for himself.

4

You don't have to be crazy to shoot at people and to kill yourself; you just have to be pretty upset about something.

Believe me, I'm not saying this just to dramatize the point I want to make. I just want to convey to you the extreme limits of what can happen if you're *very* shy, do nothing about changing, and so withdraw more and more into isolation, loneliness, and depression. Don't be frightened; maybe the odds are one in a million that you could regress to the point where you get desperate, but it does happen.

What Price Privacy?

Bob was eighteen years old when he committed his final act on that cloudy Monday of October 27, 1975. The pieces of his psychological puzzle were left behind in the form of a diary and other documents. We can now get a pretty good picture of what his last six months of loneliness and anguish were like.

He was a high school senior that year. His teachers were unanimous in their appraisal of him: he was efficient in his academic pursuits and had an excellent work record. He was good, quiet, cooperative, amiable, pleasant and a good fellow in class. He was clever, conscientious, worked hard, and obtained good grades, according to the principal.

His schoolmates, all of whom were just acquaintances, couldn't believe that Bob would do such a thing. "We all thought he was a regular guy" about sums it up.

Equally shocked and amazed at the event of that day, his father couldn't believe that Bob could have acted that way. "He was a quiet, happy boy. He was a normal boy —just a quiet, happy kid," he repeated.

This picture of a normal adolescent with all the privileges of a middle-class upbringing is complemented by other concrete evidence. He lived with his parents in their $125,000 home. Six years before they had let him take over the basement to fix up his own room any way he wanted. The basement room had a private garage entrance, and his mother agreed not to poke around downstairs as long as he assumed responsibility for keeping the area clean and neat. There, Bob had an electric typewriter, a calculator, a radio, and his own phone. He proudly displayed models of ships and aircraft around the room.

He received a small allowance from his father and he supplemented it with a newspaper route and occasional part-time work at a pizza parlor. He had saved enough money the year before to buy a ten-speed bicycle. While alcohol was kept around the house, Bob showed no interest in either drugs or liquor. Everything pointed to a normal, cooperative and easygoing disposition in the boy. At the coroner's inquest, expert psychiatric opinion testified that there was probably something in his personality makeup that could have led to his act of violence on that day, but that it would not have been apparent to those around him or even detectable by the trained mental health observer.

But the evidence of a cool, easygoing, and placid exterior was betrayed by what he wrote in his diary and by a reconstruction of his activities in the six months prior to the shooting. Testimony from two hundred fifty witnesses at the inquest documented that he didn't have any friends, that he never said much, and always kept to himself. Psychiatrists testified that there was evidence that in early adolescence "Bob made attempts to establish heterosexual and other peer relationships, and that these efforts failed and he progressively withdrew from people, became a loner, and isolated himself from social reality." As the picture of a private, isolated, and slowly withdrawing person began to emerge, others volunteered their own corroborative opinions. Classmates said he was "a loner, all brain, never seemed to fit in." His father couldn't recall Bob showing any great emotion. He couldn't remember ever seeing him with a girl. Bob's diary entries confirmed this, and more.

In the six months before that fateful October day, Bob wrote about how difficult it was to make friends at school, of the many thoughts he had about girls at school, and how he could never succeed in making contact with them. He spoke of loneliness, periodic depression, and concern that these feelings of misery might return. He indexed boxes of "girlie magazines" he bought in an attempt to enrich his fantasy life. He became more and more interested in having his fantasies substitute for real social relations, and he wrote about how a mail-order purchase of a life-sized inflatable sex doll broke his savings account. Later, another entry revealed that even that expensive effort at an alternative to real-life relations was a failure. "The inflatable doll is a big disappointment," he wrote despairingly.

The thought of returning to school in September and having to face more failure and frustration in his desperate need for friends and an involvement in a social network became too frightening. He tried something else. In October, the classified advertising department of the city newspaper received his letter:

Dear sirs:
Please insert my ad for seven days. Please find enclosed $5.04.

The ad, placed two days later, read:

Male, 18, looking for companionship.
Post Office Box 4021, Station E.

The police testified that Bob's appeal for friendship resulted in three replies. In their search they discovered that these came from homosexuals and that Bob did not make contact with any of them. He had reached his end point. With no prospects for new avenues to try out, with no hope that his loneliness and depression could disappear or could lift itself through a lucky social encounter, he bought a Winchester shotgun from a downtown store. At home he sawed off the barrel to twelve inches. A fantasy for a dramatic exclamation of his misery had been fomenting in his mind for a while, and he made all the preparation for a sensational and final social experience, in which all needs, wishes, and fantasies would be realized in one tragic moment.

On that Monday morning he approached a seventeen-year-old girl whom he recognized from school. She was waiting for a bus. He told her he had something very important to show her in his house. She hesitated but went along with him after he assured her that he would drive

7

her to school on time. In his room he tied her on the bed with ski harnesses. He stabbed her several times and raped her. He then poured kerosene over her body and all around his room, lit a match to it, then bicycled to school with the sawed-off shotgun under his arm.

He strode up the steps leading to the main entrance, burst through the front doors with a hard commando-like kick, and fired one round, which struck a student coming down the hall. He opened the door to a room where a class was in progress, raised the shotgun to his shoulder, paused to take aim, and fired several rounds into panic-stricken and dumbfounded students. He stepped out of the classroom and into the hall, where he spent the last round on himself.

The total cost for his loneliness: three dead, five injured.

Very few shyness reactions are this severe and end so tragically, but they can happen. You really can't leave your social well-being to chance.

But to be fair, now I'm going to tell you about another case of shyness in which the outcome was positive. The odds of this happening to you are about the same as the odds that you'll end up like Bob.

Somebody Up There Likes Me

A number of years ago a psychology professor friend at a large Northeastern university decided to conduct a kind of "experiment." For some time, he had noticed that a bright and hard-working woman student in one of his classes was acting in a manner that was much too introverted to be considered healthy and proper for her emotional well-being. She seemed to be a terribly shy person, speaking rarely to classmates and participating in no social activities outside of class. She was completely devoted to her studies—in fact, she was dedicated to the point where for quite some time she had managed to survive without any friends at all.

The professor felt a great compassion toward her and he was concerned about the excessive preoccupation she had with maintaining her straight "A" average. Recalling how difficult it was for him to socialize with ease and skill when he himself was a student, he developed an elaborate plan to make sure that she would be drawn out of her shell before it was too late. He approached five reliable and self-confident men students whom he knew well and he asked them to cooperate in his "experiment." Determined to help the young woman become more socially active, alive, and spontaneous, he got his group of men students to cooperate in establishing her as a social favorite throughout the year. The men saw to it that she was invited out to all college affairs that were considered important and that she always had partners to dance with at Friday night mixes. They all agreed that they would treat her as if she were the reigning college favorite. No desire or wish of hers was denied, and nothing would ever be said or done that might put her in an embarrassing situation. The men paid attention to her whenever they were near her. They often went out of their way to make sure that they had the chance to say hello to her at some time during the day. She had their company for coffee, lunch, and at least three different kinds of evening social entertainment throughout the week.

A few months later the professor noticed the young woman started to dress differently. He was also pleased to see that she spoke up more in class and that she was less fearful about volunteering her own opinions. Her whole attitude toward life seemed changed. She smiled more easily and carried herself with greater ease and comfort. She even felt free to come late for class without having to give lengthy explanations. Before the year was over she had developed an easy manner, and by the end of the year, when the men in the "experiment" stopped making efforts on her behalf, her new social habits and the self-confidence she had acquired during the "experiment" stayed with her. It continued over the years and the men themselves accepted her as a success.

It is difficult, if not impossible, to say what this woman's career would have been like if someone had not decided to intervene on her behalf. It is fairly certain, however, that she would have resigned all social ambitions and would undoubtedly have found interests that were compatible with her social ineptitude. The last two years of her college career were the happiest she had ever spent.

For her, as for most people, all she needed was the opportunity to test out her "social life" in the reality of interpersonal exchanges. By trial and error, by looking and copying, and by gradually taking more and more risks in the social challenges that were being presented to her, she acquired a large array of social habits and a positive mental attitude toward the complex question of what to do when you are in an unpredictable social situation. Gradually she acquired confidence, poise, and an easy manner in all her social relations. Because the men treated her as a success, she started to *believe* that she had potential to be socially successful on her own. When she adopted this attitude and behaved accordingly, the men were surprised to discover that their own reactions vis-à-vis her had changed. As she accepted herself more as a social success, so did they.

This woman was lucky to have had five men to make all these efforts on her behalf and draw her out of her shell. But the odds of something like this happening are probably one in a million. There are many lessons that can be learned from this experiment, but one of the most important is that you can't rely on chance. You can't wait for other people to help you out of your shyness problems. You have to make an effort on your own. This, unfortunately, is doubly difficult for shy people who tend to believe that the good or bad things that happen to them are governed by external events and tend to adopt a "wait and see" attitude.

A good example of this comes firsthand from a woman student with whom I had been studying the problem of shyness. She remembers how shy she used to be when she was eighteen—and this, not only with persons of the opposite sex, but with girls her own age. She describes it this way:

> It was my first year at college. I first saw her when we were all standing in line in the cafeteria. She was quite outstanding. Not only was she very physically attractive, with dark skin and long black hair, but she also wore a very "in" outfit and carried herself with great confidence and poise. She was with three other girls, all extremely good looking, all "with it." I envied her and her friends. She represented all the

things that I wanted to be. Because she was so outstanding in these respects, I thought I could never be
like her or associate with her and with her group.

I thought it would be impossible ever to become a
friend of hers because she probably wouldn't even
consider associating with a person like me. It was as
if her "beauty" cast her into a social class I could
never be a part of. She was one of the "beautiful
people," and I was just plain. I didn't even bother to
entertain the idea of approaching her because I was
afraid she would laugh at me, discard me, and make
me feel like a fool for thinking I could be part of her
group. For a whole year I watched her, trying to as-
similate all her mannerisms, taking notice of how
she dressed, walked, talked, wore makeup, *etc*. I
really wanted to be like her. She was even in one of
my classes, but I didn't dare speak to her.

The next year at school I noticed she was again in
one of my classes. That made me feel good because
it was a special class for students in the same program
—very small and selective—so I thought that not only
did we have something in common, but more important to me was the thought that I was suddenly
more equal to her, at least in one regard. I hoped
that maybe she could think about becoming a friend
of mine because she would not see me as intellectu-
ally inferior. I was also happy about her being in the
same class with me because I could watch her more
closely and incorporate more of her into myself
and somehow perhaps become a "beautiful person"
myself.

One day she came late to class and sat down next
to me. After class she asked me about what had
gone on before she arrived, and I told her. Then she
continued the conversation by asking me what program I was in, my name, where I was from, *etc*. I
was shocked that she would even consider this kind of
interest. We discovered we had a lot of things in
common and that we were in the same program and
would be in all the same classes that year. In speaking to her, she came across much differently than I
had expected. My biggest shock was the gradual
awareness that she was just an ordinary person like

me—nervous about the program and adjusting to a new year of school. She was friendly, open, outgoing, but sometimes she even seemed a bit self-conscious and insecure. We started meeting for coffee and sitting together in all our classes. I couldn't believe this, but she was as shy about sitting beside a stranger as I was. Later I found out that her perception of herself was totally different from how I saw her. She saw herself as a regular person and perceived me as being as attractive as I thought her to be. I met her friends and found that they were just regular people. I also discovered that the fantasy I had about her social class and background was totally false. I had this image of her as coming from a very high class and from a well-to-do family. I was surprised to discover none of this was true.

I was lucky that she came up and spoke to me that day in class. I know I would never have had the nerve to go up and begin a conversation with her. Since that time, there have been a number of other occasions in which I have overrated people, and I guess my tendency to perceive people as better than me is something that I have to work on. I'm much better at it now—not that I tend to berate people, but I think I tend to accept myself more and see myself more as an equal to those around me. It's really hard to get rid of this "halo effect," where you generalize all kinds of other positive characteristics about a person on the basis of one or two appealing aspects of the way they look or how they behave. It's sort of funny, but the more that I see myself in a positive light and learn to accept myself, the less I compare myself with those who are different from me. This has had a lot of positive consequences. Now I'm much less hesitant about approaching someone for the first time and beginning a conversation with them.

As you can see, it was *lucky* for her that the fellow student she so greatly admired came in late to a class one day and found an empty seat beside her. That one lucky break gave her the opportunity to question, check, and correct a major misconception she had about people she was afraid of approaching. That one single event was strong enough and significant enough to alter many assumptions and perceptions that made her anxious to talk to certain people. Freed from these fears, she was more willing to initiate social transactions with people she wanted to meet.

Having good luck does play a part, but it plays only a minor role compared with the potential and power that lie behind a decision to take action and to do something on your own for yourself. Whether you have good or bad luck is not within your own control. And a situation that is only a matter of good luck does not contribute to your sense of self-esteem. Increases in self-esteem are only derived from those successes that are brought on as a result of *your own efforts*. Shy people have the greatest difficulty in learning how to give themselves credit for their successes. In so doing, they rob themselves of the essential ingredients that feed into self-esteem and happiness.

From the Club to the Clinic

There have been quite a number of times over the past fifteen years when I've been preoccupied with the problem of shyness. At times I have focused on my own shyness, and also I've been concerned with the problem of shyness in others and with learning as much as I can about how this almost universal problem is experienced and handled.

Plans for our Shyness Clinic began quite unexpectedly when a group of students and I decided to study how well we could predict who would sit where and with whom during lunch in the cafeteria. Every day at 11:30 we'd wait in the cafeteria for people to sit down with their meals and we'd record with whom, where, and for how long various interactions lasted. We got tired of monitoring and recording what we saw from afar and decided to step right into small groups at a table and look more closely at who did the talking, what was said and who asked questions. There was no purpose in our research except to see if people had consistent or reliable styles of relating to others.

More often than not things got pretty dull at the tables

13

and while we found that shy people tended to associate with other shy people, these groupings were not active enough to provide us with a wide enough variety of social responses. So we decided to move into social contexts that had a greater potential for social action—singles bars, discotheques, and social clubs of all descriptions. There, we had many opportunities to watch people socializing and to study the plays, strategies, and maneuvers that were used to meet others and to relate with them successfully and unsuccessfully. Since we got to be "regulars" at some of these places, we became well acquainted with a large number of people who frequented them on a weekly and sometimes daily basis.

We interviewed many single people over a six-month period of time, asking such questions as what constitutes having a good time at such and such a place, what they did to try to make new friends, how they presented themselves, what kind of people they preferred to meet, and when are they most nervous.

About the same time we were amusing ourselves collecting this information, we were also running "assertiveness training" groups for people who wanted to learn how to be more emotionally independent and stand up for themselves. The emphasis of these groups changed as we became more aware of the importance of being socially skilled in getting what you want out of social transactions, and we gradually shifted our training focus onto the problems associated with socializing more easily and effectively.

For the next two years, we studied shyness and experimented with a wide variety of techniques for overcoming social anxiety and building self-confidence. Then we began to offer workshops and a ten-week social-learning program designed to teach people what to do if they wanted to feel more at ease with people of the opposite sex and if they wanted to increase their social self-esteem generally. We developed a twelve-week social-skills-training program and revised it many times to take into account a greater variety of shyness problems in people of a wider age group. Our treatment techniques were being continuously refined and broadened to include a greater diversity of men and women and to make sure that the gains that

14

were made in the Shyness Clinic were going to be maintained after the end of the program.

This is where we discovered the importance of having each person become his own "therapist," and we found that it is only when people continue to strive and test out social reality on their own and then alter their beliefs, develop new skills, and change their perception of themselves that durable and beneficial changes were obtained from what they had learned with us.

By and large, the material that I am going to present to you in this book parallels the method we use in the Clinic. For this reason, it is important that you gain a clear and thorough understanding of all the concepts and principles that will be presented. You may go through this book in one sitting, but remember that the participants in the Clinic spend an average of twelve weeks. So don't skip or gloss over a chapter that you may not think is all that relevant or interesting to you. If *you* are going to be the active agent in changing, make sure you are thoroughly equipped to handle what you're going to get into.

How Long Will It Take?

Some shy people can see dramatic increases in their confidence and changes in their social life from seven to ten days after applying the principles described in this book. Others prefer to move more gradually with social risks and reach the same level of change after a year. There are basically two reasons for this. People differ in terms of their motivation to change. Some people would give anything to stop feeling shy, while others would really like to conquer their shyness but don't want to put in the sustained effort required. In fact, this is another characteristic that distinguishes shy from non-shy people. Many shy people have unrealistic notions about how hard they should try if they want to be successful in a social encounter. Not surprisingly, when only average effort is put into making a social episode pleasant and rewarding, the outcome usually falls short of expectations and desires. And, of course, when this happens they give up trying and complain about how miserable and impoverished their social life is.

A second reason why people progress at different rates has to do with the different levels of shyness they began with. The deficiencies in social skills, the degree of social anxiety, and the extent and range of mental bias can all be represented in various degrees. While one person may have all the social skills at his disposal and suffer primarily from social anxiety, another may have problems in all three areas. Often when all three components are involved, you can suspect that the shyness has existed for quite some time and that there are mixed-up feelings about how to relate with persons of the opposite sex. I remember one case particularly well because I worked with this young man for about a year, trying to sort all the complex feelings he had about girls. The story of Jack is a good one. It illustrates a number of shyness components and describes how adolescent experiences can cause the social anxiety of later years.

Jack was twenty-six years old and extremely shy when he came to see me, complaining of intense fears and anxieties in social situations. Both his parents seemed to stress the importance of academic achievement, and Jack found that the only way he could obtain their approval and a moderate degree of attention was by excelling in school. He never dated during high school or at the university. His older brother somehow fared much better than he in that he could easily establish friendships and date with facility. Jack would confide a great deal to his brother about his frustrations and looked up to him as a model. His brother went to medical school, while Jack completed a graduate degree in library science. Jack spent most of his time reading and studying, wanting to do well in all of his subjects. His major source of self-esteem was his intellect, yet he was afraid to speak up in class. He had few friends at college and never had a date because he was too shy.

Toward the end of his second graduate year, when he knew he was going to make it all right, Jack started going with men friends to college activities. One Friday evening, after a few drinks at the college pub, he spontaneously struck up a conversation with a girl, Joan, and she in turn responded with interest. The next day he waited for Joan outside her residence, and they spent the afternoon walking around the campus and through the city parks, getting to know each other. They did the same thing the next day. By Monday Jack was convinced that he was in love and that he was sure that Joan felt the same way. The last two months of college were the most emotionally involving and the happiest days he had ever spent. While they didn't live together, it seemed as if they might as well have. Jack would call Joan early and they would have breakfast together. They would meet for lunch, and after classes they had supper together and studied together. They would go out every evening for some kind of activity—either a movie, a dance, or a social gathering with Joan's friends. Jack stopped worrying about whether he would have his assignments in on time, because he managed to work more efficiently in half the usual time.

Because of Joan, Jack was afraid of nothing. In class he would ask questions, volunteer information, make presentations, and talk with fellow students as never before. He didn't seem to worry about what other people might think of him. He could walk into a room full of people and not feel at all concerned. He could socialize freely, talk openly, and express himself with confidence. He found he could initiate conversations with people he had never met before and carry off a social exchange successfully. He was jubilant and overjoyed at having found Joan and at having freed himself from the fear of being rejected and unloved. His inhibitedness and shyness were no longer there. Jack sent Joan flowers twice a week and brought candy when she least expected it. Jack believed that "love conquers all."

But these feelings and patterns of behavior were not reciprocated by Joan. While it was interesting, amusing, and fun for her to receive all this attention for the first few weeks, she soon tired of it and felt the pressure of the emotional demands being placed upon her. She understood the depth of what Jack was into and was very much afraid of hurting him. She was happy to have all this attention, but, Jack was asking for a degree of attachment and commitment that she simply was not ready to make. And she couldn't tell him. (Or perhaps she tried to drop subtle hints, which Jack failed to pick up.)

Joan waited until the end of the semester, when she would be leaving college to go back home before telling him. She felt that the distance would make it easier for her when she told Jack it was all over and that she was sorry.

When Jack came to see me he had been working in his present job as a reference librarian for about six months before he began having anxiety and panic attacks in social situations. His affair with Joan had been over for about eight months but it was evident that it had left its mark on him. He could not speak comfortably with women, nor could he be appropriately assertive or expressive in any manner whatsoever. He felt that people were criticizing him and judging him. Things made him angry very easily and he could not deal with this anger either by asserting himself in the situation or by ventilating it during our sessions.

While it took a long time and lots of talking before he could deal with his strong emotional needs, especially those that focused on his mixed reactions of anger and affection, it didn't solve his social loneliness and shyness problems. So I got him involved in assertive-training workshops and later in our social skills clinic and our Shyness Clinic. Prior to this he had been living a solitary existence, never socializing, avoiding coffee breaks and lunch hours in which large groups of people met, and he had no men or women friends. From his social-skills-training and Shyness Clinic participation, he learned to join a number of clubs and how to make a solid group of friendships. His biggest concern, however, was that he would find a woman that he would like and that he would become too deeply involved with her and that the same cycle would repeat itself.

He would get terribly anxious when dancing with a woman, thinking that he might get to like her. It was only after he found himself dating three or four women on a regular basis over a period of four months that he felt he could gradually let himself go emotionally with one woman. He felt that he could risk this because he had other good friendships and relationships with women to which he could always turn. He learned to become more aware of his feelings and to discriminate between various needs that were being satisfied or unsatisfied. He became more self-confident, more socially skilled, less afraid of negative evaluations, and less preoccupied with negative thoughts about himself.

Jack's social history and reactions to his first experience in relating with a woman are not untypical of the problems many shy people have to face. With few social contacts and relations with the opposite sex, the need for this kind of interpersonal involvement increases steadily and builds up to the point where the first positive relationship takes on incredible importance. Everyone at one time or another gets snubbed, turned down, or cast aside for one reason or another, and people who have had an adolescent social life that has been filled with numerous encounters with a wide variety of people in different circumstances somehow inoculate themselves against an overwhelming emotional disturbance when an emotional relationship takes a turn for the worse in early adulthood. Jack had a lot of catching up to do before he could stop overreacting to the uncertainty of adult social encounters.

You may have noticed that the case descriptions presented so far have dealt exclusively with shyness problems of adolescents and early adulthood. The rules for overcoming shyness apply to all age groups and to both sexes, but in this chapter I have singled out illustrations from this thirteen-to-twenty age group in order to highlight what may not be immediately obvious—specifically, that shyness reactions are first encountered in adolescence. This is the time when peer groups and the development of friendships and a network of social relations can have the greatest impact on social security. Depending upon the success or failure of these courageous attempts, a psychological bias away from or toward adult shyness dispositions is established.

Recognizing Your Own Shyness

There is no such thing as a "typically shy" person. When we take a group of shy people and examine their behavior, their thinking, and their reasons for emotional upset, we find that no two are exactly alike. Now, while these psychological components of behaving, thinking, and feeling are all interrelated, it is still possible—even neces-

sary—to speak of each one independently. Some shy
people may have their greatest deficiencies in behavior.
Others may have all of the behavioral skills but suffer
from an incapacitating thinking style. Still others may
have only moderate deficits in one or all of these components. Nevertheless, the best approach that I can take
in this book is to describe the behavior, thinking, and
emotional reactions of a very shy person who has problems in all three areas, keeping in mind that there are
differences in degree and differences in kind when individual problems of shyness are considered.

My hypothetical, "typical" shy person will be presented
with deficiencies in all the shyness components, and there
may be the tendency for you to begin attributing to
yourself a degree of maladjustment that is unwarranted.
As you progress from chapter to chapter and recognize
the relevance of one or more of the shyness components
as they apply to you personally, you may inadvertently
paint a most unfavorable picture of yourself. I caution
you against this. The severely shy person who is markedly
deficient in all three psychological components is not common.

To confuse the issue a little more, let me say that a
completely opposite process can take place when you're
reading through the chapters of this book. For reasons
that will become clear to you later, there are many people
who claim that they are not shy generally; however, when
we test their feelings, examine their thinking styles, and
look at their behavior closely, they seem to behave not
unlike many shy people. Consequently, it is only by monitoring closely how you behave, how you think, and how
you feel that you can come to be more aware of your
own functioning and assess more rationally to what
extent the descriptions provided in this book are applicable to you. There are a number of exercises, question-
naires, and inventories you will be asked to complete.
Be prepared to alter your position on how shy you consider yourself to be and why. Try to keep an open mind
about how relevant each of the components may be in
your particular case, and make an effort to complete the
inventories and to take part in the exercises recommended
—whether or not you think they are relevant for you at
the time.

As you read on, many distinctions will be made between shy and non-shy people—how they differ, how they compare, and how non-shy people would normally behave, think, and feel in certain situations. As I continue to refer to the non-shy person throughout our discussions and illustrations, it may seem as if this non-shy character is being glorified or idealized in some manner. He may seem to you like a super-competent social hero who can master any task, overcome all social discomforts, and behave appropriately in all social circumstances. I don't believe that such a person exists anywhere, and, if he did, his excellence in every personal domain and his superiority in every avenue of social functioning would make him unwelcome and disliked by most people. Like the shy person, the non-shy person also experiences lapses in social competence and he gets upset. But he doesn't discourage easily and he won't withdraw from the challenges inherent in new transactions. Rather, he will continue trying. He remains unflappable, with undiminished hopes of future social success.

chapter 2

HELP YOURSELF
TO SOCIAL REALITY

WE ALWAYS START THE FIRST MEETING OF THE SHYNESS Clinic with a discussion of how difficult it is to fit in socially. Absolutely everyone we have ever seen has reported at least two—and usually many more—personal examples of problems in meeting people and anxiety in social encounters. And just about everyone handled these difficulties in the same way, by staying away from potentially embarrassing social situations.

But staying away from groups and avoiding meeting people is the beginning of a downward spiral composed of feelings of loneliness, exclusion, and boredom with life. Before we talk about how important social adjustment and emotional well-being are, we have to assess your own individual tendency to cut off social reality because of the distress it causes. Each person experiences a different level of social anxiety, and some tendencies to avoid social contacts are stronger than others.

What is *your* Social Penetration and Stress Index? To what extent do you get upset and anxious in social situations? How strong is your need to avoid social contacts or of various kinds? Take the following test and find out how you compare with other people.

SOCIAL PENETRATION AND STRESS INDEX

Reply to the following questions by indicating either TRUE or FALSE with respect to how you usually feel or behave.

1). I feel relaxed even in unfamiliar social situations.
2). I try to avoid situations that force me to be very sociable.
3). It is easy for me to relax when I am with strangers.
4). I have no particular desire to avoid people.
5). I often find social occasions upsetting.
6). I usually feel calm and comfortable at social occasions.
7). I am usually at ease when talking to someone of the opposite sex.
8). I try to avoid talking to people unless I know them well.
9). If the chance comes to meet new people, I often take it.
10). I often feel nervous or tense in casual get-togethers in which both sexes are present.
11). I am usually nervous with people unless I know them well.
12). I usually feel relaxed when I am with a group of people.
13). I often want to get away from people.
14). I usually feel uncomfortable when I am in a group of people I don't know.
15). I usually feel relaxed when I meet someone for the first time.
16). Being introduced to people makes me tense and nervous.
17). Even though a room is full of strangers, I may enter it, anyway.
18). I would avoid walking up and joining a large group of people.

19). When my superiors want to talk to me, I talk willingly.

20). I often feel on edge when I am with a group of people.

21). I tend to withdraw from people.

22). I don't mind talking to people at parties or social gatherings.

23). I am seldom at ease in a large group of people.

24). I often think up excuses in order to avoid social engagements.

25). I sometimes take the responsibility for introducing people to each other.

26). I've tried to avoid formal social occasions.

27). I usually go to whatever social engagements I have.

28). I find it easy to relax with other people.

You'll find the key to the scoring of the test on page 227.

On the average, women score about eight and men about eleven on this scale. The higher the score, the more anxious you tend to feel in social situations and the more you are inclined to avoid groups. It's interesting to see that men are more socially anxious than are women, and cultural differences with respect to what men are expected to do and perform in social groups seems to account for this. Generally, if you score two or three above average, you are a person who is uncomfortable in social situations and who prefers to be alone. Even thinking about the prospects of social interaction in the future is enough to make you anxious. Scores that are a few points higher, indicate that you worry a lot about social events and how they're going to turn out for you. Even *higher* scores mean that you are generally isolated and fearful of having to be with others.

If you score below the average, you are calm and confident in groups and you don't purposely avoid social company because of anxiety.

Some of the more salient modes of behavior that distinguish the shy from the non-shy are: 1). a marked tendency to avoid others and social situations; 2). a tendency to avoid taking action or initiating social contacts;

3). once in a social situation, an inclination to remain silent; 4). a tendency to avoid eye contact; 5). a habit of speaking in a soft or low voice. The common factor in all of these behavioral tendencies can be said to reflect non-action, or, at best, minimal action—*not* to initiate, *not* to behave, *not* to respond, or, more generally, *not to do anything in social situations.* Researchers at the University of Ohio found that about sixteen percent of the men and twelve percent of the women at that school admit to some degree of fear of simply being with a member of the opposite sex, and thirty-two percent of the men and thirty-nine percent of the women expressed fear of meeting someone for the first time. These are certainly large and striking figures. If you number among these men and women and if your fear is intense, I can understand why you might use the simplest psychological mechanism for managing your emotional state—that is, avoiding social situations altogether. But as we've already seen, the consequences of this mode of adjustment can be severe.

When shyness is prolonged from adolescence into adulthood, it produces what has been called *social loneliness,* a feeling of boredom, aimlessness, and exclusion that is generally caused by the absence of an engaging social network.

Social loneliness should be distinguished from emotional loneliness. The latter is derived from a failure to have a close emotional and intimate relationship to someone, and the psychological prescription for this focuses on the acquisition of personal and other skills that enhance relationships by promoting intimacy through self-disclosure. The cure for social loneliness, however, is not to be found in applying the principles of humanistic psychology or in encounter or sensitivity groups. Social loneliness is an unfortunate by-product of shyness, and it can be overcome only by acquiring the social skills needed to establish friendships, maintain casual relationships, make new acquaintances, and to provide the basis for informal transactions with people.

The *number* of social contacts and friendships a person has is closely related to his emotional well-being. Even among children aged between four and eleven, those who have few or no friends are often found to be emotionally disturbed. Among adolescents, a response of "never" "sometimes" to the question of "How often do you go out with friends?" indicates poor social and emotional adjustment. In the adult population, social contacts and friendships are exceedingly important in promoting well-being and happiness. In a recent North American survey involving over fifty thousand people, both single men and single women ranked "social life and friends" first above sixteen other aspects of life that they felt contributed to their general happiness. Having friends and a good social life is more important for single people than personal growth, physical health, an adequate sex life, or even a good financial situation. Among married men and women, "being in love" ranked as the highest component in contributing to their general happiness, and "friends and social life" was relegated to a comparatively low degree of importance, in the eighth position.

But don't be deceived! Getting married will not prevent feelings of isolation, social loneliness, and depression. Even among those who are married, involvement in activities of a social nature outside of marriage, such as "membership in voluntary organizations," is what distinguishes between those who feel socially isolated and those who don't. *Social* loneliness and *emotional* loneliness are two independent and separate components leading to positive feelings in life and emotional well-being. Having a successful marriage and enjoying a deep and involving relationship with someone does not necessarily mean you will escape social isolation and loneliness. Participating in a social network *outside* of a primary relationship is what contributes to positive feelings about living. Forty percent of the fifty thousand people surveyed admitted to often feeling lonely, and these frequent feelings of loneliness were not limited to single people, but were just as characteristic of those who were married.

In retirement, too, the relationship between the absence of social contacts and social alienation and loneliness holds. Having social contact only with relatives or with persons in the same dwelling or with people only to obtain the basic necessities leads to feelings of depression, isolation, as well as poor health. In all age groups, regardless of wealth, marital status, or sex, low social interaction is related to loneliness and maladjustment. Involving yourself in social arenas of *various forms* is what contributes in a concrete and powerful manner to a feeling of emotional adjustment, health, and a positive attitude toward life.

Social Conditions That Help

You're not alone in believing that there are difficulties associated with making new contacts and meeting new people. Most people admit to this, and society at large acknowledges it. Institutions try to ease the problem by arranging social conditions and structuring environments to make it easier for people to meet and enjoy each other's company. Do you take advantage of these opportunities?

Virtually all schools and businesses offer a variety of activities that are specifically designed to facilitate social contact. Large cities, communities, religious and cultural groups, as well as a host of other special-interest groups make available to all those who are interested a variety of activities that tend to encourage social interactions. Boys' clubs, sewing circles, dance clubs, organized sports events, religious fellowship groups, professional associations, arts and crafts groups, drama clubs, and more are available everywhere. If you avoid using these facilities which are valuable resources for social contacts, is it because you are afraid to initiate contacts, or do you feel unskilled at facilitating social interactions? I wonder if maybe you simply have no appreciation of the social rewards and positive consequences that can be derived from these activities.

Somehow, we seem to be ashamed of admitting to and even recognizing that we do have a *need* for human contact and social affiliation outside of marriage, kinship, and work activities. For some embarrassing reason, the process of making friends and establishing social contacts for the simple reason of social interaction has failed to become as acceptable as "task forces," "work groups," or as institutionalized as marriage and parenting.

In our society, we tend to hide the real motives for bringing people together. Clubs in school and at work set themselves up under titles that present a *practical* rationale for their existence, but the *social* benefits serve as a primary motive for membership. For example, "Single Parents' Groups" meet every month to discuss how single and divorced men and women with children can learn to cope with the various problems their condition promotes. The most socially satisfying aspect of membership in such a group, however, quickly becomes the dinners, parties, dances, and social gatherings that emerge later. The annual meetings of various local and national associations of interest groups allegedly exist for the express purpose of discussing common objectives, but many are motivated to attend these annual meetings by the desire to meet old friends and make new ones. Drama clubs, archery clubs, hiking clubs, camping clubs, and work- and school-sponsored clubs all provide a convenient title or label to attract members who are interested in socializing. In fact, in our inquiry among college students, depending upon the club or organization involved, we found that between forty percent and sixty-five percent of recent members joined because they wanted to meet new people and make new friends. All groups need to have a purpose for bringing people together. What better purpose than sports, hobbies, or other leisure activities? People gravitate to them for their real rewards—social interaction and human contact. Don't be embarrassed or ashamed to admit that *you* have few friends or want to make new friends.

Social Conditions That Hinder

Avenues and opportunities for "social contacts" appear every day in the entertainment and the want-ad sections of the newspaper. Singles bars, singles nightclubs, singles dances, and discothèques clearly advertise to the unattached with one purpose in mind. As you might suspect, the opportunities provided by these social avenues cannot only be the most threatening and anxiety-provoking if you are shy, but they can also make for the kind of failure experiences that can aggravate your shyness condition.

Lonely hearts' clubs never really caught on, possibly because the label "loneliness" was too close to a reflection of some social-psychological disease. Dating services that charge exorbitant fees abound in every city and try, usually with little success, to get people to do what they are afraid of doing on their own. Getting people to make new friendships under the guise of matchmaking simply doesn't work. Fortunately, the shy are often too inhibited to participate in the social encounters made available by singles clubs and dating services. Singles bars, nightclubs, discothèques, and arranged date contexts carry with them a great deal of defensiveness and anxiety and are "artificial" forms of social contact that make the prospects for new friendships very difficult, if not depressing.

Maybe your shyness is the kind that can be conquered through social-skills training. Do you want to learn about how to initiate a conversation, how to maintain conversation, and how to terminate a social transaction? On the other hand, maybe you have some, if not most, of these social competencies but are debilitated by anxiety, and by the time you muster enough courage to initiate a new contact you find yourself so incapacitated by fear that you flounder badly and wish you had never started the interaction. Or do both components apply? Whatever the case, I'll be guiding you through this maze of uncertainty and showing you step by step all the experiences and skills you will need to find your way out of your present condition. But before describing the social skills and emotional resources that are necessary for meeting this challenge, let's take a look at what you're going to miss out on—if you decide not to act on the problem.

If You Stay Shy—The Dangers

When we look at the reasons for separation and divorce, we quickly see that one of the major causes of couples breaking up is that one has outgrown the other emotionally, or that the personal development of one partner has gone off in a direction opposite that of the other, making their partnership unfulfilling. When two people decide they want to form a long-lasting relationship, you'd think that they would make this decision on the basis of good judgment arrived at from a broad base of experience and knowledge. But too often a decision to form a long-term relationship is taken without having had an adequate opportunity for testing out and experiencing different kinds of *persons* and different kinds of *relationships*. With an intoxication of the central nervous system masquerading as "love," the governing principle seems to be an intense feeling for one another. While it is fashionable today to believe in trying out different kinds of relationships with different people, still most of us end up by paying lip service to this advice and marry just as quickly and as irrationally as ever before.

If you are the kind of shy person who lacks social skills, self-confidence, and the courage to initiate a variety of social contacts, you may be destined to make this mistake about a marriage partner, and the reasons for this are understandable, if regrettable. For the shy person to stumble across someone who shows interest in him may be very gratifying, and it may reflect a rare opportunity not to be passed up. In addition, there is the problem of knowing whether social loneliness or emotional loneliness is being alleviated by these infatuations. When people experience intense emotions, the chances are high that the cause of these feelings will be misattributed, and, in the case of shy people, friendship feelings are inclined to be inadvertently labeled as "love" feelings. If you are shy and have few social contacts, be forewarned that the feelings that accompany friendship can become inextricably mixed up and confused with the feelings that belong to "romatic love" relationships. Only after you're built up a storehouse of friendship experiences can you learn to discriminate between which need is being satisfied. Only after you've participated in a large enough sampling of different relationships, with different kinds of people, and in different situations can your decision to settle down in one relationship be considered a wise choice.

The problem of getting a representative sampling of different people and different situations that engage different kinds of skills is made more difficult by being shy. Being shy also means that the social contacts you have are with few people, in limited situations, and require few skills. Going to a movie is a relatively simple situation that entails few conversational episodes. Having dinner in a fancy restaurant is a completely different situation, requiring different responses for easy and comfortable transactions. Swimming, dancing, walking, or sleeping with the person all require different kinds of behavior and skills. If you increase the range of social contexts, then in each new situation you are allowed to witness a different component of the personality of the other. This is a major problem among those who are shy: they do not generally avail themselves of the opportunities for seeing different aspects of *one* person in different situations, and, similarly, they do not pick up on the opportunity for interacting with *different* persons in any one situation. Shyness can default you on two fronts, then. Not only will you not experience different persons and learn about what makes people tick, but if you don't get involved in different situations, you may never develop an easy manner and a confident attitude that will make social situations fun.

If you're shy, another more extreme tendency may occur, and that has to do with not seeking out any personal or social contacts whatsoever. In a study of why some people never marry, the majority of five hundred unmarried women over thirty considered their difficulties to be mainly those associated with being too shy. They had feelings of inferiority, fears of rejection, and then were inclined to pursue hobbies and leisure activities that were unrelated to the possibilities of finding companions. Most of these women had few or no dates and hardly even socialized with men. Even after having left the sphere of parental influence, extremely few of these women did anything about their social condition. Here is where the lack of social striving and the absence of sustained effort in seeking companionship have their biggest impact on life decisions. A lack of motivation and drive curtails effort, and erodes natural ability. It fuels social fears, and it adds weight to passivity and dampens hopes for social success. Do *you* have little motivation in trying to solve your own social problems? While the need for social contact may be strong and dominant, unless there is a motive to succeed, social experiences will be meager and fraught with frustration and despair.

Stop Being a Social Pain and Drain on Others

Did you know that shy people can be the most boring people on earth? Unknown to themselves, many shy people are dull, uninteresting, and a real pain to have around. If you listen to a conversation between a shy and a non-shy person, the odds are high that it was the non-shy person who *initiated* the conversation. And if you follow the course of the transaction between the two, you'll probably find that the non-shy person asks most of the questions, responds in greater length, is more animated, shows more enthusiasm and recognition of the other, and for all intents and purposes carries the responsibility for maintaining the conversation. If we could videotape such typical social episodes and play them back slowly, we'd see that the non-shy person shows a degree of social competence and a knack for filling in between pauses. He does this through the use of a variety of non-verbal and verbal communications. In his closing ritual, prior to finishing the conversation, we'd see that the non-shy person was the one to provide all the clues necessary to smooth out the end of the transaction prior to his taking leave. The non-shy person often senses the timidity and inhibitedness of the other and shoulders the responsibility for making the task of relating easy and natural. If this happens several times between the same two people, what would normally be a pleasant, ritual social episode turns into a chore and eventually a social burden for the non-shy person, a situation to be avoided if at all possible or to be quickly ended if accidentally begun.

As part of a field program for studying shyness, some of our researchers would go out to specific social gatherings and take detailed notes on the behavior of many of the people they met. Often they felt a certain amount of sympathy toward shy people and many times they would try to "bring them out" socially. This led to some successes and to some failures. One researcher, who finally got tired of feeling sorry for one shy person, told me:

> I used to see this guy at a discothèque almost every weekend. What was funny about him was that he

didn't hesitate to come up to me and say hello after the first time I met him. What really bugged me about him was that after he said hello he would simply stand there and look at me and wait for me to carry on everything. He'd never ask me any questions; I never heard him express an opinion about anything, and whenever I asked him anything, his answers were always so short and matter-of-fact that I never really got to know him. Not only did he say nothing, but his face was always expressionless. He would just stand there and look at me. It was a real drag, and he eventually got to be a pain in the ass. Really, I didn't mind the guy that much . . . he seemed all right . . . it was just that he made so many demands on me for dealing with his embarrassment and social difficulty, and the fact that he didn't know what to do or say.

Ending a conversation with him also was a great effort. I mean, I'd have to think about what I was going to say to him in order not to hurt his feelings if I felt like moving on to another table. You know, with other people you sort of just say "see you later," or somehow you just know when to end your conversation by how you sort of look or what you do, but with him it was another thing. I'd have to tell him clearly something like, "Well, excuse me for a minute, I have to go to the bathroom." I remember one time he looked at me with such big eyes when I said that to him and I felt so sorry for him that I added, ". . . but don't worry, I'll come right back, and if you don't see me right away, I'll keep an eye out for you." It was a real pain to have to think about what I should say to him, and I got really tired of giving this guy reassurance and support.

Most people are usually not unwilling to try to help "bring out" the shy person and make him feel more comfortable in a given social situation, but what happened in the case just described clearly shows that certain behavioral and verbal deficits can make some shy people very unpleasant people to have around. Possibly, this shy person didn't recognize that his behavior needed some kind of change, or maybe he didn't know how to change.

SHY?

Ask yourself these questions: What is it that I do or say when I'm with someone that would make them want to speak with me again? What do *I* contribute to making the episode a fun or rewarding one for the *other* person?

Often It's Who You Know That Counts

If you still want to stay shy, then think about how it might affect your career.

Insurance, automobile, and real estate salesmen know of the importance of social contacts in finding new customers and in making sales. Obviously, a career in sales is definitely out if you are shy—and not *only* sales. While many lower-level jobs are obtained on the basis of filling out an application and presenting concrete credentials to a personnel officer, many higher-level jobs and promotions are obtained on the basis of "who you know" and how you work with other people. Advancement and promotion tend to be biased in favor of people who are better acquainted with those who hold the power for granting such advancement. Democratic systems exist in many organizations, equal-opportunity programs exist, and unions exert a great deal of power in assuring that merit and time on the job are considered in advancement, but the human factor always makes the essential difference

Everything being equal, those who are more visible, more popular, more sociable, and carry themselves with an easy social manner are those who are preferred and selected over those who are not. It's perhaps not too surprising to find that shy people compensate for their lack of social skill by working very hard at perfecting their work skills and to see that they find employment in areas that don't involve extended social interactions.

Getting Out of the Shyness Rut: Build Social and Psychological Muscle

By far, the most important reasons for wanting to get out of the shyness rut have to do with gaining the person-

34

ality strengths that come from the new thinking styles that replace and defeat those of the shyness condition. Rehearsing, practicing, and applying these social and mental skills lead to increased self-confidence, making it easy to move in and out of different social contexts. You will feel a sense of control over the good things that happen to you, and, at the same time, you'll know you can do a great deal to avert the negative things that might come your way. The worry, apprehension, and anxiety that are experienced in social situations are derived from the fear of being seen as inept, inadequate—a pawn in a large social chess game. But learning to overcome shyness by acquiring personal and social skills will mean gradual gains in self-confidence. As your power to use these skills freely, spontaneously, and at a moment's notice increases, so will your self-confidence and your personal-social power. You won't feel worried or anxious anymore.

We have found that as the person applies the correct social and mental skills, he feels more secure and comfortable in moving into new social environments, and these new social situations in turn provide him with a great deal of personal satisfaction and social rewards. With increased confidence and a healthy thinking style, he learns not to be afraid of meeting up with unsuccessful social encounters. He learns to discriminate clearly between what is a failure and what is a successful experience. His perception of other people changes, and he learns to see himself differently. He learns to accept himself, as well as others. The self-confidence he acquires is directly proportional to the number of social successes he has, and these depend upon the number of new social situations he has tested.

When you move from shyness toward self-confidence, you'll see that your self-esteem increases with each new social success. You'll be perceived more favorably by others, and as you sense this, you'll begin to see yourself more positively. You'll be more relaxed in general, since you won't be worried about the social contacts of the following day. You won't have to worry about the possibility of being socially embarrassed because you'll know what to do, where to go, and how to act and react in social company. What was once "learned helplessness" will turn into an adult way of assuming responsibility for your own social well-being. You will have unlocked the door that leads to a flexible, healthy style of self-exploration. Are anxiety, apprehension and worry, lack of social skill, and heightened self-preoccupation the dominant features of a frustrating social life for you? If so, they are the most severe roadblocks against believing that you can exercise a beneficial influence on your own behalf. This learned helplessness can be overcome only by participating in a structured series of social experiences—experiences that lead to self-confidence, renewed strength, and which help develop the psychological tools needed to brave the challenges of social reality. Only then can you freely indulge in the great benefits social reality offers.

chapter 3

THERE IS NOTHING SO BAD IN YOURSELF; ONLY YOUR THINKING WILL MAKE IT SO

WE'VE ALREADY TALKED A LITTLE ABOUT THE *kind* OF anxiety shy people experience, and you'll recall that shy people experience the same symptoms as non-shy people when in an unfamiliar social situation, except that these are more intense. We are now ready to explore the nature of this fear more specifically and to determine how much you are affected by worry and apprehension about being embarrassed, ignored, compared with others, or about being just generally "negatively evaluated."

Are Shy People Really That Different?

If you ask a group of shy people and a group of non-shy people to make a list of the various social situations in which they find themselves uneasy and then ask them to indicate the various symptoms they experience in each of these situations, the lists will be virtually identical. Both shy and non-shy people experience a pounding heart, perspiration, trembling, irregular breathing, clammy hands, and other internal symptoms. Strange as it may seem, the shy and the non-shy are very much alike in that they both experience the same physiological reactions when they are in potentially socially difficult situations. The only distinguishing characteristic is the *intensity* with which these feelings are experienced. Shy people all have the same symptoms, but to a much greater degree.

The immediate question that springs to mind is: What is it about the shy person that should make him react more intensely than another? And, of course, the first place to look for an answer is in the personality or character of the shy person in the hopes that some unusual pattern of traits will emerge. And, indeed, we do find mental biases, exaggerated fears, and irrational beliefs that serve to partly explain why the shy person reacts with such heightened fear.

But first let's understand that the same situation may be experienced in different ways by the shy and the non-shy person, and that the key to knowing where self-confidence comes from is in knowing how situations are perceived. The more unfamiliar the social environment, the more intense shyness reactions become. The person doesn't feel he "knows" the social situation, meaning that he doesn't understand the patterns and the interconnected forms in that social theater. And so he doesn't feel much, if any, self-confidence.

But to get to "know" social situations, you have to be in them long enough. Building confidence about presenting yourself socially comes only by repeatedly testing out your social self and waiting for an echo that confirms and reinforces what you've presented yourself to be. And what stands in the shy person's way? One of the most severe roadblocks of all: fear, and, in this case, it is a fear of being judged or evaluated unfavorably.

Are you excessively concerned about what people *might* think about you? Do you sometimes feel that people are looking at you and just waiting for you to make a mistake? Are other people's opinions of you so important that you feel the safest thing to do is not to do anything? How strong is this concern for you? Take the following test and find out where you stand among shy and non-shy people.

There Is Nothing So Bad in Yourself

Complete the following questionnaire by answering TRUE or FALSE to each of the questions.

1). I rarely worry about seeming foolish to others.
2). I worry about what people will think of me even when I know it doesn't make any difference.
3). I become tense and jittery if I know someone is sizing me up.
4). I am unconcerned even if I know people are forming an unfavorable impression of me.
5). I feel very upset when I commit some social error.
6). The opinions that important people have of me cause me little concern.
7). I'm often afraid that I may look ridiculous or make a fool of myself.
8). I react very little when other people disapprove of me.
9). I am frequently afraid of other people noticing my shortcomings.
10). The disapproval of others would have little effect on me.
11). If someone is evaluating me, I tend to expect the worst.
12). I rarely worry about what kind of impression I am making on someone.
13). I am afraid that others will not approve of me.
14). I am afraid that people will find fault with me.
15). Other people's opinions of me do not bother me.
16). I am not necessarily upset if I do not please someone.
17). When I am talking to someone, I worry about what they may be thinking about me.
18). I feel that you can't help making social errors sometimes, so why worry about it?
19). I am usually worried about what kind of impression I make.
20). I worry a lot about what my superiors think of me.
21). If I know someone is judging me, it has little effect on me.

22). I worry that others will think I am not worthwhile.

23). I worry very little about what others may think of me.

24). Sometimes I think I am too concerned with what other people think of me.

25). I often worry that I will say or do the wrong thing.

26). I am often indifferent to the opinions others have of me.

27). I am usually confident that others will have a favorable impression of me.

28). I often worry that people who are important to me don't think very much of me.

29). I brood about the opinions my friends have about me.

30). I become tense and jittery if I know I am being judged by my superiors.

You will find the scoring key to this questionnaire on page 227 in the back of the book.

On the average, men usually get a score of fourteen, while women get scores around sixteen. If you score two or three points above the average for the population, you're getting into a range of people who have a "fear of negative evaluation." People who fear the evaluation they might get from others don't want to be the center of attention. If you score high on this scale, you tend to be defensive, not dominant, not autonomous, and possibly self-effacing to the point of underestimating yourself and putting yourself down. You are overly concerned with the opinions of others and are nervous in situations in which people might evaluate you. You have a strong need to be liked and approved of in social settings. You may expect and fear the worst and think that you *are* being evaluated when no judgment is ever intended.

For all of these reasons you may be choosing social situations in which little evaluation is possible. You may be refusing to put yourself on the line in relations with others because you feel people will evaluate you and think the worst. With this defensive attitude, you're simply not going to risk testing yourself out in social situations, and while this strategy may offer some protection, you are forfeiting the chance to find out that you're okay.

Humpty Dumpty Ego

This concept of the Humpty Dumpty ego is closely tied to the ones discussed previously. People who have a high need for approval and a fear of negative evaluation are also fragile and respond to failure as if it were a catastrophe. The underlying mental processes responsible for this fear of failure are different from those that cause a fear of negative evaluation and high need for approval, but both occur in the same people.

Many shy people have failed to take part in a significant number of social experiences of any kind, and they have a meager history of social interactions with people. The majority of their social experiences are derived from parents, relatives, a roommate, a few classmates, and immediate co-workers. Any change in the regular and patterned routine of customary interactions with familiar people becomes a new social situation. With every new encounter in every new social context, the shy person doubts his ability to meet the social demands of the unfamiliar. He views novel situations as trials, much like the experimenter's rat when thrust into a maze. At each intersection there are two or more choice points: Where shall I turn? What shall I do? Where do I go from here? Did I make a mistake? Fortunately, for the rat, it has little to suffer except the expenditure of effort and energy in getting to its goal, where its reward lies. For the shy person, however, the situation is a little more complex. He can think and he can wonder what the people with whom he is interacting are thinking about him. And he becomes afraid. For the rat, success is obtained when it has reached the reward, and with repeated trials, the rat learns to expend the least amount of effort in getting to its goal. In interpersonal relations, however, success is measured at each choice point: "Someone said hello. Should I turn around to see who it was? Oh, it's that girl from yesterday. Should I stop, pause, pretend I didn't hear her? No, she knows I heard her. I can't show I'm shy. I'll turn around and answer her. Should I smile? What should I say?

41

Should I shake her hand? Oh, no, she wants to hang around to talk. What do I talk about? She's asking me questions. How can I end this conversation? I think I'll tell her I'm in a hurry to get to a meeting. Whew! I'm glad that's over."

Thus goes the stream of thought when you're concerned with maintaining a public image, when you have a high need for approval, and when you are preoccupied about being negatively evaluated. Each new situation becomes a series of trials, and the success of each is decided on the basis of whether you can avoid any blunders or shows of ineptitude and nervousness.

In cases in which the severely shy person has been ridiculed, or in which he has been emotionally wounded in a vain attempt at trying to establish communication, his immediate reaction is to withdraw from any further attempts at social contact and to compensate through other social activities that are more regular and predictable on the basis of stable roles or tasks. The following description of a severely shy person is a capsule of his thinking and behaving over a period of time.

As an adolescent he spends large amounts of time watching television and developing interests in reading and in other solitary activities. He fantasizes vividly an image of himself as popular, the center of attention, or even a hero. His strength lies in his I.Q., an intellect derived partly from native ability, but mainly from reading and hard work. With time, his friends come to know him as "quiet, introverted, minds his own business, friendly but not too sociable, *but—intelligent, honest, and trustworthy.*" When he eventually moves away from home and takes his own apartment, feelings of loneliness, isolation, alienation, and even depression slowly begin to settle over him. He has few friends outside of his work environment. When the situation becomes desperate enough, he risks trying to establish social contact, hoping that somewhere someone will be kind enough to see that he is all right, acceptable, and likable. He goes to a singles bar, hangs around, has a few drinks, watches other people, and finds that nothing happens. He goes home despondent, and his hopes for future possibilities diminish.

He marries the first person who shows any interest in him. He is overjoyed at the prospect of establishing a relationship with someone who is safe, who loves him and accepts him, someone who will never reject him, no matter how rough the going gets. In the months that follow there is a positive glow about him and it seems to change his behavior somewhat. He seems a little more sociable, more willing to help others; in fact, he is quite generous in this way. He feels good about himself and is comforted by the fact that someone has found him acceptable, lovable, and a worthy person. He appears to talk more at the office, especially to those secretaries he used to avoid. Somehow, it all seems much easier now. He is less anxious and worried about what the girls think about his motives for approaching them. This change lasts only a few months. While still very happy in his marriage, the glow from his newfound self quickly fades and before long he is back where he started, wondering what it was that ever gave him the nerve to behave in the courageous way he would at one time have thought too bold.

He works hard on the job and minds his own business. He saves his money, takes his vacation at the beach in the last two weeks of August, and, as the story goes, he moves into a nice house with a flower garden and a picket fence, raises three children, and has a dog named Rover that just never seems to bark loud enough to disturb the neighborhood. His friends and neighbors consider him to be intelligent, honest, trustworthy, and a good citizen.

Too melodramatic, you say? Not when you consider that those who are deficient in a number of behavioral and personality components are afraid of trying and know few of the skills required to meet the challenges of social reality. Fortunately, many of us are not too deficient in too many of the shyness components, and we do seek out social relations, go to social gatherings, join various groups, and have friends who introduce us to their friends, and we even risk initiating a first encounter with someone to whom we think we may be attracted. We don't really try very hard, but we try just hard enough to produce an effect, to shake up our social entourage, to wait and see where the pieces fall. More certain of ourselves, we try again and wait to see if a familiar echo comes back. We profit from our social successes and, to preserve our egos, quickly dismiss as personally irrelevant whatever reason caused us to fail.

Nothing Succeeds Like Success

In some vague and general way, we believe that adage to be true. The successes of businessmen, industrialists, salesmen, and others seem to open up new doors and opportunities so that they can take new risks and succeed again.

In strict psychological terms, following a successful experience most people have a "positive glow" about them —some internal aura that for a minute, an hour, or a day changes their behavior, their thinking, and their mood. Following successful experiences, people momentarily become more charitable to others, more willing to help others, and are more willing to give of themselves. In social terms, these are positive by-products of having had a successful experience. But what are the personal consequences of success? The most immediate one is increased self-esteem. There is no denying that successful experiences contribute heavily to how we view ourselves and to how we feel about ourselves. This is true for virtually all kinds of achievements, whether in business, academic work, or in personal self-management when we succeed in losing weight, stopping smoking, or in becoming more physically fit. Self-esteem can come from many avenues of endeavor, but the source that concerns us most here is *social* self-esteem. The best measure of shyness comes from the social self-esteem level.

How is your social self-esteem?

Social Self-Esteem Inventory

Complete the following inventory by assigning a number from 1 to 6 to each of the following statements. If you feel that the statement describes you exactly, you should place a 6 beside that item. If the statement is completely unlike you, then you should place a 1 against the item. The numbers 2 through 5 represent varying degrees of the concept "like me."

1). COMPLETELY UNLIKE ME
2). _____
3). _____
4). _____
5). _____
6). EXACTLY LIKE ME

1). I find it hard to talk to strangers.
2). I lack confidence with people.
3). I am socially effective.
4). I feel confident in social situations.
5). I am easy to like.
6). I get along with other people.
7). I make friends easily.
8). I am lively and witty in social situations.
9). When I am with other people, I lose self-confidence.
10). I find it difficult to make friends.
11). I am no good at all from a social standpoint.
12). I am a reasonably good conversationalist.
13). I am popular with people my own age.
14). I am afraid of large parties.
15). I truly enjoy myself at social functions.
16). I usually say the wrong thing when I talk with people.
17). I am confident at parties.
18). I am usually unable to think of anything interesting to say to people.
19). I am a bore with most people.
20). People do not find me interesting.
21). I am nervous with people who are not close friends.
22). I am quite good at making people feel at ease with me.
23). I am more shy than most people.
24). I am a friendly person.

25). I can hold people's interest easily.
26). I don't have much "personality."
27). I am a lot of fun to be with.
28). I am quite content with myself as a person.
29). I am quite awkward in social situations.
30). I do not feel at ease with other people.

The scoring key is found on page 228 in the back of the book. A score of 130 to 134 is about average. The higher your score, the greater your social self-esteem. Those people who have a high social self-esteem, but still consider themselves to be shy, will easily overcome their problem by going through the basic step-by-step social calisthenics presented in this book. But for those who have much lower social self-esteem, the issue is a little more complicated. With a score of 80 and below, you are easily depressed, often feel lonely, tend to withdraw from social contacts, and to feel quite pessimistic about ever having a bright, active social life. Scores below 90 may also mean you have a mental bias *against* easily overcoming shyness problems and in developing confidence in yourself. The lower your score, the more likely this is true. However, don't despair. If you take one problem at a time, work hard at understanding the issues presented, and put real and sustained effort into the social exercises in this book, you'll pull through readily enough.

If I asked you to make a list of all the *good* things you considered to be true about yourself—such as, being honest, intelligent, strong, capable, hard working, attractive, or good looking—and to make a list containing those things that you consider *negative*—for example, being impatient, miserly, dull, boring, anxious, hard to please— your self-esteem at that moment would be decided on the basis of which list outweighs the other more in number and value. This way of arriving at self-esteem is a true indicator for the majority of people, and, indeed, most people have a heavier "positive" list and do have some degree of self-esteem.

But suppose your list of positive and negative characteristics resembles very much the list described above, and yet we see a big difference between the level of your self-esteem and that of another person with a similar list. Is there another factor? Yes. It is how *often* you think positive and negative thoughts about yourself and how much of the real positive or negative things you can *remember* about yourself at any one time. Simply put, it is the extent to which positive things as opposed to negative things are foremost in your mind that determines your level of self-esteem at any moment.

Treatment programs for people with low self-esteem have operated on the basis of this simple psychological fact alone. Self-esteem is increased when each person purposely reminds himself of his good qualities. This can be done by writing out on a series of cards those things that are valued positively and then reading through these at various times during the day. This very simple device has been successful in increasing scores on the social self-esteem scale by as much as thirty points after only two weeks of such daily repeated reminders. But there are limits to the effectiveness and advisability of this technique. Also you have to make sure that these thoughts don't end up by feeding pretensions that can't be backed up in social life.

Doing It Naturally

The best way to make your positive qualities become foremost in your mind is to have successful experiences. For the best psychological effect, you can't beat something that is rooted in social reality. Succeeding at a particular task is often enough to get people to suddenly (sometimes unconsciously) recall and think about many more personal attributes, while "not remembering" those things that are negative or unflattering. In this way, successful experiences have a way of "naturally" doing what self-esteem treatment techniques do by direct intervention and forcing thinking patterns. So, the adage, "nothing succeeds like success," is true primarily because successful experiences have a natural and enduring psychological effect.

Let's go a little further: people who have successful experiences create hope in themselves. This is important, because it is this *hope for success* in the future that provides the motivation to face new challenges and to brave the demands of social reality with confidence. Experiences of failure lower hope for success; they tend to depress motivation and make it more difficult to maintain goals. The result is depression, apathy, and resignation.

"Okay," you may say, "this is all well and good, but how do I go about increasing my chance for success?"

The answer to this question is presented in the forthcoming chapters in the book, and as you will see, involves changing your irrational beliefs about social reality, developing the social skills of verbal and non-verbal behavior, and testing these out in a series of specified encounters. But first I must warn you about something that can make the whole series of exercises and tasks completely useless and non-productive for you. I am referring to mental bias. Unless this bias is changed, no amount of work or flexing of your social muscles will give you strength and confidence.

If you scored below 132 on the Social Self-Esteem test, then the chances are that you have this mental bias, and if so, pay close attention. One of the first steps in changing this mental bias is to fully understand what it is and what it does.

What Does It Mean to Be Socially Successful?

Success has to do with the outcome of our efforts. Now, while many people with low social self-esteem do have successful experiences, they simply do not *experience* the psychological impact of the success; and here lies the root cause of chronic low self-esteem, the fear of failure, and the Humpty Dumpty syndrome in shy people. We call this mental bias.

We have already said that shyness is associated with a fear of negative evaluation and failure. Failure can be defined along lines that suggest that a person is inept at coping with social relations, and that his social encounters are unsuccessful because he feels too anxious and nervous or because he obtains (or thinks he obtains) a negative evaluation from the other person involved. When interpersonal transactions and all the separate components that contribute to these transactions are seen as separate trials, the shy person becomes afraid of failing at any one of these component trials. "Nothing succeeds like success" is only true for those who are not afraid of failing. Even a long series of successful experiences will not change the mental outlook and poor self-regard of a person who is afraid of failing. It is as if there is something in his head that prevents him from developing the calm, self-assured, and confident manner of the non-shy social entrepreneur.

Let's look more closely. Self-esteem and positive self-evaluations can rise or fall following an event depending on *what* the person thinks was responsible for the success or failure. Not only does a person ask, "Have I been successful or have I failed in this social task?" He also asks, "What has caused my failure, or what was responsible for my success?" The answer he gives to these questions will determine whether or not there will be an increase in self-esteem and whether or not it will contribute to an internal sense of control. Shy people tend to *blame themselves* for their lack of success, and when they do, they lower their self-esteem. Furthermore, when they are successful, they attribute their success to something *other* than themselves. Study the following table of forces.

FORCES

	STABLE	UNSTABLE
LOCUS OF CONTROL — INTERNAL	ABILITY	EFFORT
LOCUS OF CONTROL — EXTERNAL	TASK DIFFICULTY	LUCK

As you can see, success and failure can be attributed to a combination of either internal or external sources, and these can be either stable or unstable forces. Ability is an internal-stable aspect of a person. The difficulty of the social task or the complexity of the interpersonal problem is an external-stable cause. Now, if you fail at an extremely difficult social encounter, you should attribute the failure to the task difficulty and not to a lack of ability. To do so has little implication for your self-esteem, since the failure was caused by some external condition, something you can't be held responsible for. The other two cells refer to the amount of effort you're willing to put into making a social encounter successful. While effort is an internal component of yourself (you control it), it is also something that is variable and can change from moment to moment, day to day, trial to trial. The last cell refers to luck, chance, or simply unexplained causes over which we have little control and understanding. It is a variable force, as well, since luck occurs on a random basis.

If you are shy and afraid of failing, the odds are that you also have a tendency to set very low social goals and aspire to very little, or to set unrealistically high social goals and aspire to a level that is, at present, inconsistent with your social skills and aptitudes. Now, we know that social goal-setting is very much related to personal and social adjustment. For example, the academically successful school children are those who set realistic goals for themselves, as opposed to those who are academically unsuccessful, and characteristically, set unrealistic goals. The well-adjusted person is a person who has a level of aspiration and a tendency to set goals that correspond with his ability and skill. Less well-adjusted people and those people who have a fear of failure tend to be inconsistent in their levels of aspiration, either by setting goals that are too low for themselves or unrealistically high goals.

Now, follow this reasoning very carefully. If, like most shy people, you are erratic in setting appropriate social goals for yourself, then this will have a direct impact on whether or not you are going to *experience* success. If you choose low social objectives, success is easily attained, and the credit for success goes to the *facility of the task* (an external factor) and, of course, this does not entitle you to give yourself much credit. On the other hand, if you choose a social goal that is too high, considering your social skills, your chances for success are slight, and should you happen to attain your goal, the success has to be attributed to *good luck* (again, an external factor). Thus, by taking very low risks, or very high risks, you create conditions that make it almost impossible for you to give yourself credit when you are successful.

If you are at all like this, the problem of a mental bias doesn't end here. You'll tend to blame yourself when social encounters don't go your way. This is a definite mental bias and is something not seen in non-shy, high social self-esteem people. People with high social self-esteem and greater experience with social reality attribute their failure to external factors, such as how difficult the social encounter really was, or simply to bad luck. And, if an external factor is not immediately discernible, they know to ascribe their failure to lack of effort. Now, while a lack of effort is an internal cause, it is also a variable one; so, the confident non-shy person preserves his self-esteem by avoiding the crucial "internal-stable" cell of the matrix. He turns around and says to himself, "This lack of effort that has led to failure in one social transaction is something that I can compensate for next time— *by trying harder.*"

The crucial issue here is that non-shy people with high social self-esteem are indeed more successful and they benefit more from successful experiences because they give themselves credit for their accomplishments and know to attribute failure to conditions external to them. Shy people, on the other hand, assume personal responsibility for all their failures and never give themselves credit for their successes—small wonder they have low self-esteem and feel helpless to change their lot.

The problem with being shy and afraid of failing in a social situation is compounded by a reluctance to risk and try out any aspect of the social self. The tendency to avoid social relations and social groups prevents the shy person from engaging in the kind of reality testing that could change the beliefs that cause low social self-esteem. By not risking social responses, he can only perpetuate his unhappy condition.

SHY?

We've been describing the mental processes of those who are severely shy, but do not be deceived! Moderately shy people suffer from the same fears and mental biases, but to a different degree. Even non-shy people feel some kind of apprehension and anxiety in meeting someone for the first time. Even the person with the most adequate sense of self-confidence has some concern over the possibility that his social advances will be met with rebuke, or, worse still, that he may be ignored. However, the non-shy person doesn't get discouraged and doesn't stop trying. While it's not pleasant to be turned down, to be ignored, or to be snubbed, it *is* unrealistic that these events should lead to massive anxiety, social withdrawal, and depression. The non-shy person doesn't try to be perfect in all social situations; he can admit to faults, mistakes, and to those things that make him less than heroic but that are, nevertheless, consistent with being human.

Let's look at a specific instance of shyness. Somebody in a strange town is too shy to ask his way. Let's suppose that he is interested in sightseeing and that he is not pressed for time. He knows that the logical solution to finding out where to find Fisherman's Wharf is to ask. But he is reluctant to come into contact with a stranger. Why?

First he would have to choose a particular person to approach, think of what to say, and the right way to say it. He would have to confess his ignorance and request help. Then he would have to trust the stranger and accept the help, if given. What keeps him from doing these things?

Most likely he is afraid of being misunderstood, or of putting the request incorrectly or in an improper way, or of appearing too modest, or of becoming conspicuous. He may be afraid of ridicule or embarrassment—in case the place he asks about turns out to be "just around the corner." And he may be afraid of being "snubbed," that the stranger will say to "find it yourself" and walk away. And again, he is probably basically ashamed of the actual fact of needing help, because this shows his dependence on others.

Where do these fears come from? The fear of being ridiculed, or rejected, or laughed at comes from the *irrational belief* that you must be perfect in all your endeavors, and that others think that you must be perfect, too. Not only is it irrational to believe that you *must* be perfect in your display of skill and ability and competence, but it is also a very unrealistic expectation. The end result of such a belief is inevitable failure, because any instance in which you are not perfect becomes an example of how you have not met your personal standard of excellence. The result of any social accomplishment that fails to meet a personal standard is a drop in social self-esteem.

People everywhere are filled with irrational beliefs, and these irrational beliefs are the root cause of a great deal of the emotional upset in people today. It is not other people or other things that are the cause of emotional upset and disturbance; it is irrational assumptions that people have about others and the way things should be. We can significantly reduce the amount of emotional upset that accompanies unfortunate experiences by learning how to perceive them correctly and by learning to adopt a more healthy view of them. Shy people hold a number of irrational and unproductive beliefs that not only perpetuate their anxiety and their inhibited condition, but that also serve as the most severe roadblocks against changing and trying new, more adaptive, modes of behavior. Let's look at some of the more common unproductive beliefs that preoccupy and interfere with the social adjustment of many shy people.

chapter 4

IRRATIONAL AND
UNPRODUCTIVE BELIEFS

IF YOU HOLD IRRATIONAL AND UNPRODUCTIVE BELIEFS, you can be pretty well assured of perpetuating a vicious cycle of "not trying," "fear of failure," and the whole shyness condition.

1). If I Hang Around Long Enough at a
Social Gathering, Party, or Dance,
Something Will Happen.

Waiting around for things to happen will most likely lead to nothing. We have consistently seen in social gatherings ranging from casual get-togethers, to formal parties, to lunch-hour gatherings to singles bars that to hang around and wait for things to happen produces little, if anything at all. While the issue of waiting for someone to approach and strike up a conversation is more typical of women, men also adopt the same attitude. They go to social gatherings in the hope of meeting people, especially women, and yet they do not take the initiative in this regard. These people usually leave frustrated and upset.

What is surprising, however, is that many of them will return the following day (especially to singles bars and discothèques) and do precisely the same thing—sit there like a bump on a log and wait for things to take place in their behalf. On occasion, someone will go up to them and ask them for a light, or ask them what time it is, or if they can move over a little, and the general reaction of these people when these "accidents" occur is to communicate casual uninvolvement, and to comply with whatever request was made. Often their manner makes it appear that they are preoccupied with other more important personal concerns. Or they appear depressed, or upset, or even drunk.

Sometimes it happens that the person *will* have too much to drink and slowly begin to nod while people continue to mill around him. It would be easy to infer that he was drowning his sorrows in alcohol, but our observations lead us to think that it serves as a convenient excuse for not involving himself. After all, what better reason can a person have for not initiating contact with someone when he is too drunk to carry on a normal conversation?

In all these ways, people try to camouflage their fear of trying.

On a number of occasions we decided to approach people who were the silent, "wait and see" type. Surprisingly, it was very easy to strike up a conversation with them. They were more than willing to socialize and talk. We would introduce them to other men and women who were with us and there would be a sudden personality change in them. They began smiling, chatting, and laughing, all too happy to be included.

Why this fear to initiate? What is it about this *fear of trying* that paralyses? For many people trying is the most difficult thing to do, but when they do try, all the social skills are at their command.

2). Most People Are Lucky. They Get All the Breaks. They Are Popular and Get Invited Out.

This second unproductive belief should be familiar to you by now. It focuses on the notion that good things happen to *other* people because of luck and good breaks.

But the good times and friendships we see around us are rarely created by accident, and even the initial meetings are not govened by luck. Unless you are formally introduced by a third party, someone has to make the first step and initiate contact. The belief that good things happen to other people because they are lucky or because they are at the right place at the right time does not hold true in the large majority of favorable encounters. In most cases, a person will have a strategy to make contact with others. This strategy may begin with making a decision to go to one spot as opposed to another.

Often someone will join a club, go to social gatherings, parties, singles bars, and other places with the express purpose of meeting new people. The strategies may never be fully articulated or discussed openly, but they are there. This person is not lucky; he has just taken advantage of opportunities.

If you believe that your social self-esteem will rise as a result of a fortunate circumstance, an accident, or good luck, you're clearly mistaken and you are adhering to this notion defensively because of your fear of trying. The correct belief is always that *you must go out and initiate. You must try.*

3). The Odds of Finding Someone Who Will Be Interested and Attracted to Me Are Always the Same, No Matter Where I Am.

This third irrational belief is the flip side of the second. It focuses on the notion that a person's chances of making a favorable impression with someone of the opposite sex are always fixed and stable. Common excuses are: "I'm not really lucky with girls," or, "I've never really stood a chance, and I can never really make it," or, "There aren't any good places where I can go to meet people."

These kinds of statements are usually defensive maneuvers against having to attribute personal failure to some internal quality or trait, or else the person has failed to try hard enough.

While these beliefs prevent you from suffering a loss of self-esteem, they also put up severe roadblocks against trying to seek out acquaintances using your own initiative.

4). If Someone Doesn't Show They Like You Right Away, They Really Don't Like You and Will Never Like You.

This unproductive belief is usually held by people who think that if someone is going to like them, they must prove it by a show of complete interest through verbal and non-verbal communication even in the first moments of conversation.

People who hold this belief know very little about human nature, first-time impressions, and initial encounters. In fact, it is *rare* for one person to disclose his liking and interest in the other following the first brief interchange. People need to have some history of transactions before they can feel comfortable about communicating liking, and communicating *interest* is often more difficult for people to do and for others to pick up. For example, a woman may wish to communicate interest in a man only in the hopes of finding out whether or not she might like him. The man could have difficulty picking up whether she is communicating interest cues or liking cues, even though both would seem to go hand in hand.

A good example of this irrational belief comes from our own observations. One evening, after having introduced a female acquaintance to a male friend at a social engagement, the friend asked the woman to dance and she readily agreed. After the dance was over, she also accepted someone's invitation to dance. He was upset by this. Much later, when we questioned him about the event, he admitted that he didn't think that she was interested in him. As he put it, "After all, if she had *really* been interested in me, she would have found some excuse not to dance with that other guy when he asked her." What this friend didn't know was that in this case, as in a majority of cases, even when *interest* is not immediately communicated in the other, it doesn't mean that the possiblity of *liking* may not be there.

5). If You Are Really Going to Make It With Someone, You'll Both Know It When You Meet and It Won't Be Any Problem.

If you are willing to wait for "love at first sight" as your only opportunity for any kind of relationship, don't let what is said below disabuse you of that notion. Some people really believe this, but for others it provides an easy defensive excuse against initiating contact with people and making the effort to establish real friendships out of casual acquaintances. Some people think they must be madly in love with the other person before they can show concern, interest, care, or have a friendship exchange.

Unproductive beliefs numbers 4 and 5 prevent people from making the *effort* necessary for establishing friendships and in testing out their social capacities for maintaining them. For these people, not making the effort allows them to blame their lack of success in social encounters on an external and variable cause—luck. But it doesn't help them attain those social goals and objectives that contribute to social self-esteem.

6). If I Ask a Woman Out and She Turns Me Down, It Is Because I Am Not Worthwhile or Good Enough for Her.

This irrational and unproductive belief is at the root of much social avoidance, failure to initiate, passivity and lack of responsiveness in social situations. It is this irrational belief that activates the fear of failure and perpetuates low social self-esteem. It has to do with the irrational assumption that in order to be a worthwhile and valued person, one must be liked, accepted, approved of, and be considered attractive by *everyone, all* of the time. This irrational belief is the cause of much emotional upset in everyday relations, but it takes on a special meaning in the context of social transactions with persons of the opposite sex. This fear of being turned down prevents shy people from testing reality and initiating social contacts, and it serves as the strongest inhibiting factor to initiating any social transaction, from a casual "Hello, how are you?" to a more formal request for a date or for a future meeting.

Being turned down can take on verbal and non-verbal forms. For some, a reply of "Thanks very much, but I'm busy Friday evening" is a clear indication of rejection, while for others it simply signifies a refusal of that particular request at that particular time. Or, in one of its non-verbal forms, being turned down can be "vibes." A man may send out a number of vibes to a woman that he likes her and is interested in seeing her, and if she doesn't return these non-verbal messages, he might interpret this as rejection and lack of interest. But perhaps she is just preoccupied with something else. The fear that interest and liking will not be reciprocated is based upon a fear of failure and a fear that one is not likable, worthwhile, or attractive to another. Why is this belief irrational?

Many shy people are too ready to infer that a refusal or a lack of reciprocated interest is caused by some undesirable trait in themselves. A lack of social experience together with a fear of failure invariably lead the shy person to infer the worst about *himself*. Not only does this tendency encourage emotional upset and psychological disturbance, but it also reflects an erroneous perception of the factors that lead to these kinds of refusals. In most circumstances, a person's decision to accept an invitation for a date or a future meeting is based upon: 1). how the person has gone about making the invitation —that is, the *social skill* involved; 2). the *social history* the two people have shared previously; 3). the *availability* of the other person for a future meeting; 4). the personal interest-needs of the other at that time.

Social Skill

A person's social skill often determines his success or lack of success. Asking someone out or communicating interest face to face, over the telephone, via a third party, or in writing represents different skills and each requires individual attention. But let's consider only face-to-face transactions. The various verbal and non-verbal aspects of such encounters can be executed in varying ways. Some people try to show that it really doesn't matter to them whether their request is accepted or not, or that it isn't really that important to them and it's just a "by the way, if you're not busy Friday night, how would you like to. . . ." Others are brash and arrogant: "Hey, sweetie! Let's you and I go out Friday! What do you say?" There are different ways of asking whether someone would be interested in making arrangements for a future meeting, and each of them carries with it a different probability that it will be received favorably.

When you ask people if they would like to join you for coffee, for lunch, or to go to a movie, what do you communicate about your interest, motives, and degree of liking for them in the way you phrase your request and the style in which you extend the invitation? Before automatically thinking that it is *you* that the other person doesn't like, you should consider first: What was it about the way I asked her out that communicated something unfavorable, unpleasant, or questionable about my motives? It is important to remember that often if the request had been phrased differently, the reply could have been more favorable. And, there are still *other* reasons for an unfavorable response that have nothing to do with you as a person.

Social History

Social history can mean the number of interchanges two people have had, no matter how brief, or we can talk about how familiar each is with the likes and dislikes of the other, or to what extent each has allowed the other to get to know him or her.

As a general rule, the better you know the other person, the greater your chances of being received favorably. Usually, people are more reluctant to pick up on social invitations from relative strangers. They are afraid of responding favorably to an invitation from someone with whom they have never interacted before, a caution that is not necessarily unreasonable or irrational. If you think about all the different kinds of people there are in the world, it is usually to your advantage and safety to find out at least a few basic things about the past history and character of the person who is asking to spend some time with you. Is the person interesting, bright, sociable, easy-going? What does he or she want from me? Am I in for a heavy trip? Is he or she on the make? Furthermore, people do unconsciously ask themselves the questions: "What do I want from a social episode? What can this person offer me in a social relationship?"

Having had an opportunity to spend some time getting acquainted prior to making a request for a future meeting increases the likelihood of a favorable response tenfold. This is true in almost all social contexts. Even at a singles bar or discothèque we have consistently seen people get turned down in a request for a dance, a date, or even an offer for a drink under conditions in which the request was the *first* social encounter between the two. But even in these encounters, when the two people finally have an opportunity to become better acquainted, these overtures are invariably favorably received.

The absence of social history between two people and not any absolute degree of liking of one for the other is what *causes* an unfavorable response.

Availability

The extent to which a person is available for a future meeting also tempers the kind of response to a request for a date.

Imagine the following situation: At a party, you begin talking to someone with whom you have had brief but friendly verbal interchanges in the past. You seem to be hitting it off well and you ask her if she would like to accompany you to a social event next week. She replies that she is tied up that day and thanks you for asking her. She doesn't specify what she will be doing that evening, but simply says she won't be able to make it. What should you infer from that? Does her reply mean that she's not interested in you and is simply offering a convenient excuse? That's always a possibility, but it might not be. In many cases those who have a fear of failing *immediately* infer the worst and *automatically* conclude that there is a lack of interest and liking, and *that they are not valued or worthwhile persons*. They become terribly upset and think the worst about themselves, the other person, and social relations in general. Of course, the most productive way of handling such refusals is to immediately suggest a number of other alternatives, such as getting together the following day or on another social occasion. Many people will not do this because they are afraid of being turned down a second time, if, indeed, the other person was simply being polite.

Many shy people have an unrealistic appraisal of the social lives of others. They too quickly assume that others don't have *any* social engagements or that they are *always* tied up with other commitments. Furthermore, shy people think that if the other person does have other commitments, they stand little chance of finding a spot in their social calendar.

So when a person turns down a request for a future meeting, it could be because of the *way* you phrased your request—your verbal and non-verbal style—or because you have not had a *long enough* social history to make the other person feel comfortable with the thought of spending some time with you alone. Or it could be because the person has other previous commitments. When none of these three causes is accountable, there is a fourth common cause of refusals.

Interest-Needs

Let's consider the needs of the person you have asked to see again. We have to ask the question: What do you have to offer that would fill one of his or her social interests and desires? Strictly speaking, social relationships operate under the principle of equity and exchange, *i.e.*, you hold some valued social or personal resource that can be used as barter in obtaining the other person's attention, graces, time, and social presence. It is unfortunate that the issue has to be presented in this light, but this approach is much more realistic than believing in the presence or absence of some vague romantic idea as the cause of a particular social outcome.

Irrational and Unproductive Beliefs

You hold some personal or social resource that someone else wants. Maybe it's money, social class, position, intelligence, or the social prestige derived from being seen driving around with you in your yellow Corvette. Maybe you're a sympathetic, understanding, and friendly person who would make no emotional or sexual demands upon the person. Maybe you're in a position of power and could serve to exercise a beneficial influence in his or her behalf. Maybe you're popular, sociable, extroverted, and the life of every party, and that's what's appealing. If the conditions of social skill, social history, and availability have been met, instead of attributing failure to some inadequacy in yourself, you are better off looking for causes in the other person. While you may indeed have valued personal resources to offer, it is very often the case that the other person's need orientation does not coincide with what you can offer.

People differ widely. They differ in terms of what they're "into," not only at any particular moment from day to day, but at different stages of their own personal, social, and emotional development. In adolescence, the peer group exerts a formidable influence, and what your friends think of you is exceedingly important. Being *seen* with someone who is popular, regardless of the personal traits that person may possess, is the primary social interest and strongest need satisfaction. Later on, when a person abandons these adolescent strivings, other interpersonal components become more important in promoting favorable and adequate social transactions. At various stages in life, sex is all-important. Do you communicate that you are willing to share this orientation with the other? Other times, friendships that involve the lack of attachment and commitment may preoccupy the person's social prerogatives. For another person at another time, honesty, integrity, and sympathetic understanding are highly sought after. Do you hold the attributes that could satisfy that personal orientation at that moment in time?

In adolescence and early adulthood, people have to find their own identity, and they search along various paths, common routes, up blind alleys, and in open fields. They experiment with different kinds of relationships. Often, a person involved may not even be able to articulate

63

what it is he is looking for; nevertheless, from moment to moment, day to day, and year to year, one's desires and needs change. Shy people have the unrealistic notion that they can satisfy *all* of the needs of *all* potential social partners *all* the time. Not only is this unrealistic (*no one* can ever satisfy *all* of the needs of any one person), but it is also irrational, because this attitude does not reflect the way in which social relations and personal relationships actually occur, evolve and last.

There is a distinct and healthy trend among people today to seek out clearly differentiated kinds of relationships. One person may satisfy a personal need, another may satisfy an emotional need, another a social need, and still another an intellectual need. It is important to understand that a refusal of a request for a future meeting can be caused by the fact that the person is into something else. When someone says, "I'm sorry, I think I'd like to, but I really won't be able to make it. Thanks very much," this does *not* imply some negative or undesirable characteristic in you, the one who made the request, but it is because his or her needs are peculiar and could not be met by you or even seventy percent of all other people. Your personal assets still stand; it is just that, from a simple exchange point of view, the other person is simply not in the market *at that time* for those commodities. Maybe tomorrow, or next month, but not right now. This is why it is important not to give up or stop trying, even with that same person! There will be a time when the other person will be relaxed enough to receive your goods and exchange for them what it is that you're looking for. The best way for you to verify this principle is to pursue an unwilling social partner until your invitation is accepted.

Shy people seem to have difficulty understanding these issues, perhaps because they are too constricted and do not have enough social experience. They are altogether too eager to attribute failure in social situations to some *personal* inadequacy and to infer that they are not likable, acceptable, or worthy persons.

Consider the issue of social skills and competence—not only how to make a request for a future meeting, but also how to judge when it is *appropriate* to make a request. While this may sound hard to believe, we have

met many people in the course of our investigations who
appear to have no notion whatsoever of what conditions
would lead to the acceptance of their invitation. In one
of our interviews with the people who frequented social
clubs, a twenty-two-year-old male candidly disclosed
that, on no fewer than three occasions, while dancing with
a woman he had just met a few minutes earlier he asked
her out for the following evening to have dinner at his
parents' home. Needless to say, he was politely turned
down on each occasion. Not only was the request for that
kind of date a little inappropriate for people who frequent
those social affairs, but it was also inappropriate in terms
of the *timing*. The request was made too quickly after the
initial encounter. Social skills extend to planning and timing skills, since you have to have a few clues about *when*
to speak, even after you've learned *how* to speak. Clearly,
if you are to escape the fear of failure bias that induces
you to infer the worst about yourself when social transactions don't go your way, you had better learn more
about social norms, cultural standards, and other people
—their quirks, needs, and day-to-day fluctuations.

In summary, given the social skills, the availability of
the other person, and an adequate social history, the
reason underlying the lack of success in social transactions
rests with the disharmony between what you've offered
and what the other person really wants. And you can't
be held responsible for somebody else's orientation. A
doctor doesn't think he's being rejected if you happen to
be healthy; an insurance salesman suffers no loss of prestige if you are already adequately covered; a shoe salesman doesn't become disturbed if he doesn't carry a line
of shoes that suits your taste, for, while it may be unfortunate that he didn't make a sale, he has no pretensions
about being able to satisfy *all* of his customers' needs.

Social skills include what we say, how we say it, and
when we say it, and once we have acquired these skills,
we stand a much better chance of having successful social
interactions. When an unsuccessful social transaction cannot be ascribed to poor social skills, then it is important
to *try harder*. Trying hard means making an effort to
properly use verbal and non-verbal messages. It involves
paying close attention to all the relevant cues that can tell
you which strategy and tactic to adopt. And it means

having patience and perseverance. Given the right circumstance, and the availability of such a person for social relations, if you are not successful it is because *you did not try hard enough.*

Can I Ever Be Sure?

If we made a list of all the different and varied social contexts you could get into, the list would be long. If we tried to make a list of all the different kinds of people there are in this world, that would involve continuous additions. If we generated a list of all the different kinds of verbal and non-verbal behaviors that could be made, either singly or in combination, we could never be sure that all combinations would be covered. There are simply too many social situations, too many different kinds of people with different day-to-day orientations, and too many different kinds of socially appropriate behaviors (which become algebraically more complex when we consider the combination of situations and persons together) to be able to prescribe what to say or do, with what people in which situations, in order to be successful. Even if we could give this vast number of rules, no one could learn and memorize them. There are so many external factors that just when we think we have them all under control, an exception to the rule is sure to come up.

In everyday interactions, the social reality about us consists of an interplay of personal factors, circumstances, and skills. Fortunately, we have rituals and easily learned social habits to bring order and predictability to some of this. Otherwise, even the simplest social interaction would be a formidable and uncertain task. Still, we can never control *all* the factors that can help us predict success and failure, at least not in the real world of mundane social realities. But what if we tried to construct an artificial social reality in which all these factors, except one or two, are stable? Wouldn't this allow us to manipulate those factors to our advantage? This is what organizations that arrange for singles vacations try to do for their members. Let's take a look at how a social reality is artificially created and how arranging for opportunity and the fulfillment of personal interest-needs can have positive and negative consequences.

The organized singles vacation offers a unique context in which the external factors present in everyday social settings are controlled. Every possibility for easy social contact is afforded everyone.

Private and completely self-contained, these organizations often accommodate from 800 to 1,800 people in various locations around the world. People who take advantage of these facilities are mainly singles between the ages of twenty and forty, and all are looking for social contacts of all kinds and varieties. Typically, the daily programs of singles vacations are arranged so that with very little effort you can get involved in social or sports activities. In order that there be no issue of having to carry enough money, or even concern yourself with carrying a purse or wallet, everything is paid for in advance and no money is ever exchanged. A necklace of different beads or tickets may serve as the means of exchange at the bar. Dress is very casual. The atmosphere is always friendly and relaxed, the programs exceedingly flexible, and organizers are always available to provide whatever assistance may be needed.

There is very little thinking, organizing, or preparation and planning needed on your part in this social haven. All concern and worry about having to obtain tickets, fill out forms, follow rules, or stand in line is eliminated. There is no reason to do or not do something according to protocol, since there is none. You would think this would be precisely what shy people are looking for, especially if they are unsure about their social skills and worried about "how to behave." No, this may not be the best social reality for those who are shy! And you'll see why in a moment.

The social events generally center around meals, evening entertainment, and sports and leisure activities during the day. You hardly have to lift a finger to create opportunities to meet people. The opportunities are already there and waiting to be used. Everything is arranged to maximize the chances that people will meet and interact with one another. For example in one organization, there are three hosts and/or hostesses who greet you at the door when you arrive in the dining room for a meal.

They're all very aware of the kinds of conditions necessary to make it as easy as possible to meet people. The
hostess has the responsibility of sitting people at tables
that can accommodate four, six, or eight people, and
while she has to try to fill the available spaces at any one
sitting, it is also her task to make sure that if you arrive
alone, you're seated at a table that has available members
of your own age group and of the opposite sex. Indeed,
she is more of a social facilitator than she is an usher.
The situation appears to be well managed and there is
virtually no doubt in anyone's mind that the occasion for
social contact and friendly opportunities is there to be
seized, and everyone recognizes and admits to these motives. It seems almost impossible not to begin interacting
with someone almost immediately.

The issue of a personal need orientation is also easily
taken care of. People go on singles vacations with the
express purpose of taking advantage of the various
forms of socializing available. So you can be assured that
most of the people you meet have similar motives in
mind. There is a general understanding that if you meet
someone, you do not have to remain with him or her for
any specific length of time, let alone for the remainder of
your vacation. In fact, an organized singles vacation is a
royal opportunity for all those who are looking for brief
social and sexual encounters. Little time is wasted in the
formal "get acquainted" rituals that are more fashionable
in polite but hesitant society. Even the most meager social
response is viewed as an invitation for an ongoing transaction. It seems as if almost any socially skilled behavior will
elicit a social response. Raise your eyes and smile at someone across the outdoor poolside bar and you'll be sure of a
return smile, wave, and a cheerful *"salut."*

But this experience is not the right one for the person
who has difficulty maintaining, and terminating, social
contacts. Indeed, for some shy people to participate in
this unreal social environment is to invite further aggrava-
tion of their fears of failure and feelings of unworthiness.
Why is this? Doesn't the singles vacation offer an ideal
opportunity for those who have difficulty "making it" in
this complex social reality? No, and here's why.

Imagine for a moment that you are in a social gathering back home and that you're interested in making new

acquaintances. If you initiate a conversation with someone and it doesn't seem to go very far, or if you don't find anyone in that group whom you think might be interested in pursuing some social transactions, then your lack of success can be attributed to an external condition—to the situation or to the peculiarities about the people who are there. And you will be quite correct in saying, "This place is a real drag. It's not much fun in here, so let's go somewhere else." You can say, "These people are real duds. If I'd known that these were the kind of people who came here, I wouldn't have bothered coming." While lack of success is disappointing, what prevents you from becoming emotionally upset is the fact that circumstances beyond your control are to blame and there is no threat to your self-concept.

The singles vacation, however, doesn't allow you to attribute failure to external conditions. If you don't obtain some measure of social success there, it is almost impossible to attribute this to the situation or to the people, or even to the fact that you didn't "try hard enough." If you spend two weeks under conditions in which the people are willing, the situation is easy and facilitating, and the initial investment is minimal, but you still fail to take part and are left standing alone with no excuse, then your shyness, social anxiety, and irrational fears really stand out.

The singles vacation can also be a stressful experience for many non-shy people, especially those who come with the attitude and belief that if you don't get laid the first day, and at least twice the second day, you're not making it, and if you're not making it, you're something less than the super-male some vacationers tend to idealize. Men who are on the make invariably gather together to compare notes. The bragging of conquests and victories, of group scenes that were organized, of how many times they got laid the day before, and what conquests they have planned for today are all too reminiscent of locker room or dormitory boasting—except magnified a hundred-fold.

If you have doubts about your masculinity, or if you define your sense of self through some stereotyped notion of maleness, the singles vacation can be an anxiety-provoking experience. But the fact of the matter is that in these circumstances your willingness to risk is *all* that is being tested.

For many people this experience produces mixed emotions. An outside observer comparing the amount of "social acting out" back home with what goes on during a two-week singles vacation would automatically attribute great success to the latter. The vacationer, however, may have had many more social and sexual contacts—indeed, enough to sustain him or her for the next eleven months—but the problem is that when he looked around, he saw people who were better at it. Compared with friends back home, he was a smash; compared with other vacationers, he barely made it. And, besides, although he leaves with many tales and stories to tell, he has probably discovered there's no glory in unearned gifts. When social rewards are too easily obtained, there's not much you can give yourself credit for.

No, it's far better *not* to have the one-hundred-percent guarantees the organized singles vacation provides. There is more to be gained from social contexts in which you cannot be absolutely sure you're going to meet with success—to be tested, that's where the potential for gain lies. The best social context is back home, where you can experiment with different social formula, winning most if losing a few. That is how the building blocks of self-confidence are laid.

There Is Nothing to Fear But Fear Itself

Most people have a certain amount of apprehension about how social transactions will turn out, especially when they meet someone for the first time and in a new situation. But an excessive amount of fear—that's what you should be afraid of! High levels of anxiety produce definite and distinct psychological consequences, and if there is anything that's going to curtail your success, it is going to be fear. Let's look at the reason for this.

The kind of situation in which you find yourself can determine the ease of your social interactions. If the context is old and familiar, the odds are that whatever your social competence and skills are, they will be displayed without too much difficulty or distress. However, if the situation is new, or if there are significant changes in an otherwise customary and familiar setting, this may create a certain amount of stress. And this stress may be enough to interfere with the mental effort needed to assess and judge the social situation, or to inhibit the use of what you know to be the inappropriate social skills for that social context.

In a familiar setting, you respond to social cues without really thinking, in the manner of habits. This gives us the opportunity to think of other things that may concern us, or to polish our verbal and non-verbal skills, to develop tact, grace, and a pleasant social manner. Consider verbal behavior. Many of our replies consist of well-learned ritual expressions, phrases, answers, and verbal fillers that tumble out effortlessly, with little thought. Someone asks you a question: "Hello. How are you?" The question goes to your mind and almost unconsciously you search out whether the question is a familiar or unfamiliar one. If you recognize it as familiar, as this one definitely is, you unconsciously decide what the appropriate answer is by selecting one of at least half a dozen or more verbal responses that can come spilling out without thinking. But the one that is selected is the one that is appropriate to the situation and the person who asked the question, depending upon whether you're standing, walking, sitting, or whether the transaction takes place with the expectation that nothing more is to follow or more interchanges are to occur. This all takes place unconsciously, quickly, and smoothly when it comes from habit.

Habits are only acquired on the basis of practice. Think about how you learn to drive a golf ball with skill. At first you have to instruct yourself: stand up straight, keep your left arm straight, swing back smoothly, bend your right wrist, keep your eye on the ball, swing down, follow through. But after many repetitions the self-instruction fades, until the golf swing is smoothly executed without the guiding influence of these internal reminders. In fact, if you have learned to execute the golf skill particularly well and you suddenly start to describe what you're doing, this self-talk will *interfere* with your skilled execution of the swing. The same thing is true for any behavioral skill, whether it is learning how to drive a car or even as simple as signing your name. It all happens automatically, and when we do it, our mind is freed to think of anticipations, consequences, future possibilities, and to monitor what is happening around us.

The same applies to verbal and non-verbal skills in social transactions. Those people who have had a wide variety of social experiences usually have acquired an equally wide variety of social responses, and with time these responses become so ingrained that they form habit assemblies. Then all that is required to trigger off these habits is the simple recognition of what is going on in any social episode. The use of these assemblies frees us to think about all those things that make social transactions easy—what we are going to say next, if we should pursue this or that line of a conversation, if we should bring up a tangential issue for comment, *etc*. Verbal and non-verbal habit assemblies free us to muse, to think. For example: "What he said just reminded me of something. I should be sure to bring it up later." Or you might say to yourself: "I see someone else I want to talk to across the room. What's the best way for me to finish this conversation smoothly?" This is just a sample of the stream of consciousness of the non-shy person within a short ten-second social episode. His social behavior remains appropriate, and the listener would never know that this thought was occupying his mind.

In contrast, shy people don't operate on the basis of socially appropriate response habits. The only thing that is habitual with a shy person is to remain quiet and uncommunicative, verbally and non-verbally. He is so preoccupied with himself—what he is saying, how he is saying it, whether it's well received—and with thoughts of how to avoid the situation that nothing else can enter his head. His mind is not free to think of those necessary things that would make for a smooth and easy-flowing social transaction. We already know that one of the reasons for this excessive self-preoccupation has to do with his fear of negative evaluation; another reason may just be that he is simply unskilled or unaccustomed to casual social situations, and so, like the novice golfer, he has to attend more closely and diligently to every component of the skills involved. Only when these skills are rehearsed both mentally and in action can they become habits.

Only then can habit assemblies develop and with them an ease and lessening of effort.

These general habit assemblies that ease casual social relations break down under one condition—when anxiety persists. While psychologists and other researchers are still investigating the nature of anxiety and stress and have yet to fully understand what these reactions are all about, there is one thing about which they are all in universal agreement—*anxiety inhibits freedom*. Under states of anxiety the freedom to respond becomes curtailed. When a person is stressed, his mind locks like a vise around fixed ideas. Under conditions of fear, there is little variability, both in thought and in action. This principle has been so well accepted that it has been applied in primary school systems. For the past fifteen years, the trend in modern education has been to foster a "low-risk" educational environment so that the child can engage in a variety of responses, make new and wild associations, and be creative about his attempts at tackling problems. Under stress, we are less flexible, and we adhere to those things we know for certain. Just about the only thing that the shy person knows for certain is that if he *doesn't* respond and *doesn't* say anything, he's not going to provide any grounds for a negative evaluation, and so the cycle perpetuates itself.

This stress phenomenon is also true for non-shy people. When a non-shy person finds himself in new social contexts, he has to react to the cues in the situation with conscious effort. "I've never been in this building before. I wonder what the people are like. Who should I know here? What shall I say to this person? I better stick with those styles that I know." Or he might say, "I've never been to a party like this before. It looks like there are a lot of embassy people here. I wonder who is who. Good heavens! There's a reception line. Where do I go from here? Who should I speak to? What shall I say?"

When people are in a new social situation and they're unsure about what is socially appropriate, they say and do whatever they are sure of, whatever can cause no offense. Even while making these social responses, a person has to be attentive to feedback that could communicate that he is or he is *not* being appropriate, or doing the right social thing. So new social situations are stressful not only because of the absence of certainty, but also because they interfere with the person's ability to free his mind to think of those things that would make an interaction easy and smoothly carried off. Verbal behavior, facial and bodily expression, and thinking processes, can be inhibited, no matter whether you are shy or non-shy. Occasionally, social stress makes a person more active, but this very activity shows their anxiety. Their talk takes a random direction, with lots of rambling, tongue wagging, and loosely connected thoughts.

The shy person has to deal with two sources of anxiety. The first stems from a fear of negative evaluation and failure. The second results from the fact that new situations occupy mental processes and prevent a casual and relaxed chaining of social behavior. If social stresses are severe enough, they can even turn a non-shy person into a shy one. A good illustration of this is seen in the following true account.

A good friend, Bob, decided to spend two months touring Europe. His plan was to start in the Scandinavian countries, fly to Paris, and then drive south into Spain, visit Barcelona, and spend a few weeks on the island of Mallorca. Bob decided to travel alone in order to have greater freedom to pick himself up and go wherever he wished, whenever he wanted. He was interested in visiting the countries and in trying to get to know the people.

Starting in Copenhagen and Oslo was a good idea, as it turned out, since the successes he had with the people there gave him great hope for success in France and Spain. Two days before he was to leave for Paris, Bob was sitting in a discothèque with friends he had met that day, and he was literally "picked up" by a very attractive Norwegian blonde about his own age. She was from Oslo and only just managed to make herself understood in English. It was evident that she was interested in spending some time with him, and she made that clear very early on in their conversation. He distinctly recalls her first words in broken English: "Hi! I sit your table with you? I'm Elsie!"

She certainly seemed to know what she wanted, and she didn't hesitate to go out and get it. This general attitude characterized her behavior throughout the hours they spent together during the next two days. Elsie was very bold, very self-confident, and very self-assured. She didn't hesitate to ask questions of him or of anyone if she felt so inclined. If Bob asked Elsie something about Oslo that she couldn't answer, without hesitation she would stop someone in the street and ask them the question. She was always smiling, jovial, and very happy about everything she did.

During a taxi ride into town one morning, the driver was going much too quickly through busy streets, weaving in and out among parked cars and cyclists. It took no time at all for Elsie to speak up and give the driver a piece of her mind, instructing him to slow down. While Bob couldn't understand the Norwegian, the tone of her voice was enough to indicate how sure of herself she was. Elsie was never rude or obnoxious, only very expressive in stating the things that she wanted. She seemed free and spontaneous and somehow in a hurry to get as much as possible into both their lives before Bob left for Paris. Soon the taxi got stuck in traffic, and, tired of waiting, Elsie told the driver this was far enough, they were getting out. She paid him, waited for her change, tipped him, leaped outside the cab, and in three steps stood at the front door of a small pub-restaurant waving at Bob to follow her inside.

The café was filled with working men drinking their morning beer before going to work. No table was available, so, without hesitation, Elsie walked over to a person sitting alone at a small table and kindly asked if he would mind sitting with others at a larger table so that she and her friend might be able to sit together quietly. Over a breakfast of cognac and eggs, she looked up at Bob and said, "You're shy, aren't you?" She glanced at him coyly and showed a broad smile.

Bob was surprised that Elsie would think this and he quickly dismissed the idea, attributing her perception to some social difference between the sociability of Swedes and the more reserved nature of an American from Minnesota. He added that the language problem did not make matters easier. Still, he didn't feel shy.

During the forty-eight hours that Bob spent with her, he saw Elsie interact with young and old people, males and females, street sweepers, clergymen, professors, and businessmen, in all kinds of contexts, from an exclusive restaurant to a skid-row tavern, from the street and to the university. She was at ease and comfortable in all situations.

This Norwegian bird of happiness seemed to have a spirit that was free and spontaneous, open to everything, comfortable with everyone, regardless of setting. Being with Elsie was a refreshing contrast with the "heavy trip." Bob had been into several months earlier with his wife. They had decided to separate, and there were still several emotional issues he hadn't fully resolved. Elsie provided a great distraction from these thoughts. He wanted to stay with Elsie longer, but he had other plans to follow and other distractions to pursue.

The greatest distraction was to be found in Mallorca, where he went on a two-week prepaid singles vacation. It was everything he had expected. After the two weeks he was exhausted from the late hours, gallons of Sangria, and just too much socializing. In a sense, he was glad it was all over; what was once a challenge with the opposite sex had turned into a mundane routine, providing little excitement or interest. He decided to spend a few days recuperating quietly at the other end of the island.

Bob had three weeks left and he didn't quite know how he wanted to spend the time. The image of Elsie kept returning to his mind, so one afternoon he picked up the telephone and in two minutes the operator had dialed the Oslo number.

"Yankee friend!" Elsie cried.

Bob told her he had been thinking about her and would very much like to see her again. If she went to the SAS office in Oslo, he said, she'd find a ticket for Mallorca waiting for her. Elsie was ecstatic. She agreed to come and said she'd call him when she knew exactly when she would be arriving.

Later that evening, the head waiter approached Bob at his table and said there was a long-distance call for him. On the phone he heard a Spanish and Swedish garbled interchange and finally heard the familiar "Hello ... Yankee?"

The words spilled out of him, "Yes, yes! Elsie?"

"I come tomorrow ... five o'clock, okay?"

By some luck she had managed to pick up a direct flight from Copenhagen to Barcelona, and from there she would take a twenty-minute flight to the island. The airport scene was one filled with embraces and excitement —both of them completely overjoyed at their reunion. They walked out of the airport arm in arm. How could Bob have imagined that in three days he'd be back in that airport saying good-bye to her as she returned to Oslo?

The taxi drive to the hotel was quiet and uneventful. Elsie tried to read billboard signs along the highway and asked what some of them meant. Bob, as best as he could, translated into simple English the gist of what they were advertising.

Elsie wasn't used to five-star hotels or the social form that accompanies such extravagance. She didn't know what to say, let alone what language to say it in. Elsie looked to Bob for guidance, trying to get a hint about how to react. She was quiet, almost sullen. She followed behind him as he carried her bag to their room.

At dinner that evening Elsie had to ask about every item on the menu, and she wondered why there was none that appeared familiar to her. This was the first time she had been outside of Scandinavia, and evidently it was her first exposure to non-Nordic people, customs, and language. She wasn't pleased with the situation. It was much too new for her, much too different, much too strange. She became very quiet and passive. She looked in Bob's direction every time she moved, wondering if he had caught her doing something wrong. Bob thought this would pass pretty quickly—culture shock and all that. Tomorrow they would go into Palma, rent a scooter, and go tearing through the streets. Then they would rent a motor-sailer for the day and pick up where they had left off in Oslo a few weeks before. But that was just a hope.

Elsie seemed to be paralyzed with fear. She turned out to be a strange bird in a strange land, for she had lost her familiar environment and her sense of self-direction. In the past, she'd reacted to her social condition in any way she wished, and there was always a confirming reply that came back. Those traditional boundaries and that familiar echo that for so long had reinforced her social self were no longer there. Two days—that's all it took. Then she was lost, once more an adolescent, insecure, unsure about everything.

As Bob described the situation to me and related the specific components of her behavior in Spain, it was astounding to realize how similar were her deportment, thinking, and feeling style to that which prevails among those who are very shy. Elsie was obviously disturbed and upset. As stated previously, anxiety and emotional distress suppress relaxed behavior and free thinking, and this was true for Elsie. Her anxiety was quite real. Back home, in the familiar, stable, and dependable environment, she could act freely and spontaneously and be her own person. But in Spain, there were too many social cues that were new and different, too many things that were untested, and too many reactions she felt unsure of. Like a shy person, fear of negative evaluation not only from her friend, but from the whole social context, preoccupied her and made her anxious. As a defensive measure, she withdrew from any attempt at expressiveness, from any spontaneous social activity. She became inhibited, timid, and unresponsive.

By the end of the second day, Bob began to feel the demands that were being placed upon him. They weren't concrete demands in the sense of overt requests for help or support; rather, they were very subtle demands. Elsie needed to be assisted, and she needed him to behave in a manner that could serve as a model for her to follow. Bob had to initiate, he had to originate. It was up to him to carry the weight of transactions, introductions to others, and to be vigilant about whether or not Elsie had correctly interpreted the loudness or tone of voice in a waiter or attendant. While he had to look after her social well-being, he also felt some responsibility for looking after her emotional welfare. That was something he had never expected, and for him, at that particular time, it was something he did not at all want to cope with—especially after a two-week rampage of cosmetic relationships on his packaged vacation, especially after what he had left behind in Minnesota.

Originally, Elsie's stay in Spain was to be as long as his. The plans were to drive back to Paris together and there Elsie could take a plane to Oslo. But Bob knew that if this situation continued for very much longer he'd become angry, resentful, and eventually hostile toward her for being such a burden. He knew that he'd have to send her back before it was time for them to make their return trip. That night he told her.

It was a somber scene at the airport the next morning. They said little to each other and avoided each other's gaze. Elsie got up from the table where they had been drinking beer to go and get something. Before she left, she wanted to make sure that he'd stay at the table and that he'd be there when she returned. He reassured her that he would watch her bags and that he would stay right there. She came back minutes later with a small box in her hand. She handed it to him, saying, "Here, for you. It is me." Bob opened up the box and found in the middle of neatly wrapped tissue paper a small blown-glass bird. As he looked at it, Elsie said, "Little gray sparrow . . . should be careful."

Bob was moved by the present. It obviously represented something about the way Elsie saw herself and perhaps also something she wished from him. For a moment he thought about how he could get it back home without breaking it. Then he wondered whether he should even hold on to it.

During the drive back into town, Bob was still disbelieving that Elsie could be so different away from home, and he was disturbed by what he had done. He looked at the little glass sparrow. How fragile it was! He wrapped it up again and put it in his pocket for safe keeping.

chapter 5

POSTURES AND POSES

IN LOOKING AT MY PICTURE IN THE BOARDING SCHOOL yearbooks, I have to admit that I was a cute kid. My head was crowned with girlish locks that framed a cherub's face, the effect of which, I guess, was just too angelic to be held responsible for any misdeeds. I wore short pants in good weather, and baggy jeans (with turned-up cuffs of the kind that shows a flannelette mackintosh pattern fashionable today with Bay City Rollers' fans) in the winter. I was cute in those early years, and I think that served as the major cause for my getting away with lateness, not making my bed, occasional tantrums, and the granting of such peculiar privileges as sitting at a girls' table with the house mother while 124 envious school-mates sat segregated at their own tables. Being the young-est and smallest, I led all single files into the chapel, the dining room, classes, and lines for all assemblies. I also placed first in my class from grades one to five.

Cuteness and the benefits derived from it were not under my control, however. They finally got a school uniform to fit me (I grew into one) and made me get a haircut. And during my third year there, the house mother got this crazy notion about making me become more independent. She got me to make my own bed, and she banished me from her all-girls table, where I had become comfortably nested, and she made me join the rat packs across the dining hall. That wouldn't have been too damaging to my primitive ego were it not for the fact that I was being displaced by another cuter and younger kid that had arrived that year. It's not much fun being cast away like a satellite after spending two years at the center of the universe.

The problem with being a cute kid has to do with the fact that it is a temporary condition; but nobody tells you that. The problem with the temporary condition has also to do with seeing your rival occupy the seat you thought was forever yours and wear the green zippered pullover given to you by the house mother a year before. The problem with being young is that you can't help outgrowing costumes that were really never meant to fit in the first place.

The absence of class distinctions at school kept social comparisons to a minimum, and with that was removed the basis for the anxious competition I have seen elsewhere, particularly among upwardly mobile, achievement-oriented kids. No one had status where I was. No one could claim a corner on the social forces that led to prestige, power, dominance, and other social-ego assets. Whatever social gains I was to obtain were without a doubt to be attributed to developed skill and learned ability. If anyone was to "rate" socially, it wasn't going to be derived from external and unearned factors. For that I was thankful. I'm glad we were not allowed social stratification or the display of any element, such as fancy clothes, that would have elevated anyone's social scale. I couldn't have competed on those counts (there were too many kids from well-to-do-families), and if I had tried, I would have been constantly frustrated, or, worse still, a failure.

I think about how young men and women were deemed desirable and how they attained social success in some rigidly stratified social environments in the Thirties. Many universities encouraged social class distinctions that meant that if you didn't "rate," you didn't date. For example, at Pennsylvania State at that time, you had to have a Class-A rating in order to stand a chance in the social scramble every September. You had to belong to one of the better fraternities, be prominent and visible in social activities, have money, be well dressed, have a car, and only date popular students if you were to rate. The social prestige factors that defined success at Penn State were all external and not determined by skill, ability, or social effort.

Women at Penn State had to be popular to make it socially. It sounds paradoxical, but in order to succeed socially you had to be a social success to begin with. Social form and appearances were the determining factors. Since their social prestige depended upon dating more than anything else, clever coeds contrived to give the impression of being much sought after even when they weren't. Campus prestige meant that you must never be available for last-minute dates, never be seen too often with the same boy, arrange to be seen at expensive places, have many partners at the dances, and be called often to the telephone (a situation which, if it did not occur "naturally," could be, and, indeed, often was, contrived with a sympathetic accomplice).

Now, while most of these factors were determined by the socio-economic position of the parents and could never serve as something for which personal credit could be given, there were some personal elements that were under direct individual control: to dance well, to be "smooth" in manners and style, and to have a "good line"—those were the skills to be acquired—but, again, all at the service of prestige and social form in an arena where public display was the sole vehicle of commodity exchanges. There was enough social injustice, inequity, unearned privilege, and emotional distress brought on by these social conditions that eventually caused fraternities and sororities to be banned in many state colleges and universities. This has effectively resulted in the equivalent to an "equal opportunities act," except that friendship is what's in the marketplace, not jobs.

I can't really remember what it was that made us "rate" at boarding school. Sometimes physical attractiveness increased our desirability, but sometimes it worked against us. I know that in the first month of every school year physical attractiveness made you rate, but as the year wore on it seemed to play a less important role. Perhaps this was because those who were physically desirable were not available, anyway, and we may have resented being constantly reminded of the institutional religious barriers, and school rules from which an extended glance at sexy Mary made our guardians automatically suspect Freudian smolderings. For those of us who participated in the social process, anyone who was physically attractive and did not hide it was labeled conceited, egotistical, snobbish, and stuck up.

Mirror, Mirror, on the Wall

Everyone knows that physical attractiveness plays an important role in meeting someone of the opposite sex for the first time, but let's look closely at how it can sometimes help and sometimes interfere with social transactions and self-esteem.

While you may think that we all have different tastes, you'd be surprised to find that people generally agree on who is attractive and who is not. Physical attractiveness has its greatest impact on initial encounters and gradually loses its effect in subsequent get-togethers. As we start to interact with people and more information becomes available, our impression of them changes. We find out about their past history, their interests, and their personality traits, and suddenly physical appearance no longer matters. How many of us have disliked a person on the basis of their physical appearance only to have them become our closest and most valued friend later on? How many of us have been completely enchanted and enthralled by the attractiveness of people upon first meeting them, only to develop a dislike for them once other features of their personality are made evident?

When we look at the preferences, patterns, and dating habits of men and women, we find that a person's decision to date a person the first and second time is largely based upon that person's physical attractiveness. This is not surprising, since at the level of first encounters, the more physically attractive a person is, the more he or she is liked. However, it is important to remember that it is the person's *perception* of the physical attractiveness that determines whether they date that person again. In first encounters and first encounters only, the perceived physical attractiveness of the other far outweighs in importance other characteristics, such as whether the other person has similar interests, is of good character, *etc*. As they date more frequently, a person's character or personality and behavior become more important and salient in deciding whether he or she will be dated again.

How attractive or good looking do *you think* you are? The answer to this question may determine who you approach and select as a possible dating partner. In general, both men and women who believe themselves to be unattractive are more likely to think about dating unattractive partners than attractive ones. Similarly, highly attractive people tend to think about dating very attractive partners. Men generally think that their chances of being accepted are less with a very attractive woman, and this "inferred probability" is what determines whether they approach them or not. Given the opportunity, however, men will prefer to date the most physically attractive women *if* they are assured they will be accepted by them. Otherwise, men will turn their desires toward moderately attractive or even unattractive women, with whom they think they can succeed.

If you are shy, you tend to have a lower sense of social self-esteem. You also have a tendency to devalue yourself and your importance in a social context. For example, if I were to show you segments of your social behavior on videotape and ask you to evaluate different aspects of your performance, chances are you'll be much more critical and self-debasing than will a person who is not shy and, therefore, has a higher social self-esteem. Shy people are much more self-critical not only about their behavior, but also about their physical appearance, and when it comes time to figure the odds of being accepted on a date, they typically underestimate their real chances.

Are the physically attractive preferred? Do they have an edge on the rest of us? The answer to the first question is an unequivocal "yes." Those who are physically attractive generally tend to be preferred, but only in a particular sense. People want to be associated with physically attractive and beautiful people for extrinsic reasons and for the external rewards that are obtained when they are seen publicly with them. We tend to prefer to associate with physically attractive people primarily for prestige reasons. If a man is seen with a very attractive woman, people tend to attribute a large number of favorable characteristics to him. If his girl friend is not physically attractive, people tend to view him in a more negative manner overall. Thus, simply being associated with someone who is physically attractive tends to create a more favorable reaction in the public eye.

For many, dating is a very public affair—public in the sense that a person puts his ego on the line when he presents himself with someone in full view of others. And often it is not good enough merely to be seen in physical proximity of a physically attractive person; observers must be led to believe that there is some tie or connection between one and the other. But, as we'll see later, this public spectacle provides few rewards in terms of friendship or social relationships.

People often assume that physically attractive men and women are more likely to possess socially desirable personality characteristics, and this bias tends to be accentuated in shy people. They also tend to think that physically attractive people lead more successful lives than their unattractive counterparts. Physically attractive people are often perceived by others as "masters of their own fate" and as behaving with a sense of purpose and out of their own free will and desire. Unattractive people, on the other hand, tend to be seen as coerced into things and generally influenced by others or by environmental conditions. Fortunately, this physical attractiveness stereotype exists only for people who are at the extreme ends of the attractiveness scale.

We cannot deny the fact that physical attractiveness does contribute to self-esteem and a feeling of well-being. Think, for a moment, about the effect of facial plastic surgery or even the simple use of cosmetics. Improving physical appearance has a dramatic effect upon the person because it leads him to evaluate himself more positively and to "feel good about himself," and this raises self-esteem. Losing weight, being physically fit, and wearing contact lenses instead of glasses can all serve these positive ends. One dramatic illustration of the effects of improved physical appearance on self-concept will suffice.

A group of inmates in a penitentiary, many of whom had been jailed on drug-related charges, underwent plastic surgery to correct disfigurements and to get rid of burns, scars, lop-ears, and tattoos. Following their release from prison, this cosmetic social rehabilitation proved to be the most successful program for keeping them out of jail, for finding and keeping a job, as well as for their overall social and personal adjustment, compared with a similar group of inmates who had not received the cosmetic surgery. Clearly, facial features and general appearance have a strong impact upon how we perceive ourselves and how others will perceive us. While there are limits to how much we can improve our physical appearance, it is a wonder to find how many shy people don't seem to be aware of styles, fashion, and ways of highlighting positive aspects of their appearance—perhaps not *too* surprising, though, since shy people are reluctant to shine in the first place.

Even though you may be reluctant to be "on stage," the center of attention, or to have people look at you, think a little bit about what you can do to make yourself look and feel good: dressing differently, losing a bit of weight, trying different makeup, or maybe just cleaning yourself up. Do this not to put on airs, but more for yourself. You'll see the difference.

While physical attractiveness has a lot to do with an initial encounter, it has very little to do with maintaining a conversation or sustaining an interaction over time and in repeated encounters. What makes a person socially rewarding has little to do with his physical appearance; it has everything to do with how he behaves and whether or not he has the social competence for making an enjoyable interaction possible. Women who are beautiful easily attract men's fancy, but the absence of social skills that would make interchanges equitable and mutually rewarding will guarantee these men will not return. The same principle applies for physically attractive men. Throughout the course of our interviews with shy and non-shy people, we asked questions concerning who they would like to date, why, where, and whether they would like to date that person again, and we repeatedly found that while physically attractive partners were generally preferred, their decision to date a person a second and a third time was based upon the rewards that were obtained in the dating experience. We found that the physically attractive were abandoned if they didn't provide for a mutually rewarding social relationship. The following commentary from a thirty-year-old single male who dated relatively frequently is not untypical.

"I'm not sure how much of a general rule this is, but I've found that the women who are very attractive often are those that are the least fun to be with. In fact, now I hesitate to go out with very attractive women more than once because I know that very little in terms of friendship or a mutually satisfying relationship is likely to evolve. I don't know what it is about sexy women, but some of them are such bores that I'd rather not approach them at all in a social situation. I have gone out with several beautiful women who only seem interested in being entertained—I mean this literally. They like to be taken out to fancy restaurants, to go to the best social functions, and to real high-class joints. They just like to be *seen* in public. Many of them don't really care about you as a person. I'd say that they do want your friendship, but only because you can serve as an escort for them.

"Now, what I usually do is, if I see someone who is really sharp and good looking, I'll go up and start a conversation with her. If I see that she's really full of herself and has little to offer in being interested in me, I won't even pursue her any longer than five minutes. I've gotten into the habit of dropping the whole idea of getting to know a woman if she gives me the slightest indication that she is using her attractiveness in coyish and egotistical ways. I used to be into going out with women so I could show off, but I got tired of that. Now I like to go out with someone who is interested in showing her grace rather than her charms."

Following is a statement from a twenty-seven-year-old woman who, during the year following her marital separation, dated frequently and with a wide variety of men.

"In listening to what John [the person whose descriptions are given above] had to say about dating very attractive women, I guess a similar idea applies with me, at least as far as my experience is concerned. I, too, have found that very attractive men, and especially those who *know* they are good looking, have a way of being too preoccupied and concerned with their egos. Don't get me wrong; I don't want to put down anyone who's boosting his own ego, but I find that there's a big difference between those who are attractive and those who you wouldn't necessarily consider attractive. Now, I've got to tell you, when I moved out on my own I was . . . I guess you could say . . . I was trying to find out whether I still had it or not. Well, if I saw a good-looking male, I'd find some way of getting to know him, and eventually he'd ask me out. I found that really gratifying, and in a sense it was nice to be seen with him because I wanted others to know that I still had it. But it's funny, after a while that really becomes boring. I don't know if it's their vanity, their egoism, or their conceit that gets in the way of even a casual date where you can simply talk about each other, but I've found that some of these men are too interested in showing off. I mean, this is crazy, but, at least twice that I can remember, these guys seemed to take great delight in telling me about all the other women they had gone out with, and how one had dated this beauty queen, gone out to this embassy party and had breakfast with the ambassador's daughter, ugh! Really, I'd rather be by myself when they come across that way. I'm not really down on good-looking men . . . [laugh] at least not as much as John is down on his beautiful women. I'd rather give them a chance, but, boy, I won't accept a second invitation from a guy who is only into himself . . . especially a date where the two of us are going to be alone. If there's a group of us, I don't mind that much because I can talk with other people. I don't know, now that I think about it, part of me wants to flirt with attractive men only so that it makes me feel good when they ask me out, but I always have second thoughts about what the evening is going to be like with them."

Following is a statement from a twenty-three-year-old woman who, while never having any difficulty obtaining dates, somehow never seemed satisfied with the men she dated.

"The kind of guys I like to go out with are those who are really sharp dressers, you know, nice suit and modern clothes and all that. I like guys with dark hair, not too long, but guys who are well put together, you know. They've got to have nice bodies, too—not naked, you know, but like tall and tapered with their clothes on. I like a guy who can really be strong and sure of himself. I think it's a guy's role to take the lead and to be aggressive and on top of things . . . [laugh] if you know what I mean. I like it when they're polite and open doors for you and offer you a cigarette and look after you . . . to see if you have a drink and things like that. I want the guy to be popular and the boss. Sometimes I think I've gotten pretty good at telling the kind of car a guy drives and whether it's clean or not by looking at his fingernails. If they're clean and cut, it's usually a good sign."

This person is obviously attending to external form and is not much concerned with substance or the process of interchanges between herself and her date. The kind of skills that are required to get her to agree to a date are those that have everything to do with coming across like a masculine stereotype. In discussing other possible qualities she might want to find in men, especially those characteristics that facilitate an ongoing casual relationship and that focus on verbal communication and equitable interchanges, she admitted that she wasn't too concerned about getting into that kind of relationship, at least not with those men who were to serve as dating partners. At the end of our interview, it finally came out that she preferred to be submissive and to be dominated in a relationship because she wouldn't know how to go about making a relationship equitable and wouldn't know what to say or what to talk about if her date ever wanted to pursue questions about her. She thought that maybe she might be missing out on some rewarding facets of friendships and she was prepared to try to learn. The fact that she volunteered the last comment suggests she wasn't entirely happy with her friendship habits.

Not all women prefer men who are very physically attractive. Consider the following statement from a twenty-five-year-old woman who, while preferring attractive men to date, qualified the nature of this attractiveness.

"Sure I like to go out with men who are good looking. Doesn't everyone? I don't like men who are *too* attractive, though. Well, now I don't really mean that; what I mean

89

is that I like men who are attractive but don't appear to be [laugh]. No, really, let me tell you what I mean. I don't like a man who has every hair in place. I don't like a guy with polished shoes. I really prefer the average good-looking guy, if there is such a thing. Let me describe how I see the kind of attractiveness I prefer. Okay, now it all depends on the place, but I think I'd prefer a person who is underdressed for the occasion. For example, I'd prefer a person wearing a turtleneck and jacket at a party where shirt and tie are what is being worn. In class, I'd rather see a man in jeans than one who's neatly dressed in slacks. I'd rather see a person's hair out of place than neatly combed. Really, I like to see a man who has one or two things out of place or is wearing things that don't go together than to see someone who is perfectly co-ordinated. I'd rather go with someone who makes mistakes and doesn't appear too concerned with putting himself together perfectly."

The observations from this woman are consistent with what we know is the best way for presenting a favorable image. Often, when we see people who are trying to make themselves look too good, we become skeptical, and because of this we tend to prefer people who present themselves in a more "modest" fashion. People who are superior in certain traits or personal characteristics, such as physical attractiveness or intelligence, are much better liked if they present themselves as people who are something less than medalists. And this carries over into behavior itself, since a superior person who makes a mistake is better liked than a superior person who is perfect. People who show that they are only human even when they have strong positive qualities are much better liked than those who appear to be super-human and select. But this isn't true for a person who *doesn't* have good qualities. The person who doesn't have at least one outstanding characteristic and who makes mistakes only proves that he's clumsy and inept.

Physical attractiveness can pose serious difficulties because people in groups tend to compare themselves to the others there. On college campuses, in business, factories, communities, or in any situation where people gather together for some common purpose, unnecessary frustrations and disappointments or false self-exaltation and self-esteem are likely to arise, depending simply upon the ratio of physically attractive to unattractive people in the group. Consider the severe problems encountered by a "typical female college student" whose social environment consisted of a high proportion of physically attractive women.

"One of the greatest troubles is that men here, as everywhere, I guess, are easily overwhelmed by physical beauty. Campus glamour girls have countless beaus flocking around them, whereas many friendly, sympathetic girls who want very much to be companions and, eventually, wives and mothers, but who are not physically dazzling, go without dates and male companionship. Many who could blossom and be very charming never have the opportunity. Eventually, they decide that they are unattractive and become discouraged to the point that often they will not attend no-date functions where they have their best [and perhaps only] opportunity to meet men. I will never understand why so many men [even, or maybe particularly, those who are the least personally attractive themselves] seem to think that they may degrade themselves by dating or even dancing with the girl who does not measure up to their beauty standard."

Clearly, the physical attractiveness and popularity of people around you can have a strong psychological impact and can moderate the extent to which you will be sought after and perceived as desirable. And it's impossible to escape these social comparison processes in any real and healthy way. People compare themselves with those who are immediately around them, and it seems tragic that their social self-esteem so often depends upon who happens to belong to the group. But this fact is the all-important reason behind *not* relying upon physical attractiveness for your self-esteem. Instead, develop those social and personal skills that are more immune from social comparison effects.

The person who is unsure and insecure about his social self and needs to develop his social self-esteem is better off learning the truth to the saying:

STOP COMPARING YOURSELF WITH OTHER PEOPLE. THERE WILL ALWAYS BE SOMEONE WHO IS BETTER THAN YOU.

SHY?

If your social environment is one in which it is difficult for you to be selected as a social partner, there is no point in continuing to expose yourself to this high-risk, low-social-probability situation.

FIND A SOCIAL ENVIRONMENT THAT HAS A HIGHER PROBABILITY OF LEADING TO SOCIAL CONTACT.

Some people may be unwilling to do this, not because they don't know where to look for a different social group, but because they have an attachment to "making it" with their present social clique. No matter how unfortunate this may seem, if you're not obtaining social rewards from your current social group because of too much competition or because your personal or social commodities are being out-ranked by others' status, you would do well to revise your pretensions downward slightly and find a social environment that can accommodate your personal resources. Your self-esteem and social adjustment depend on it.

Shy people more than others tend to be very susceptible to social comparison effects. Because they remain in limited social settings and tend not to have broad social experiences, the social reality presented to them by the people and places they frequent is all the more crucial to their self-evaluations. With only one social environment from which to derive social rewards, shy people invest a great deal of hope in what that social group can offer. When they place themselves in the rank of others in terms of attractiveness, intelligence, popularity, status, sociability, *etc.*, they tend to act and react as if these were absolute standards of comparison that have universal and constant application. The shy person doesn't give himself the opportunity to participate in a wide enough variety of social groups, and so he can't see that self-evaluations are based on social comparison processes and that he is wrong in making an absolute judgment about himself on the basis of any one social group.

Physically attractive people have little difficulty in getting attention. All they have to do is present themselves in public and all eyes are on them. Even after someone who had exchanged pleasantries with them leaves, they are pretty well assured that someone else will come along to go through the same ritual. Very attractive people rarely give themselves the opportunity for developing social skills, communicative skills, and those interpersonal capabilities that facilitate the formation of longer-lasting friendships. Many of them obtain too much ego gain from being the center of attention and from not expending much effort in making the first social contact. When this attitude and pattern of behavior become habit, the door opens to feelings of frustration and depression. And when physical attractiveness decreases with age and so does the amount of attention the person receives, the consequences can be severe. For many, it leads to withdrawal from social settings, social loneliness and depression. If the physically attractive person has never had to initiate interactions, the absence of practice and skill provides unstable grounds for self-confidence, and this places him or her in the same category as the shy and fearful, who are also unskilled and unsure of themselves.

Sometimes our assessment of our physical attractiveness depends on some ideal standard. Aside from grooming, cosmetics, and coordinated styles of dress, weight loss, *etc.*, there is very little that anyone can do to increase their attractiveness. Absolute standards of physical attractiveness seem to reside more in the mind and imagination of the person, and they are too often derived from movie stars, magazines, advertisements, and television, where unrealistic ideals are portrayed. Attractiveness at a church tea, in a work environment, on the beach, at a party, bar, discothèque, on the ski slopes, or in one's backyard varies with the observer and the situation. Among adolescents, only the peer group can provide recognition, approval, and acceptance, but later these components of popularity and acceptance play a less important role. Then the way a person *interacts* with another says a great deal about who he is, what he is, his traits, qualities, and his potential for supplying one kind or another of interpersonal satisfactions.

Should I Play Hard to Get?

The general intention of playing hard to get is to increase desirability. But it is a risky strategy that can have the opposite effect, and, in the long run, produce worse consequences.

A prostitute was once asked to act normally with half her customers and to play hard to get with the other half. When playing hard to get, she would say, "Just because I see you this time doesn't mean you can have my phone number or see me again. I am going to start school soon, so I won't have much free time. I'll only be able to see the people I like best." When she played hard to get, the men involved appeared to like her less and they were also less likely to call on her again in the future than when she didn't use that line.

After carefully interviewing the men who were involved in the "hard-to-get" and "easy-to-get" experience, it was found that playing hard to get often raised self-doubts in the man. The best way to guarantee that a person will not like you and not call you up again is to come across in a way that threatens him and makes him lose his self-confidence. Women who are hard to get for everyone create the impression of being cold, unfriendly, and stubborn. The women who play hard to get but who make themselves available to that one person in question create the impression that they are selective and popular, with great potential for being friendly, warm, and easygoing. So if the "hard-to-get" strategy is to be used, the person should indicate that while she is generally unavailable ("I usually don't go out with men unless I've had a chance to know them better."), she is, however, willing to make an exception to her principles for this time, for this one man.

Playing hard to get may increase the momentary appeal and perceived general attractiveness of the person, but the person who uses this strategy successfully must then exercise some social skills in order to maintain the level of perceived attractiveness. If this strategy is used among those who lack skills to maximize social rewards, eventually there can only be a letdown and a loss of interest in that person.

Have you ever played hard to get as a defensive reaction against revealing to others that you have a need for social contact? Are you worried that if you respond in positive terms to a social invitation that this will be seen as an admission of your need for new acquaintances and friendships? Be careful not to typecast yourself as aloof, uninvolved, and independent. Guard against remaining unresponsive to social overtures, because people will quickly stop asking.

Or do you sometimes play hard to get in order to cover up your shyness? This condition is much more prevalent than you might suspect. Among those who are shy, being unresponsive and playing hard to get provide an easy cover under which to hide a shyness problem. This can produce two reactions: first, it can extinguish further attempts at initiating transactions (thereby satisfying all needs in the shy to escape these situations); second, it can worsen the shyness condition when the person recognizes the role-playing and tries all the harder.

We met many shy women who had mixed feelings about being in a social group. In a social gathering such as a singles bar or discothèque, these women can normally be found standing at the bar or by some table or other fixed structure. They occasionally sit at a table but always in close proximity to a heavily trafficked area. They seem to like to be seen as available. Often, they will come in with another girl friend. They never initiate anything with a stranger. They rarely send non-verbal cues (vibes) of interest, let alone communicate that they are aware of the presence of others around them. They stare blankly at the wall or pretend to follow the image of an imaginary person walking across their field of vision. Sometimes they appear deep in thought as they gaze into a drink. The outside picture of calm and assuredness is only betrayed by an inner fear that either they would not be approached by anyone, or that a stranger would come up and ask them to dance or be brazen enough to start a conversation with them.

Someone's nearby. She senses a hand near her elbow and hears a voice saying, "Hi, did you just get here?" She turns her head and glances to see who dares to intrude into her private world. It's a man, attractive, genial. What does he want? Trying to pick me up? Ignore him. She replies with a dull and non-expressive "hi" and turns away to resume her Mount Rushmore posture, pretending to be more occupied with other matters and showing no evidence that there is a trace of his memory left in her mind.

On another occasion, depending on her mood, she'd try a different tactic. She'd turn away completely without responding but give away in her facial expression an attitude of disdain and contempt, as if to say: "Who do you think you are, anyway? I don't talk to creeps." Two or three other males may approach her, either from the side or directly, and make the same ritualistic but polite invitation for conversation. She'll treat them in the same cold way, perhaps lighting up another cigarette. Forty-five minutes and two Margueritas later she'll whisper something to her friend and they'll both get their coats and leave. Her memories of the experience will be filled with scorn and anger at the place and at the people who go there. She'll call them "jerks, hustlers on the make," and console herself with the thought that there are other places where a person can go and be treated with more respect and courtesy.

This attitude and behavior in women is not uncommon. The basic underlying cause of the disdain that is but a mask for social fear is anxiety over being in a social situation where the roles are unfamiliar and where there is the erroneous belief that everyone is looking to see how you're doing.

Being unfamiliar with customary modes of initiating transactions and of the usual forms of social relations stifles any possibility of social engagement. Some people are afraid of being talked to. They're unsure about what a response on their part will lead to. They're unsure about how to interpret the motives behind polite but appropriate remarks made in their direction. They're afraid of being used, conned, manipulated, and sucked into something that they're afraid may prove to be too embarrassing. They are shy. They are unfamiliar with the rules of this "interaction ritual" and form of social exchange.

Often, shy people have no understanding whatsoever of the fundamental methods of making new acquaintances—for example, the need for someone to initiate a conversation. It's not uncommon to find that, when seeing someone they know but may never have exchanged more than a few words with in the past, shy people immediately begin a conversation as if they were long-lost bosom buddies. The enthusiasm revealed in these interchanges communicates their sense of relief at having found someone with whom they can interact socially and thereby scotch any notion of the fact that they are alone or unsure of how to behave.

There can be a sharp contrast in the behavior and attitude of shy women according to their situation. The same man who approached them at a bar may approach them in a "safe" context, such as at work or school, and obtain a dramatically different response. We have seen this kind of "split personality" in people often enough to make the point worth mentioning again: unusual or new social contexts have the effect of elevating anxiety and fear to the point where defensive reactions, rather than genuine manifestations of interests, likes, and dislikes, predominate.

On one occasion, a male in our study group approached a young woman at a bar very politely and appropriately in the hopes of initiating a social transaction. She had clearly heard him and seen him, but instead of replying in a socially competent manner, she simply turned her back on him as if he were not there. The man, more upset at the fact that she had been rude than at being turned down, leaned over her shoulder and quietly said to her, "Excuse me, I'm sorry if I upset you. You know, if you're having difficulty coping with the scene, you'd feel less anxious if you didn't come to a place like this."

The tendency among some women who do not show any interest in a person who approaches them is occasionally derived from the belief that it will be embarrassing for them if the man should leave. This last attitude was well exemplified in one woman we came to know quite well. She would come to the singles bar at least once a week over a period of eight to nine months. Sometimes she'd make an appearance two or three times a week. She would usually come with a girl friend and they would park themselves by the side of the bar. Every now and then she'd walk around the full length of the bar and then return to her spot, never once stopping to talk to anyone. She was trying to tell others that she was there, that she was present, and that if anyone was interested they would have to approach her and speak to her. This strategy was relatively effective for her, not only because she was attractive, but also because she was known by a good number of the regulars.

The interesting thing about her, however, was that whenever a man approached her for conversation, the first five or ten seconds would seem most cordial and pleasant, but that's only how long it lasted. She took very little time to change her body orientation away from the person, to stop gazing in his direction, and she began to answer questions in as brief a manner as possible, never asking any questions in turn. She did everything possible to show a lack of interest and involvement with the other person, no matter who approached her. She seemed to be deliberately inviting rejection.

We questioned her about this some months later, asking about what kind of things she would like other people to do when she arrived at the bar. She said that she secretly wished that people would come up to her and say, "Hi! Where have you been? Haven't seen you for a long time." She said that if anyone came up to her and said this, it would mean that he had noticed her absence and that he was happy to see her again. She wished that everybody who was there would go up to her and greet her and say that they had missed her. It was evident that her primary motive focused on getting as many people as possible to notice her and that spending too much time with any one person would reduce the chances of obtaining widespread, albeit brief, attention.

There was an interesting paradox about this woman's motives and her behavior. She had a strong need to develop a good friendship and a need to have a lot of attention. She explained that she didn't want to be stuck with any one guy for more than five minutes or so, fearing that if someone else was interested in her he might be discouraged and not approach her. What was ironic was that she would be consistently left standing alone, unhappy and miserable. People did go up to her and greet her, but over a period of time they came to know her style pretty well and they quickly lost interest. We asked her whether she thought she was, perhaps, inviting the lack of attention, and that maybe it was her behavior that was responsible for her own lack of solid friendships. She was initially taken aback and quite astounded by the question. So were we when we heard her reply. She maintained that she felt she went overboard and did everything possible to establish contact and to maintain it once someone approached her. In reality, not once did we see her initiate contact with anyone, and, in fact, she did everything possible to assure that people would not be encouraged to continue conversations with her. When this was pointed out to her in a very gentle manner, she became tearful and was visibly hurt. Then she admitted to her fear of showing too much interest in one person. She was afraid she would be left standing alone, looking foolish and "taken in" when the person decided to move elsewhere. For her, it was important to appear cool, uninvolved, and not too interested in becoming attached to anyone. "That way," she said, "when people come and go and talk to you just to say hello, it doesn't look as if you were ever really interested in that person, and people won't think you're hurt."

Going to a singles bar or a discothèque is the worst place for a shy person to gain self-confidence. Self-confidence comes from two sources: the belief that you have an internal capacity to relate with skill and aplomb, and the opportunity to test your "self" out on repeated occasions. Neither of these is enhanced or even offered in the social settings of bars and discothèques. Go there and have fun, but never rely on the outcome of your efforts to indicate anything about yourself.

chapter 6

COMMUNICATING
WITHOUT WORDS

IF YOU THINK ABOUT IT, I'M SURE THERE ARE TIMES
when you feel so tense and nervous that your mind freezes
and you block completely. Anxiety can also affect action,
and when it does, the result is frozen and stilted movements and expressions.

The solution to becoming more expressive in social
situations is twofold: first, you have to become less worried and apprehensive about what people may be thinking
about you; second, you must learn the behavior appropriate to social transactions. You can easily learn to make
yourself more attractive by behaving in the way that
makes you most interesting and alive. The specific tactics
and strategies for reducing anxiety and for acquiring these
verbal and non-verbal modes of behavior will be dealt
with explicitly in the later chapers of this book, but first,
let's make sure you understand the major components of
non-verbal expressive communications.

When you talk with someone face to face, the impression you create is made up of three separate components.
First, there's the verbal component, the actual words and
the meaning of what you say. Second is the vocal com-

ponent, the stylistic way in which the words are spoken—
tone of voice, loudness, intensity, and the feeling communicated form the basis of "vibes" that are sent out.
Third are the non-verbal communications that accompany all messages.

In this chapter we'll be concerned mainly with this last,
the non-verbal aspects of your presentation. Very few
people are really aware of how much their body language
and facial expressions reveal about them. The more shy
you are, the more you need to become aware of what
you are telling someone when you stand as straight as a
board, or when you stare at the ground during a conversation. So read about what this type of communication is
all about, find out how the various illustrations apply to
you, and then set your mind to do something about changing your frozen self into a style that is more pleasing and
meaningful.

We communicate through facial expressions, which involve the mouth for smiling and grimacing, the forehead
for frowning, and the eyebrows in order to show a variety
of emotional states. The way in which we position our
bodies or generally orient ourselves toward or away from
the person with whom we are talking is another form of
body-talk. When you're conversing with someone, you can
cross your legs at the ankles or at the knees, you can
fold your arms, put your hands on your hips, or bend the
elbow and support your head on your hand; you can place
your feet up on a desk, table, or chair; you can sit up-
right in a chair with both feet firmly planted on the floor
with hands on your lap; you can lean forward, backward,
sideways, or support yourself on an armrest or the wall.
Depending on what you do and how you do it, you will
reveal a great deal about yourself, your interest, your
anxiety, your tiredness, your boredom, as well as your
like or dislike for the person.

Imagine that you're having lunch with a person of the
opposite sex whom you find attractive and would like to
get to know better. You decide to pay the person a compliment by saying, "That outfit you're wearing really looks
nice on you." While the words are proper and the manner
in which they were phrased all seem designed to communicate liking, whether or not your comment will be

understood to be a compliment will depend little on your actual words. Rather, your voice characteristics and your facial features will communicate your genuineness and your extent of the liking. In fact, your words account for only seven percent of the positiveness that is picked up by the listener. Voice characteristics such as tone, inflection, loudness, *etc.*, determine about thirty-eight percent of the positiveness, and facial characteristics, such as eye contact, smiling, and the use of eyebrows and head orientation are responsible for fifty-five percent of the impact.

Have you ever thought that maybe you're so unresponsive non-verbally that you tend to give conflicting messages? If your verbal and non-verbal messages are in conflict, the non-verbal components will override the verbal in their effect. So when you say, "I really like that outfit on you," but your eyes are staring into your plate and you're chewing on a ham and cheese sandwich, chances are the result will be a negative one. Knowing how to properly balance verbal and non-verbal messages will make you more effective in communicating what you really intend and it will make you a more interesting and rewarding person to be with.

The extent to which you maintain eye contact or gaze at people when you're interacting with them reveals a great deal about yourself. Do you look at the floor when you're talking with someone? Do you stare out the window when you're listening to what is being said? Do you tend to avoid the other person's gaze?

Your use of hands also provides non-verbal communications. What do you do with your hands when you're standing and talking with someone? Do you keep them in your pockets, behind your back, clutch your purse, fuss with your hair, or gesture with them? Do you find one place for them and leave them glued there until the episode is over?

When should you smile or frown? When should you lean forward or relax comfortably in your chair? At which point does gazing turn to staring? What do you do with your legs and feet? If you take a group of ten non-shy and socially competent people and ask them these questions, their replies might surprise you. You would find that each of them has a different "rule" as to when it is appropriate to make use of these components of non-verbal communication. You wouldn't get a satisfactory answer to your question, primarily because those who are appropriately expressive and non-shy really don't think about when, how, and where to use what non-verbal components in their communications; they just seem to do it naturally. Well, if the only thing you're doing naturally is freezing into an immovable wooden block, the first step will be to become aware of what you're *not* doing. The second will be to force movements and body-talk—even to the point of exaggeration. And the third step will involve practicing different styles in simple social contexts and then in more complex situations.

Let's look more closely at the way non-shy people use body-talk. We interviewed ten non-shy people and found each of them to use a different combination of non-verbal cues in their transactions with others. For example, one non-shy person would engage in good eye contact together with head movements and occasional smiling; another person in a similar situation would express himself primarily by hand gestures and body orientation; still another spent a disproportionate amount of time gazing at his hands or at the floor while listening to someone, but he balanced out this introverted behavior by nodding his head and at the same time uttering an occasional "uh-huh" throughout the course of the conversation. While all these non-shy people differ in the way in which they use non-verbal cues, they are all the same in one major respect: they all feel free to be themselves. And whatever combination of non-verbal cues they end up using, they communicate that they are at ease, relaxed, self-confident, and assured.

But don't be misled. There is rarely a conscious effort on the part of non-shy people to use body language to purposefully manage the impression they create. Remember that every attempt at "impression management" is just another indication of the fear of being yourself. In most social situations, non-shy people are simply not consciously aware of the discrete and separate components of their combined non-verbal behavior. For them it simply comes out naturally, and the general rule seems to be a tendency to *balance out* all of the components that go into a particular display.

What do we reveal by the distance we establish between ourselves and another person? How close should we get to someone? If you stand from 0 to 1 1/2 feet from the other person, you're revealing a degree of intimate liking for him or her; 1 1/2 to 4 feet assumes a personal relationship; 4 to 12 feet signifies a social relationship; and if you stand more than 12 feet away, you are probably engaged in some sort of lecture or in public affairs. It should be noted that these principles hold true in North America and would surely be much less relevant for social relations in Europe or other parts of the world.

The more you touch another person, the more you disclose a liking for that person. The more eye contact you have, the more you behave like two people who really like each other. Leaning forward toward the person means you have some liking for him or her, and a body orientation facing the person also gives evidence of liking for him or her. Can you imagine the impact it would have if you combined all four elements into one demonstration? In most social encounters it's best to pick out one element to display and to go very easy on the other three. This balancing-out should give you the intensity you want.

Most non-shy and appropriately expressive people know these general principles. They know how to behave not because they have been formally instructed in these mechanics and general principles, but more because they have had a wide variety of social experiences in which they've been able to watch others act in various ways, and from these they have adopted what they consider to be the most appropriate and most suitable behaviors. If you haven't had a representative sample of social experiences from which to draw appropriate models, then you will have to be instructed into how to behave.

How are you to make use of the non-verbal cues listed above? The least threatening non-verbal element ought to serve as the first vehicle for communicating liking and interest. After successful interchanges, you should then consider moving to the next least threatening non-verbal sign. Distance from another person is the least threatening component. Since getting closer than 1 1/2 feet presumes an intimate distance, it should not be done in an initial meeting. Distances from 1 1/2 to 4 feet reflect a personal distance that again implies a degree of familiarity that may be unwarranted at a first meeting. Four to 12 feet would appear to be the appropriate distance from which to begin a social transaction.

A body orientation facing the other person and eye contact would rank together in the category of second least threatening non-verbal vibes. However, in order to maintain the underlying rule of balancing-out, it's wise to use only one of these at a time unless you want to risk transmitting with double-barreled force. Leaning forward is the next most direct way of communicating interest and liking, while the non-verbal message that ranks as the most direct way of telling a person that you have strong positive feelings toward them is touching.

We also evaluate people on the basis of voice characteristics. The sound of flatness in the voice often signifies a person who is sluggish and cold. Nasal qualities in the voice are undesirable. Men who speak with a tense voice tell others that they are unyielding and cantankerous, and tenseness in women is associated with immaturity, emotionality, and nervousness. People who speak quickly in the course of general conversation convey that they are animated and extroverted, but people who speak quickly when asking for a favor, asking for a date, or when expressing compliments or speaking on a personal basis are evaluated less positively.

Speech disturbances such as repeating the same word twice, stuttering, omitting part of the word, not completing sentences, slips of the tongue, *etc.*, are seen as signs of nervousness and anxiety, and they are seen as unfavorable qualities in the speaker. When the voice is confident, the person reveals that he is enthusiastic, forceful, active, competent, dominant, and self-assured.

The amount of emotion communicated in the voice is usually very easy to pick up. The emotions of anger, fear, happiness, jealousy, love, nervousness, pride, sadness, satisfaction, and sympathy can be judged on the basis of tone of voice alone. People who are good at conveying emotions in their speech are also very adept at judging the emotions of others. But if you're shy, inhibited, and non-expressive and don't convey much emotion in your own voice, you will probably have more difficulty assessing the emotions in the speech of others. It's as if: "If your vibes transmitter isn't working, your receiver isn't, either." This is an important thing to note since the implications can be significant, especially when you realize that a lot of the successful conversations operate on the basis of picking up and sending these vibes. So it's essential to learn how to transmit these if you want to pick them up correctly.

A calm voice usually has a smaller range of inflection. It is more consistent in rate and is generally lower in volume and tone than the excited voice. People who speak in an objective and calm manner are seen as more trustworthy and likable than those who speak in an emotional manner. Also, "objective" speakers are seen as better educated, more honest, and more people-oriented then emotional speakers. Emotional speakers create the impression of being tough-minded, certain, and dogmatic.

It is the social context more than anything else that decides how appropriate it is for you to be calm or animated. If you are out having dinner with a person of the opposite sex and you want to be seen as trustworthy and likable, then a calm voice with a small range of inflection and consistent rate of speech and volume will do more to giving that impression. Eye contact and facial expressions will do the rest. However, if you find yourself at a social gathering with large groups of people around you, speaking in this objective and calm manner will very quickly result in a less favorable evaluation. Let the social context guide you in deciding what voice qualities you should use. And don't be afraid to act on your judgment.

The amount of talking you do in the course of a normal conversation leads to different impressions. Both men and women evaluate a person as warm, friendly, intelligent, and outgoing if he talks about sixty to eighty percent of the time in the course of a conversation. Males and females who speak less than twenty percent of the time are thought to be cold, unfriendly, unintelligent, and introverted. Again, amount of "talk time" has to be balanced out with non-verbal messages in such a way that you don't dominate the conversation, but rather use non-verbal talk such as head nods, eye contact, and body orientation to signal that you understand, you appreciate, you're surprised, *etc.* If someone is telling a long story, it's still important that you stay in the picture and stay involved in the social episode. You can keep your "talk time" up to normal levels by using non-verbal messages such as head nods and eye contact, with the occasional interjection of such fillers as "I see," or "uh-huh," or "hmm," or "Is that right!?" combined carefully and varied with other body-talk messages.

How often you make eye contact with someone will create various impressions. If a social context is friendly and relaxed, gazing at someone conveys a message of liking and positive feeling. In conversations where you're talking about some interesting event, you should of course establish and maintain eye contact with the person listening, and if the listener leans forward and gazes a lot while you're telling your story, you're going to like him more than if he didn't look at you very much. But if what you're saying has a chance of being interpreted negatively, then you should consider not gazing at your listener, or this will result in less liking of you. On the other hand, the listener will like you much more if you do look at him when you're making a positive personal evaluation of him. A good rule to keep in mind is that if the statements you're making are evaluative in nature, and if the evaluation is general, a most favorable impression results by looking often at the person. If a personal evaluation is what you're going to make and you're not quite sure if it's going to be taken favorably, you're better off keeping eye contact.

The length of time (as opposed to how often) you spend looking at someone when talking to him or her reveals a great deal about how genuine you are. When a person tells a lie, he generally looks at the person for shorter periods of time than when he tells the truth. If you want to be believed and are trying to be persuasive, then look steadily at the person who's listening. A rule of thumb here is: looking steadily at someone serves to accentuate whatever feelings are present in that particular situation. In a pleasant social interchange, the pleasantness is increased by gazing; in an unpleasant encounter gazing serves to increase feelings of discomfort.

We've already said that the face and the various expressions it can hold is a major source of non-verbal vibes. How, then, can you learn to manage facial expressions in such a way that you communicate exactly what you want? If you're like most shy people, then you hide the expression in your face. You may do this not only because you're not in the habit of being expressive, but because of the anxiety and stress you wish to conceal. But a shy person really doesn't succeed at this. Often he can't maintain the stone-faced silence for very long before he starts to blush. Or other vibes, such as the lack of eye contact, inappropriate positioning of the body, or the head in a direction away from the person will give away his embarrassment, timidity, and nervousness. When a person tries to conceal his emotional state by neutralizing the facial expression, he usually does one of two things: 1). relax the facial muscles, inhibiting any muscular contraction; or 2). freeze the facial muscles into a nonemotional poker face, setting the jaw, tightening but not pressing the lips, and staring but not tensing the eyelids.

Neutralizing emotions in this way is very hard, especially if the social experience is strongly emotional. When trying to neutralize strong emotions, you can look so wooden and tense that you immediately give away the fact that you're trying to falsify, even if the actual emotion is not directly revealed. So make up your mind that you're better off *expressing* your emotions. Not only will you be a much more interesting person to be with, but you'll also start to feel more comfortable about being the "real" self you should be in a social situation.

A smile is a beautiful thing. It's a beam of warm sunshine that breaks through a chaotic social atmosphere. A smile is used to express happiness, pleasure, joy, understanding, or stability. Smiling tells the person that you're still in control and that you're not going to get carried away by anything that's said. I don't want you to think I'm overdramatizing the importance and significance of smiling, but I'd like you to consider it as carrying the greatest non-verbal potential for making someone happy. A smile is a gift that you give, and everyone has an appetite for it. But be careful! If you go around with a grin constantly on your face, people will think either you woke up with a coat hanger in your mouth or there is something just not quite genuine about you.

Smiling at someone only once or twice during a social encounter with brightened eyes looking directly at the person will do more for your social image than any series of carefully contrived phrases of affection or positive regard.

In addition to smiling, you can modulate your facial expression in a number of ways. You can adjust the intensity of the expression to show either more or less of what you feel by: 1). increasing or decreasing the number of facial areas involved (eyes, eyebrows, forehead muscles, mouth, and lips; 2). varying the duration in which the expression is held; 3). by increasing or decreasing the strength of the muscles that are pulled.

When Do I Use What, Where, and with Whom?

Aha! If only we had the blueprint, that map that would tell us where to navigate in uncharted social encounters. But, unfortunately, the study of social behavior has not advanced to that point. In fact, the odds are very high against ever being able to specify precisely what you ought to do, with whom, and under what circumstances if you want to be sure of the effect you have on a person. There are simply too many contexts, too many different kinds of people with different histories, and too many different kinds of verbal and non-verbal combinations of cues that can be delivered to put all of these into one gigantic equation. And even if an equation could be developed, it would be so complex that it would be virtually impossible to memorize.

Consider books of etiquette, for example. Volumes upon volumes have been written and are being continually revised in order to record what is socially appropriate or polite behavior, but no one can ever have each and every one of these fresh and ready to use. Or consider the laws that civilized communities have adopted to govern the behavior of their citizens. Law books are so complex that even the best judge or lawyer can recall only a small percentage of the law as it applies in a particular situation. Fortunately, lawyers and judges can refer to textbooks, legal precedence, and other material before passing judgment concerning violations.

But in social transactions, specific rules don't apply, and even if they did, they would be of little use, since the moment-to-moment decisions you have to make in a social situation don't allow you much time to search out your mental index to see where the rule might be found. All we have are broad guidelines concerning the effect your general behavior has in certain situations, and it's up to you to apply these guidelines, monitor the social outcome, and then alter the specific elements as they apply to the context.

How can you become socially competent and appropriately expressive and rid yourself of your social shyness? What rules are you to apply? What strategies should you adopt? First, you have to understand that even the most socially competent, non-shy person is only "successful" in social transactions about eighty percent of the time. This means, of course, that no matter how competent you are in applying your social skills in situations, at least twenty percent of the time you will feel somewhat less than perfectly satisfied with the outcome. But the crucial issue is how you understand the reasons for the failure experience. Attributing the failure to some personal inadequacy will only discourage you from trying again. It may leave a negative impact on your sense of self-esteem. On the other hand, if you attribute the failure to the fact that you didn't try hard enough to properly assess and evaluate, you may continue to challenge your social environment and success will be more easily attained.

Now, let's consider first encounters. In such meetings, it is both inappropriate and unwise to display strong feelings. It's just not the custom to communicate large amounts of liking or intense feelings on the basis of a first series of brief exchanges, and often the fact that something is not the norm is enough to make it socially inappropriate. So suppose you communicate your liking verbally, such as in the statement, "You know, you're a nice person to be with. You make me feel comfortable and at ease." If your tone of voice is soft and full of feeling, and if you are standing very close, looking into the other person's eyes, the person will pick up intense liking. And if it's a first meeting, chances are you'll be seen as weird, or, at best, as a person with strange, if not peculiar, ways of relating—just because of overloaded nonverbal messages.

Initial encounters or those that involve brief and periodic exchanges develop more smoothly when they follow the "reciprocity norm." This norm specifies that there should be an equal amount of give and take in communication of liking, preferences, and in the disclosing of feelings. The example given above shows too much self-disclosure at a time when the relationship is not ready to sustain such information. People who tell too much too soon make it embarrassing and uncomfortable for others. Discomfort is caused not only because the other person might not know how to cope with intense feelings, but because expectations are that the liking be reciprocated. The person receiving an excess of self-disclosure comes to resent your having communicated this way, and what was intended to be a friendly compliment designed to communicate attraction and positive evaluation may unfortunately turn out to be an unhappy and unpleasant exchange.

You should know, too, that if you fail to be expressive either verbally or non-verbally and remain like a mummy throughout the course of a social episode, you will be quickly labeled shy, timid, and inhibited. Similarly, if you overreact and communicate too much with your hands, body, face, and tone of voice you may be stigmatized as immature and possibly hysterical.

How can you avoid both, over-communicating and under-communicating? The solution rests with the principle of balancing-out. The non-shy person has a knack for balancing out verbal and non-verbal messages in a very natural manner, without thinking. For example, to communicate a certain amount of liking, the non-shy person might move closer, but at the same time you would lower your eyes. Or in carrying on a friendly conversation with someone of the opposite sex, he or she might gently touch that person's elbow or arm, while changing body position away from the person or taking a step backward. This mixing or balancing out of the verbal and non-verbal components of communication allows for variety and expressiveness and guards against coming across too strongly. To be socially skilled means that you not only know how to balance out these cues, but you also know how to mix each in various combinations, depending on the situation and the person involved.

Here are two examples of the appropriate use of verbal

and non-verbal communication in two different circumstances. Imagine that you're walking down the corridor and you see a friend approaching. You are headed in opposite directions and both of you have destinations you are in a hurry to get to. Chances are you're going to pause only momentarily and say hello in a conversation that will last no longer than five seconds. This is the time needed to exchange rituals and formalities, such as: "Hi! How are you? Haven't seen you in a long time. How are you doing? See you later." So you will most likely want to capitalize upon non-verbal cues to communicate interest, surprise, liking, and other positive states in relative abundance. But now suppose that you're sitting down having coffee with a friend and you expect to be together for fifteen or twenty minutes. Then your use of non-verbal cues will be moderated by virtue of the amount of time you'll be spending together. In this situation, the occasional use of one or more non-verbal cues properly mixed, but never too intense, would be best.

The socially skilled person can clearly assess the nature of the social interchange within a matter of seconds. He will unconsciously ask himself: Is this a formal gathering of people? Is it a casual meeting of old friends? How long has it been since I've seen this person last? How long will our conversation last? Once these questions are answered, the non-shy person will know what social behavior is appropriate. He will not only balance out his verbal and non-verbal cues, but he will mix these in what seems to be a random order over the course of transactions. Only a person free from anxiety and worry can fully participate in this way.

Begin to learn social skills by doing the following learning tasks:

1). Become aware of the wide variety of verbal and non-verbal ways of communicating.
2). Practice each and every one of these verbal and non-verbal manners.
3). Over-learn by over-practicing and over-rehearsing various combinations of social responding.
4). Overcome undue worry and anxiety about being

evaluated by applying rational and productive beliefs.
5). Use these non-verbal and verbal reactions in real
social contexts and monitor the reaction you get.

chapter 7

GETTING YOUR
ACT TOGETHER

DEVELOPING VERBAL SKILLS IS IMPORTANT, BUT, AGAIN, what you say and how you say it depends upon the context, the person spoken to, and which phase of an interaction you are into. Interactions can be broken down into three phases: greeting, conversing, and leave-taking. They can be of two kinds: brief, or extended in time. The verbal skills for meeting someone for the first time or for greeting a friend the first time during the day all involve minimal verbal fluency. This first phase places few demands on mental capacity and verbal ability, and it generally involves only ritual forms of exchange. Even someone with very poor verbal fluency or communication skills can easily and smoothly execute greeting, conversing, and leave-taking in brief encounters.

What makes such initial verbal transactions at greeting and leave-taking smooth and natural is the combination of verbal and non-verbal skills used. Let's consider some of the verbal components of greetings, as if there were no non-verbal elements accompanying them. Here are a few illustrations:

1). "Hello." [Sometimes this one word will suffice.]
2). "Hi!" [This is slightly different, implying greater informality.]
3). "Hi! How are you doing?" [This is very casual and informal.]

In more formal circumstances, the verbal content can change slightly such as:

1). "How do you do?"
2). "Hello, good to meet you."
3). "Pleased to make your acquaintance."

In most cases, ritual introductions such as "How do you do?" do not require a reply that really answers the question. The more ritual reply is a similar "How do you do?" or, simply, "And you?"

Informal greetings such as those that take place among acquaintances and casual friends use similar rituals of greeting; however, depending on the length of the conversation, the replies to the question "Hi! How are you?" can vary. In cases in which no more than perhaps thirty seconds will elapse, the following kinds of replies are appropriate:

1). "Fine! How are you doing?"
2). "Not bad. And you?"
3). "Pretty good. How are you doing?"
4). "A little tired after the weekend, but okay. And you?" [This is used in cases in which there is an anticipated further interchange.]
5). "Great! I'm really looking forward to tonight! [Again, this is used with the possibility of further interchanges.]
6). "Fine! Working hard?" [Expect a reply.]
7). "Pretty good! Haven't seen you for a while."

Sometimes greetings are very brief, as in the case when two people are passing each other going in opposite directions. These can be foreseen far in advance by noting how quickly the person is traveling in your direction, whether he seems preoccupied with something, or if he's walking with someone. On these occasions, it may be inappropriate to invite the person into a transaction that is going to last more than a few seconds. Occasionally, two people may approach each other at an angle and then head off in a similar direction, causing the interchange to extend from what would have been a brief five-second greeting into something that may turn into a thirty- or sixty-second social episode. At work, school, or other settings where socializing is not the primary goal, people may, upon meeting and exchanging ritualized forms of recognition, realize that the transaction is going to be prolonged for a while longer as they are heading in the same direction, *i.e.*, toward the elevator, washroom, exit, coffee machine, *etc*. Here, neither may be interested in engaging one another in a conversation at a level other than simply extending the ritual greeting and exchange. In such cases, the initial greeting of "Hi! How are you?" is prolonged either by *slowing down* the verbal exchange or by pausing before replying. This has the effect of filling in the time spent together. Another tactic includes ritual forms of exchange on such topics as the weather, sports, current events, or other noninvolving and lightly engaging topics. For example:

1). "Isn't this great weather we're having?" [You have to expect this to be followed by: "Yes. Let's hope it keeps up", or some other ritual reply.]
2). "Boy, I sure hope this weather changes soon." [This could be followed by: "You're right. It really gets depressing when it's like this."]
3). "How's the golf game coming along?"
4). "Well, getting ready for your vacation?"
5). "Got all your Christmas shopping done?"
6). "Did you watch the game on television last night?"
7). "Boy, I'll be glad when this week is over."
8). "How's the work coming along?" [Expect a reply related to the question; however, don't pursue the remark in the hopes of communicating interest by a follow-up question that would delve into specifics.]

9). "Say, I haven't seen you wear that tie before. Is it new?"

All of these are extended ritual interchanges that don't engage the person into conversational lines that make it difficult to terminate the conversation once both are ready to go their own ways. You should be careful about what you are saying to whom in these extended ritual interchanges. It may be all right for the boss of a firm to greet the elevator operator by saying, "Good morning, Joe!"

This would usually be followed by, "Good morning, sir. Beautiful day, isn't it?"

The initiative to pursue the extended ritual is usually left up to the person who is formally dominant in the relationship, and in this case the boss may ask, "How are the wife and kids, Joe?" This kind of question is a "filler" until the elevator reaches the office floor. It is also a personal question and is reserved for those interaction rituals in which "superior-subordinate" or "dominant-submissive" roles are the postural norms usually assumed. On the other hand, it would be inappropriate for the elevator operator to ask the boss a question about his wife and kids.

Terminating conversations and taking leave also involve ritual verbal exchanges. Again, the exact words used depend upon the person spoken to, the context, and possibly the length of the conversation that has just preceded. So, following a brief exchange in the corridor or on the street with a friend, or during an elevator ride, standard leave-taking expressions such as the following are appropriate ritualized forms of exchange:

1). "Bye. See you later."
2). "See you." Or, "See you around."
3). "Catch you later."
4). "Well, be seeing you."

But before making these leave-taking statements, there are a number of rituals that involve smoothly closing off a conversation. These are crucial preparatory messages that inform the other person that you are about to make a finishing statement and leave. You don't want to make a sudden exit and leave the person dangling in the middle of a sentence or leave unresolved issues in the conversation. You have to wait for an appropriate moment when the other person has finished talking before interjecting preparatory leave-taking statements. Sometimes the person may be so engrossed in explaining a point that it's hard to find any opportunity to step in, but these moments can be handled well by waiting.

Preparatory communications prior to saying good-bye are of the following kind:

1). "Well, I think I had better be going."
2). "Well, there are some things I think I'd better get to."
3). "Well, we should talk about this again later."
4). "Well, you'll have to excuse me."
5). "Okay, gotta get going."
6). "Okay, nice talking with you."
7). "Nice to see you again."

All of the preceding are preparatory communications designed to help in facilitating a smooth exit. Without this ritual of smoothly timing our departure, exits could be awkward or even rude. One of the most important reasons for these rituals is to prevent the other person from infering that you are bored with the conversation, that you found him dull, or that you don't like him.

These ritualized statements are not difficult to learn and memorize. Perhaps you simply don't know about these ritual forms of exchange or that they have very little meaning, except to smooth out greetings and leavings. You shouldn't get hung up on exactly what you should say in greeting someone or on what is being said to you in greeting. The more of these verbal ritual statements you have available to deliver in various social contexts, the easier it is to feel comfortable about entering and leaving interactions when you want to. These verbal rituals, however, can't stand by themselves. They have to be accompanied by non-verbal communications if they are to be truly effective.

Perhaps you have trouble with these rituals because of one of the following reasons: 1). you fail to establish or maintain eye contact for even a brief period of time;

2). you are usually not loud enough in your verbal exchanges, or your tone of voice doesn't indicate that you understand or acknowledge what is being said; 3). the expression on your face is usually one of restraint and apprehension, and you don't smile, so you don't communicate how pleased you are to see the other person; 4). you maintain eye contact for an extremely brief moment and then quickly look down before the other person has a chance to reply.

In European countries, it is traditional to exchange greetings even after an absence of twenty-four hours with kisses on each cheek; unfortunately, this custom is not fashionable in North America. In more formal introductions, we shake hands. To become socially adept at this, glance quickly at the person to see whether he or she is encumbered by a bag, purse, cigarettes, or other items that would make hand-shaking difficult. If your handshake resembles a limp rag, you communicate passivity and timidity, while a handshake that holds the other like a machine making a milkshake suggests boldness and aggressiveness. Your handshake should be firm enough to help direct the movement of the hand up and down, but not controlling. Think for a second about what other non-verbal messages you could make use of if you wanted to appear assertive and confident. How would you use eye contact, facial expressions, body orientation, distance, or leaning in modulating the effect you want? How would you use the same non-verbal cues if you were being introduced to a shy person and you didn't want to embarrass him or come on too strong? Think about it for a second.

What did you imagine? In order to appear assertive and confident, did you think about looking longer at the person while shaking hands? Did you consider facing the person squarely? How about greeting the shy person? What would be the effect if you didn't gaze as long, if you spoke softer (leaning forward, of course, to balance the loss of volume)? How about presenting a facial expression that is kind and gentle? If you're like most people who are learning to use non-verbal cues in a coordinated and balanced fashion, then you probably thought of reducing or changing only *one* non-verbal component. Don't be satisfied with this. Alter and modulate two, three, or four together. The picture you present then will be more what you intend.

Let's consider the non-verbal cues necessary in terminating a conversation. The best way to indicate that you're about to make preparatory statements is by providing a sudden *change* in either the topic of conversation, rate of exchange, loudness of voice, body orientation, gazing, or, perhaps, getting ready to stand up if you're seated. If you're standing, turn your body away from the person and briefly glance in another direction for a moment. These are sufficient non-verbal cues to prepare the other for a leave-taking ritual. The change in posture and/or tone of voice will be enough to draw the person's attention to the fact that something different is about to happen.

Verbal and non-verbal cues have to be timed and co-ordinated. In turning your body away from the person, you would *at the same time* say something such as, "Well, I think I should get going," and the timing of such a remark should occur at a point where the other has finished a sentence. What people respond to is *change:* change in posture, body orientation, tone of voice, or facial expression. Seeing this change is enough to get the person to reply with similar non-verbal cues or to take the lead himself in terminating the conversation.

While greeting and leave-taking involve ritual forms of exchange, maintaining a conversation involves slightly different processes. The problem of how to maintain a conversation may be one of your biggest worries and concerns. In fact, you may be reluctant to initiate a conversation, not because that portion of a transaction is difficult, but because you simply don't know what to say (or how to say it) once you have someone's attention.

Most shy people prefer stable, predictable, and structured situations to unstructured ones. Structured situations are role-specific, such as talking to your secretary or to your boss, or talking to a waitress, or to a teacher. In these structured situations there are certain rules (or roles) that are followed. As a waiter, you behave like a waiter; as a subordinate, you behave like one and follow certain role-prescribed guidelines. A teacher who is shy may prefer to relate to his students in the classroom rather than outside, where the roles may not apply. The problem is, however, that in *casual* social relations there is often very little structure, role adoption, or specific rules to follow. And usually it is in casual social encounters that your shyness sticks out like a sore thumb.

What do you say after you say hello? Can you get along by memorizing two or three pat questions that you can ask of another person in the hopes that you can maintain the conversation? Some shy people think so. In applying this rule, however, do you find that you throw out questions so fast that the other person doesn't know if you're cross-examining him or if you are on the run? How do you reply to a question that is asked of you? Do you have trouble staying calm when the attention focuses on you?

In one-to-one situations like dating, conversation can be a major problem. The reasons for this are simple. First of all, the ability to keep a conversation going has to do with being able to bring up related topics or to momentarily go off on a tangent and then to come back once more to the main track, and this "agility" requires a certain freedom in thinking and associating. If you are anxious and your mental faculties are frozen by your own self-preoccupation, then this will not be easy. Wouldn't it be nice to be able to volunteer information freely about yourself, to talk about your interests, your past, what you've done, and what you plan to do without getting nervous and feeling self-conscious? When you talk about yourself, you are the center not only of the other person's attention, but of your own. If you have enough of a problem with self-consciousness when you're asked questions about yourself, volunteering information about yourself will probably seem like jumping from the frying pan into the line of fire. But this doesn't have to be so!

Some people use the tactic of preparing a series of questions to ask. This has the net affect of not only filling the embarrassing silences, but it also serves to direct attention away from themselves. The problem with this, however, is that the other person ends up by doing most of the talking, and, unless you're with someone who likes to talk about himself, the social episode may become inequitable, burdensome, and eventually unrewarding for the other person. Here are some questions that are specific, yet broad enough to let the conversation continue and remain two-way.

SHY?

1). "Are you originally from the city?"
2). "Where do you work [study, live]?"
3). "Do you like dancing, swimming [other sports or leisure activities]?"
4). "How long do you plan to stay at this job?"
5). "Where do you plan to go after you are through here?"
6). "What did you do last summer?"
7). "Where are you going on your vacation?"

In replying to a specific question, the person often offers "free information" about himself. This free information can serve as the basis for subsequent topics of conversation and suggests follow-up questions that you can ask. By listening for this free information and pursuing even tangentially related lines of thought, a smooth and even conversational flow will result. Don't be like many shy people who are so preoccupied with what is going to happen next that they don't notice the free information being given out.

Don't be so intent on waiting for the person to finish his sentence so that you can leap into the three-second void with your rehearsed question that you miss more natural topics. Spend time listening to the wealth of information being disclosed and offer interesting points, thoughts, or feelings that these evoke in you.

Free Association

You have a natural mental ability that requires little conscious rehearsal or special training, and yet it can make for the cornerstone of many smooth and unpressured verbal exchanges. I am referring to free association, the ability to follow lines of thought and to answer or solicit information that is relevant to the main theme of the conversation. Think of a tree with limbs and branches leading out from the trunk, with smaller branches and twigs stemming from these. Now consider these branches as extensions and ideas that spring from the major source of the content, and you will see that these associations are all linked to the theme originally expressed.

Socially skilled people pursue lines of conversation that

flow directly from these associations, and they do so without concern about ever returning to the main subject. Being mentally relaxed allows them to free-associate, even while they are listening to what is being said and communicating non-verbally by nodding, smiling, and maybe an occasional "uh-huh." But if you are anxious and nervous, your fear will stifle mental faculties, making it difficult to remember, to plan, and to free-associate. Anxiety prevents people from smoothly carrying out verbal interchanges and from discharging an appropriate combination of non-verbal messages. Even people who have the verbal and social skills to keep a conversation going won't be able to use their faculties if they become anxious for one reason or another.

General Talk

Offering an opinion or making a statement about what you believe can be a little difficult at first. This is especially true if you aren't accustomed to asserting an opinion for fear that it will be challenged, or that you will look foolish or appear unintelligent. But there are ways of expressing an opinion by making statements that seem less dogmatic. Instead of saying, "I know that the movie is a good one," you can say, "I've heard that movie is a good one," or, "Some people think that . . . ," or, "I don't know, but I expect that. . . ." Prefacing statements in this way guarantees that your opinion will be considered a public opinion and not a strong personal belief. As you become more comfortable expressing opinions of this kind, you can begin to use more assertive and affirmative statements of belief that would begin with, "My views are . . . ," or, "I personally feel that . . . ," or, "I don't know what you think about this, but when *I* look at it I find that. . . ." Mixing statements of opinion and information and asking a question at the end is a successful strategy for keeping a conversation going, as well as for making it equitable and interesting for both you and the other person.

The verbal skills for keeping a conversation going can be broken down into three specific categories: minimal encourages, open-ended questions, and stating parallel experiences. Let's look at each of these and consider what value each can have for you.

Minimal encourages are usually in the form of a word, exclamation of feeling, or a short phrase that indicates interest, surprise, amazement, or a simple acknowledgment and reflection of what has been heard. Tone of voice and facial expressions are used to modulate the intensity of what is communicated. For example:

1). "Uh-huh!"
2). "No kidding!"
3). "Hmm."
4). "Wow!"
5). "Did you really?"
6). "How about *that!*"
7). "That must have been good."
8). "Sounds like you really had a good time."
9). "That must have been something else!"
10). "That's wild! Sounds like you had a lot of fun."

The non-verbal (vocal and facial) cues can be varied to communicate interest and involvement in what the person is saying. Words or phrases can prompt him to continue. When used effectively, minimal encourages not only help maintain a conversation, but they also serve to make the act of storytelling or recounting more rewarding and pleasurable for the speaker.

Open-ended questions are designed to persuade the speaker to elaborate on some point or topic. These questions cannot be answered by a simple "yes" or "no" or in single words. Open-ended questions have to have some bearing on what was just said by the speaker. To illustrate, imagine the following open-ended questions in the context of an on-going conversation:

1). "Do you get a chance to travel much?" [as opposed to: "Have you ever been to Florida?"]
2). "What's it like living on the west side?" [as opposed to: "Do you like living on the west side?"]
3). "What kinds of restaurants do you like to go to?" [as opposed to: "Do you like Chinese food?"]
4). "That's a nice car you've got. What's it like to drive?" [as opposed to: "Does it corner well?"]

5). "I've never been there myself. What's it like?" [as opposed to: "Is it warm?"]

Parallel experiences are more difficult for shy people. Describing a situation or personal event that resembles something just said involves some disclosure and talking about yourself. It means maybe having to "shine," maybe having to be the focus of attention, or maybe being asked other questions about the experience. Don't be preoccupied with the fear of being embarrassed or shamed or thought silly or foolish. Stop thinking that your experiences don't count, that you're insignificant, or that you're going to be so boring that no one wants to hear your story. In fact, quite the reverse is true. In relating parallel experiences, you are confirming to the other person the authenticity and validity of his or her own story. Making your story less dramatic may be necessary in order not to steal away from the uniqueness of the other's, and playing down some of your own elements is another useful tactic that brings the other's experience into bolder relief.

Compliments vs. Flattery

Paying compliments, giving positive feedback, and even flattery are all tactics that are effective in getting someone to like you and in making social exchanges rewarding. For example, all of the following statements serve to increase liking: "I really like the way you do your hair," or, "That's a really nice necklace you have," or, "I like your taste in cars. Have you been driving that one long?" Other traditional positive feedback methods include nonverbal messages, such as nodding, eye contact, leaning forward, body orientation toward the person, and verbal habit sequences, such as, "I see," or, "Yes, I know what you mean." All are forms of feedback that communicate that you have heard, that you understand, that you're interested, and that you agree with whatever has been said. You have to learn to give out these verbal and non-verbal habit sequences and, of course, to contribute to what should be positive, pleasant, and rewarding exchanges.

Flattery, now, is another matter. Flattery means bestowing overgenerous praise and is used primarily to obtain benefits or goods rather than to make you more attractive or liked. What we call "ingratiation" has to do with strategies that are specifically designed to make yourself more attractive and liked. "Praise" involves positive personal evaluations, and when given freely and sincerely, praise serves to increase liking.

But when praise and compliments come across as flattery, there is the unpleasant suspicion that an ulterior motive is hidden in the statement. How can you give compliments and deliver positive evaluations without misleading the other person into thinking that you want something? How can you sound more credible? How can you appear more sincere?

A number of verbal strategies can be used to increase the chances that a positive evaluation will be well received.

1). If the listener has the impression that you're discriminating or discerning and that you don't give compliments to just anybody, your message will be more believable and credible. Then, if you can create the impression that the compliment applies *uniquely* to that person and not to just anyone, chances are your statement will be well received. For example, perhaps you want to compliment a friend on how she looks or how cheerful she is. You can say, "You know something, Helen? I've been thinking, out of all the people in the office here, you seem to be the one who always dresses the nicest. It's really nice to see you every day. It really cheers this place up." Or you might remark, "Mary, there's something I really like about you. Unlike most other people around here, you have a way of being cheerful and of making people around you really happy all the time. That's really nice."

2). If you're giving a positive evaluation and the person senses an ulterior motive, he will, of course, like you *less* than if the ulterior motive is not suspected. One way of minimizing this suspicion is to have the compliment or positive evaluation delivered by an uninvolved third party, such as a friend who says, "By the way, Mary, did you know that John was really impressed by the way you handled yourself in class yesterday? He thinks you can fend for yourself pretty well." So, to set it up, you can approach Joan, Mary's best friend, and tell her what you think of Mary's performance in class. While this will do very little for getting Joan to like you, the chances are high that Joan will pass the information on to Mary. Another technique is to ensure that the compliment directed to someone is "inadvertently" overheard by the person. This is usually done in the context of a small group of people where the remarks are addressed to someone else and the target person is close by.

3). Mixing a few neutral or mildly negative evaluations with the compliment is another way of amplifying the effect of liking. The important thing, however, is to discover the relatively minor attributes of the person that are to serve as the focus for the negative evaluation. For example, "Hey, John, I've been meaning to tell you, I really like that suit on you. I'm not too crazy about the tie, but that suit really looks sharp." Or, "Thanks for lending me those notes, Bill. They were really helpful. All the stuff I needed was in there. I had trouble making out your handwriting . . . you should work on that [laugh or smile] . . . but, boy, you sure put a lot of work on those notes, and the stuff you had in there was great."

4). Another way of making yourself more liked is to show that there is some similarity or shared component between you and the other person. Try making comments such as: "You're right, I feel the same way," or, "You know, that's funny, I had the same problems with that, too," or, "Well, you know, I'm from out of town too, and, like you, I've only been here for three months," or, "That's the way I do it, too. I do exactly the same thing in those situations."

5). You can get a person to like you more if you can show you agree with the opinions he expresses. Still, there is always the possibility that ulterior motives will be inferred. One way to escape this possibility is to initially *disagree* with the opinion expressed and then to slowly come around and finally state that you now agree.

6). A person will find greater affinity and liking for you if you can be the first to express opinions on issues you know are those that are held by that person. Again, to reduce the suspicion of ulterior motives, you have to be able to show that you were never in the position to know how that person stood on a particular issue.

Talking About Yourself

Whenever you open your mouth to speak, you're disclosing something about yourself. The way you ask a question, the way you offer an opinion, and the general stylistic and non-verbal manner that characterizes your speaking say a lot about you. Invariably, people who listen to what you have to say make inferences not only on the basis of the logic and rationale of what you say, but on the basis of how you said it. This is not to say that they are judging or evaluating you constantly; quite the contrary—most people understand how erroneous first impressions can be, especially when they are based on very little information, and they are therefore willing to hold off until they have more information.

But people do have a tendency to judge and evaluate others with greater certainty when they communicate something extreme about themselves. A person who speaks much too softly is judged to be shy, just as a person who speaks much too loudly is judged to be aggressive or bold. A person who speaks with a moderate and appropriate tone of voice does not provide much grounds for obtaining a biased first impression. Nevertheless, getting to know someone is very much like building a house where stones are laid one atop the other. As more and more information becomes available, the structure begins to take shape. If one stone of the foundation is laid far out of line or is weak in some peculiar way, this affects how other stones will be placed upon it and determines the outcome of the structure. If, in the course of social transactions, your first mode of behavior is *extreme* in any way, this sets a bias for subsequent perceptions. While first impressions can be altered on the basis of subsequent interactions, the more these first impressions are based on extreme behavior, the more difficult they will be to change.

While there are many non-verbal ways of communicating something about yourself, what helps to keep a conversation going is what you communicate about yourself *verbally*. People want to find out where you work, where you live, where you're from, and where you're going. This gives people basic information and serves as a framework upon which they can attach more and more details. Some pieces of information carry more weight than others in forming an impression, especially at an initial meeting. In some circles, the job you hold will be given great weight. In others, your lack of self-importance or pretentions carries the day. Some people are very proud of being a professional and derive their sole sense of importance from showing off their occupation. Others are not concerned at all about their jobs, whether they are doctors, farmers, or unemployed. They know that they have other social skills and that whatever early impressions have been formed on the basis of "status" will be quickly compensated for by an ample display of human qualities—for example, amiable traits, a sense of humor, and friendliness. Status is to the elite as image management is to the shy; both spring from inadequacy and feelings of inferiority that have to be covered up through a display of status.

People are generally far better off communicating honestly about who they are than trying to paint the most favorable picture of themselves. Painting an inaccurate portrait of yourself publicly is something that always has to be undone and corrected, especially if there is the anticipation of subsequent future interactions. The kind of embarrassment that is most difficult to deal with often has to do with correcting exaggerations and misperceptions that were purposefully induced.

There is also another very grave consequence that accompanies not telling the truth about yourself in social situations. If you find that painting a favorable but false picture of yourself helps to get you positive social outcomes and a momentary favorable evaluation, you're cheating yourself. You can't give *yourself* credit for the positive social experience. In fact, what people come to accept and evaluate positively is not some true personal quality, but more some glorious, exalted, or heroic (but *false*) image you presented. From a psychological point of view, you have no right to give yourself credit for that success, and whatever increase in self-confidence and self-esteem you think you've gained is going to be shaky and unhealthy. Only *you* know you're not entitled to it. I labor this point only for the reason that I know that many shy people have difficulty accepting themselves for what they are, so they are afraid that, in turn, they will not be accepted by others. Rather than misrepresenting yourself to others, you are better off learning who you are, accepting yourself, and establishing relationships based on reality. If you let yourself open up to new experiences and if you are willing to learn, those things that you don't like about yourself can be changed. As you learn (by experience) that you won't be rejected when you disclose information that *you* feel is unacceptable to your image, you will also learn that it is easier to be yourself than it is to try to maintain a false image based on who you would like to be.

Talking about yourself can be done in several ways. You can be direct and explicit, or you can be indirect and allow the listener to infer some quality or characteristic. You can talk about your hobbies, the sports you like, your leisure activities, the movies you like to go to, the books you like to read, the television programs you like to watch, and the friends you like to be with. Talking about such matters not only reveals information about you, but it discloses your preferences and values. Again, some people tend to exaggerate, and this almost always backfires. The statement "I used to play a lot of hockey during my high school days, but I can't find the time to play now while I'm in college" is better than "I'm really crazy about hockey. I used to play a lot in high school, and I'm going to join the college team so I can make the NHL farm team later." While this latter statement may raise the esteem and opinion others have of you and get them to appraise you more highly for the moment, subsequent interactions are bound to take place, and eventually you will have to *undo* the lie. If you are honest in the first place, you won't have to live under the strain of maintaining the lie or suffer the guilt and shame that come from having the lie uncovered. On the other hand, if there are favorable things about you that *are* true and you *don't* reveal them, you have no one but yourself to blame for passing up the chance for healthy pride. Just because *you're* jealous of *others'* accomplishments doesn't mean that others will feel the same when you let your natural light shine.

How Much to Disclose

As interactions become more frequent and last longer, a different order of information about yourself has to be revealed in order to help sustain friendship arrangements. It is one thing to express what you think—interests, values, likes, and dislikes—but it is another thing to express how you *feel*. Whenever events allow for the exchange of feelings between people, the net effect is always one of binding the friendship and bringing the two people closer. The sharing or exchange of *emotional* experiences, however slight and insignificant, is tantamount to adding a nutrient quality to the relationship. Let's explore this "feeling talk" a little more closely and see precisely what it is all about.

The expression of feelings always has to be consistent with the amount of liking and intimacy between the two people involved. The development and maintenance of healthy, intimate, and long-term relationships clearly requires the disclosure of feelings. Dozens of academic and popular books have been written on this subject, and all are in general agreement that with more self-disclosure, exchange of feelings, and openness in the relationship, the more rewarding and intimate such long-term relationships become. There is a widely accepted school of thought that emphasizes complete honesty and self-disclosure of feelings as the only viable and "meaningful" form of interpersonal communication. However, in casual social relations and beginning friendships we need to qualify how and when self-disclosure is appropriate. While we know that adjustment and mental health are markedly improved by establishing the basis for intimate relationships, there is no promise that this is the universal panacea for all human ills, nor in thinking that completely open, honest, and emotional self-disclosure is the *sole* instrument of meaningful interpersonal relationships.

The person who discloses everything about himself—

his strengths, his weaknesses, problems, conflicts, and all his feelings—produces relations with others that are as disfunctional and negative as the person who discloses too little about himself and struggles to maintain a false image of himself. You are warned about too early self-disclosure and cautioned against concretely disclosing how you feel to just anyone. After assessing the nature of a relationship, you should decide how much and to what extent you should disclose innermost secrets and feelings. The healthiest level of the depth and breadth of self-disclosure is the one that is equal to the depth and breadth of the relationship presently being enjoyed.

Even when we consider intimate relationships, such as in marriage, self-disclosure may not be the most productive and unifying principle for closeness and intimacy. The principle of honesty and accurateness in revealing how you feel and what you think can be maintained with *appropriate levels* of self-disclosure. In intimate relationships, it is important for people to communicate specifically, accurately, precisely, and *concretely* what is felt and thought. But in casual friendship relationships you are better off revealing what you think and feel accurately —but in *vague* terms. Consider the following verbal exchanges between two people who have only a passing relationship or friendship.

BETTY: "You look tired today. What have you been doing?"

BILL: "I've been feeling guilty about not doing as much work as I should have done, and I'm worried about passing the exams coming up. I really hate myself for not having the discipline to keep up with the work when I know I should be."

Bill's response is an example of inappropriate self-disclosure because it pinpoints the reason for the "tired feeling" too exactly. And it is inappropriate because the relationship between Bill and Betty does not require this kind of concreteness. Bill's response is so self-disclosing that it presumes upon their friendship.

Here is an alternative and more appropriate way of replying to Betty's question:

BILL: "I've been fooling around and keeping late hours for the past two weeks and I'm getting a little uptight about the exams coming up. I've got a lot of catching up to do and I'm starting to sweat it."

This response included an appropriate form of self-disclosure. It is not concrete and doesn't specify the deep, gut-level component of the feeling. But it serves its purpose in freely and openly displaying the feeling.

Consider the following illustrations. Can you see the distinction between the vagueness and the concreteness in the content of self-disclosure in the following examples? In all examples, the relationships are defined as casual, simple friendships. Notice, too, that in all cases the replies are "honest" with respect to disclosing the feeling, but one is more appropriate than the other.

1). JOAN: "Hi! Haven't spoken to you for a while. What have you been up to?"

A. BOB: "You know, my usual work. But I'm really feeling good about myself and my spirits are really high because of a project I just finished. I had some doubts about doing a good job at first, but I stuck to it and struggled with it. Now I really feel a sense of accomplishment and achievement."

B. TED: "Not much . . . same stuff . . . just got a big project finished and I'm really relieved to get it off my back. I plugged away at that for a long time and it feels good to have it done and over with. I'm pretty happy with it too."

2). ALEX: "Say, you really look down today."

A. BRUCE: "Yes, a very dear uncle who was very close to me died last Thursday."

B. TED: "Yes, a member of my family passed away a few days ago."

3). JIM: "That certainly was a different movie last night, wasn't it?"

A. BLAKE: "Yeah, I really got upset a couple of times. Some of the things that happened to the guy reminded me of how alone I felt when my father left us when I was twelve years old. All those feelings of helplessness, confusion, and anger all came back to me last night during the movie."

B. TERRY: "It sure was. I was very moved by it. I don't think there was a dry eye in the place. It really *got* to me."

The verbal content given by Ted and Terry were all

appropriate to the nature of the friendship relationship. The content given by Bob, Bruce, and Blake reflects too much self-disclosure because their replies are too concrete and specify too clearly the reasons for the feelings. All replies were honest in that they admitted the *existence* of underlying feelings. However, the appropriate replies did so without going into precise details and concreteness normally associated with the intensity of the feeling. To be too precise and too concrete in self-disclosure is not only socially inappropriate in a casual relationship, but it also causes embarrassment and discomfort to the listener.

If you're like many shy people, then you refrain from disclosing *any* feelings. Maybe you reply in short sentences, using simple words and in a style that fails to suggest that anything is felt. These kinds of replies are also inappropriate and non-functional because they prevent a relationship from evolving and developing into a more rewarding and significant friendship. In addition, they are unhealthy because they keep different kinds of feelings hidden and force you to shoulder the weight of frustrations. The lack of appropriate verbal expression of feeling often produces misperceptions, and these are often the root cause of irritability, frustrations, and subsequent conflict. If you tend to be moody, it may well be because you have deprived yourself of any expression of feeling or only allowed yourself incomplete expressions of feeling.

Consider the following exchanges between two people whose relationship is defined as a casual, dating friendship.

1). MARY: "Well, John, how did things go with you today?"

JOHN A: "Oh, okay, I guess. Usual stuff, you know."

JOHN B: "I had this terrible migraine for most of the morning when I was at work, and it made me so angry and upset that I couldn't concentrate on what I was doing."

JOHN C: "I had a headache this morning at work and that really bugged me. It sounds crazy, but it really screwed up my morning."

The kind of statement given by John A is typical of non-expressive people. Not only does it lie about the real feeling, but it pretends that *no* feeling was there. John B, however, is much too concrete and specific about how he felt and is clearly inappropriate in his reply. John C's reply is appropriate because he is accurate about how he felt and he communicates the right amount of intensity and annoyance by the words that he chooses.

2). JOAN: "Say, Bill, I know something about what happened in class today is bugging you. What is it?"

BILL A: "No, nothing's bugging me. What makes you say that? Are you talking about that kidding that went on? That's nothing. I can take that."

BILL B: "Yeah, those guys in class really hurt me. They ridiculed me for being fat. They call me 'Tubby,' and I know they don't invite me to their parties."

BILL C: "Yeah, you're right. I didn't know that it showed. I guess it's those guys in class. They really annoy me sometimes! I really get the feeling they enjoy picking on me."

Bill A is obviously the inhibited, timid, and unexpressive one. While the relationship he has with his female friend is one that is a casual and friendship arrangement, it is appropriate to disclose, at least in vague terms, the presence of the underlying feeling she has already noticed. By maintaining a defensive image about himself, Bill A tries to show that he doesn't experience any negative feelings, that nothing gets to him. This is non-functional for two reasons: 1). not disclosing appropriately prevents the relationship from developing into a more personal affair; 2). Bill A will again have to struggle with having to live up to the image of being unaffected by feelings or conditions around him and refrain from a healthy yielding to what is being felt. Bill B is also inappropriate because he is too concrete and specific in his reply. The kind of reply he gives is appropriate for a relationship that is intimate and supportive, such as one that might exist between intimate couples or between a patient and his therapist. Bill C is more appropriate because he is willing to disclose what is being felt without creating any embarrassment or obligation on the part of the other person to support the feelings or to inquire further into the reasons why or if she can help.

Pick out what are appropriate and inappropriate responses in the following exchanges between two people who are casual friends.

3). BILL: "Hey, Mary, how's that human relations course coming along?"

MARY A: "Coming along, coming along. I'm not sure I'm getting much out of it."

MARY B: "Ah, shit! That assertive-training group is giving me a hard time. I can't help but think that I've got some way to go with that whole routine."

MARY C: "Well, since you asked, I can tell you. I feel hesitant and embarrassed whenever I try to say what I think to another member of our group. Being assertive is a basic problem with me, and it's a struggle for me to adopt this new orientation."

4). STEVE: "Well, Sue, are you getting ready for Christmas? Are you going home this year?"

SUE A: "Oh, I don't know. I've got a lot of work to do for the exams in January, and I've really got to bone up. I think maybe I'll spend only a day or two at home. I can't waste too much time, because I have so many courses."

SUE B: "Oh, I'm really troubled about Christmas this year. Spending the holidays with my mother is going to be painful, I think. I feel guilty and depressed whenever she calls and says she is lonely, so I feel obligated to go home for Christmas."

SUE C: "Ugh! Don't remind me! Christmastime is always a tough time for me. My relationship with my mother bugs me, and I'm not quite sure what I'm going to do about it this Christmas."

5). MARY: "Well, I had a good time at that discothèque tonight. How about you? It looks as if something got to you."

ALLAN A: "No, not really. I like listening to people talk. That was a good time. It's fun finding out about everybody there."

ALLAN B: "You're right. Did it show? You're right, I felt small and inept when the people I met there bragged about their accomplishments. When they're like that I clam up, and then I feel even more inadequate and miserable."

ALLAN C: "Yeah, you're right. People at that discothèque turn me off sometimes. I guess it all depends on who is there. Some nights are better than others. Tonight, though, some of those guys really annoyed me—bragging and all that."

6). MARK: "Say, Janet, do you mind if we talk a little bit? It's about something that has been going on between us for the past couple of weeks. I don't want to get into a heavy trip or anything, but I thought it might be worthwhile to talk about some of the crazy things we've been doing when we go out with a group. What do you think about last night, for example?"

JANET A: "Yeah, that was good last night. I had a good time last night. That was our best time since we've been going to that discothèque. That was good. What about you?"

JANET B: "I'm glad you brought it up. I had some different feelings about last night. I felt encouraged about how we related together. I remember that you spoke to me directly three or four times in front of other people. That made me feel good. Also, when you spoke the edge in your voice seemed to be missing, and that made me feel more comfortable. A couple of times I found the courage to give you some positive feedback on the nice things you were saying to me, and that made me feel elated because I felt you accepted it. Tell me how you feel."

JANET C: "Funny you should bring that up. I was thinking about that. Well, I thought things went pretty well between you and me last night. I know we usually tend to kid each other a lot, especially in front of other people, and sometimes we get a little sarcastic and that tends to be not too pleasant. Yesterday, though, I was really happy about how nice we were to each other. What about you? What do you think?"

The most serious problem you may have if you're shy and non-expressive has to do with your tendency *not* to speak about how you feel. But you could get carried away with the emotional experience of a sensitivity-training group, encounter session, or Gestalt workshop if you go to these for help in "getting in touch" with your feelings. There, you may learn complete self-disclosure and how to "get down to the nitty-gritty" of gut-level emotional issues, and if you do this, you may get positive feedback and be rewarded by how easy it can be to unburden a host of "hidden" feelings. But be careful not to confuse the *relief* associated with such unburdenings with the *insight* that goes with the correct prescription for good interpersonal relationships. You have to learn that undisclosure is not healthy and over-disclosure is inappropriate. The right level of self-disclosure has to be consistent with emotional growth principles and, at the same time, respect norms and principles of successful social transactions.

If people are turning away from you, it is probably because you are not allowing them to *know you,* or because you are turning them off by *over-disclosing* yourself and burdening them with requests for support, empathy, and complete understanding. In the long run, you must learn to talk about yourself and reveal yourself *appropriately* to others in order to increase their liking of you. And this is a statement you ought not to reject until you have personally tested it. In the end, its truth will seem more like a proverb. In the end, you'll have to agree with the saying: "Nothing can ever be said to be real until it has been experienced; even a proverb is not a proverb until your life has illustrated it." Go and find out for yourself.

chapter 8

STARTING A CONVERSATION

IF YOU'RE LIKE MANY SHY PEOPLE WE'VE SEEN, THEN learning how to keep a conversation going once you've got it started is a problem for you. Sometimes a person won't start a conversation precisely because of this, and not because he doesn't know how to start one. But learning all the skills for keeping a conversation going requires practice, and that's exactly what you're going to have to do if you want to develop confidence in this area. All I can provide you with is a structured series of social exercises to prepare yourself, but really, you're the one who is going to have to do all the work. People who seem to have a "natural" ability for keeping a conversation going were not born this way. Unconsciously, by watching others talk, by taking small risks at first, and through trial and error, they have gradually been able to find a style that suits them, one that they can use with ease and confidence.

In this chapter I'll be describing various components of these conversational skills and illustrating them with transcripts from real-life social episodes. After you've understood the components, I'll show you how to condense twenty years of social learning into a social program that contains the essential elements of this skill.

Remember that the way you open a conversation depends on the context—the physical situation (work, leisure activities, church, on the bus, or at a casual social gathering), the time of day (breakfast, lunchtime, coffee break, after work, week day, weekend, or the individual person (male, female, younger, same age or older, a subordinate, colleague, superior, single, attached, married, divorced). Fortunately, there are some consistencies and stable social elements that make the task of deciding what to do or say a little easier to manage. For example, the kind of person you might find at a bar-discothèque on a Thursday evening is quite different from the person you might find at a social tea on a Friday between 5 and 6:30 in the reference section of the local library. But if you are shy, you may simply lack the experience to know what these differences are.

There are a number of ways in which social transactions can begin. You may be introduced to someone, or you can approach this person yourself. Perhaps you approach the person with clearly recognized motives or under a pretext. You can ask the person a question concerning some common activity or task. For example, say, "Hi. Aren't you the person who lives across the street from me?" [Wait for a reply.] "Do you happen to know the bus schedule on this street?" Even after your question is answered, the door to a more casual and social transaction will remain open. The pretext about the bus has served its purpose. In a work-related situation, two people can get together to talk about some task or company issue. Approaching someone with a pretext is a very safe condition under which to begin relating, and it can conveniently camouflage your true motives of wanting to relate socially.

Another tactic focuses upon approaching someone more directly for social talk and making it clear from the start that these are your intentions. Consider the following very *uncustomary* way of initiating social contact.

John has noticed Rosemary in his class, and for the past two weeks he has been thinking about going up to her and asking her to have lunch. He approaches Rose-

mary after class and says the following: "Hi, Rosemary."
[He waits for a reply.] "I hope you won't think this is
too forward of me, but I've been thinking of asking you
to lunch for some time now. I've noticed that you usually
have lunch alone or with your friend Joan, and since she
isn't here today I was wondering if you would care to
have lunch with me in the cafeteria. I'm simply interested in spending some time with you. I'd like to talk for
a while together and spend a pleasant lunch hour in a very
casual and friendly atmosphere. I would really appreciate it if you would accept my offer, and I hope that you
won't think that you should feel obligated to accept."

While John's approach is honest, self-disclosing, and
genuine in that it reveals his motives completely, it is,
nevertheless, quite inappropriate. It runs counter to a
number of norms concerning initial meetings in that particular setting. If you were to receive such a request, you
might think that the person was strange and just say no,
or you might believe he was serious about his desire for
social company, and you would have every reason to suspect that you might be in for some kind of "heavy trip"
during your lunch hour. While most people like to have
company during their leisure hours, most don't want to
get involved in something that is obviously directed at
fulfilling openly acknowledged needs for human contact.
It's a biological condition that we have these needs; but
it's not your social prerogative to reveal them.

Usually, when a person is too direct about his intentions for wanting to relate socially, the other person becomes apprehensive about having to cope with such a
strong come-on. In most settings, it's appropriate to camouflage intentions in order to allow the other person to
save face and not be overwhelmed by such requests.
Furthermore, leisure-time activities ought to be pleasant,
fun, amusing, and light. Indeed, if we have to admit to
the validity and utility of the term, leisure times and
casual social periods are specifically intended to be superficial, if we mean by superficial an absence of a gut-
level, nitty-gritty, and a self-disclosing immersion in a
morass of private thoughts and feelings. Save these for
your priest, friendly psychologist, or the person with
whom you have a close, intimate, and supportive relationship.

SHY?

Now, look at the way in which Alex plans, anticipates, and successfully approaches Helen. Helen is an attractive young woman in Alex's class and he has been trying to get to meet her for some time now. He finally finds the opportunity when he thinks that he'll approach her with a statement on how he felt about her comments in class that day. As he thinks about it, he decides that his tactic will be to start by saying that he thought she was "right on" and that she gives the impression of having a great deal of knowledge about the subject matter.

After class Alex waits for Helen to leave the classroom, and while she is just outside the door, he approaches her and says "Man, you really seem to know your stuff in this area! You must be majoring in it!"

Helen replies, "Oh, yeah. After a while you get to do a lot of reading in this area and it all sort of fits in."

Alex smiles and continues with, "I hope you don't mind my saying this, but I'm not sure I agree completely with all of what you said."

Following this up, Helen replies inquisitively, "Oh? [laughs] Which part was that?"

By this time they are both walking down the hall heading off in the same direction and continuing to talk about strictly academic and intellectual matters. Alex doesn't know whether Helen is free now or if she has to rush off elsewhere. He doesn't want to ask her to join him for coffee for fear that his request might be taken as too open an invitation for socializing, and if she says she does have to run off, he won't know whether that was indeed the case or whether he had frightened her off.

Alex settles for a compromise strategy and says, "Well, I'm not sure if we have time to get into it now, but we could continue this conversation some other time. Do you have another class right now?" In this way Alex creates the impression that he is interested in continuing the discussion, but he is willing to put it off until some other time. He leaves the door open to the possibility that they could continue talking there and then by asking that tag-on question.

Helen answers, "No, I haven't got a class until later this afternoon."

So Alex says, "I'm going for coffee right now. Want

to come on down? You can explain to me what you meant." Alex had a way of appearing very casual about his request. He didn't want Helen to feel that she was being "hustled" since she barely knew him and would not want to be put in an embarrassing position where she might have to "cool it" if he started something.

Over coffee, Alex and Helen continue talking about academically related topics for about ten minutes and then Alex changes the topic of conversation slightly by asking, "Are you planning to do graduate work in this area?" This is the first lead-in for a reorientation of general mood and conversation. In a short time their general modes of communication change from a formal transaction into a more casual, friendly, and sociable affair. This was indeed what Alex had in mind from the very beginning, but in order to make it easier for himself and for Helen, he had to present an acceptable pretext for their meeting.

Unlike some schools of thought, we don't view this approach as lacking in honesty. We consider it as a very appropriate tactic that serves a functional role in initiating transactions. It is socially more appropriate and conventional, and therefore more helpful to hold back your true motives initially, and then ease the social door open, than it is to melt all social barriers by spilling over with gut-level needs too hot to handle.

Some would have allowed Alex to go up to Helen and say, "Hi. I noticed you in class today, and if you've got a few minutes, why don't we go downstairs and have a cup of coffee."

This uncommon form of initiating transactions should be reserved for communities where frankness and openness do not threaten other people, and where one person making the request will not feel rejected if the other replies, "Thanks, that's nice of you to ask, but I've only got time to go to the washroom and hurry off to catch a bus. Why don't we make it some other time, say, at noon tomorrow, okay?" These kinds of straightforward, frank, and open interchanges depend more upon the people involved than they do upon the peculiarities of social contexts. But the fact of the matter is that there are too many communities where people react with suspicion, anxiety, and occasional resentment to these kinds of open requests.

143

Consequently, the decision to use this open mode of initiating social transactions should be based upon an understanding of the predictable reactions it would elicit in another. What are stable social elements in one community may not be reliable or useful tactics in another.

The verbal skills to smoothly initiate a transaction at a bar or discothèque may, for example, contain something like the following: if you're standing beside someone of the opposite sex enjoying a drink and eager to make his or her acquaintance, all of the following may be appropriate:

1). "Boy [pause for a second], it sure is hot in here."
2). "Hey [wait for a second], that really looks like an interesting drink you've got. What is it?"
3). "Hi. Pretty good music in here, isn't it?"
4). "Excuse me [wait until you have the other person's attention], would you have a light [know what time it is, or what time this place closes]?"

In all of these initiating remarks, it's important to wait until the person you're addressing is finished talking to someone and is prepared to hear your remarks. It's also important to wait and get the person's attention once you've made your first remark, and not to hurry whatever question you have in mind. If you are shy, chances are you rush through whatever you have planned to say without waiting until the other person is looking at you. Most socially adept people feel quite at ease, and they take their time, pause, and wait for non-verbal cues to be returned before saying what they want to say. Try slowing down.

I'm sure you've seen people risk a difficult and assertive opening statement such as: "Hi. How are you doing? What's your name?" The person to whom this remark is addressed may be taken aback by such forwardness and may infer a degree of arrogant self-assurance in the person who makes it. Most people don't feel comfortable in responding to such assertiveness. Even those who are physically attractive often get nowhere with such boldness; the immediate inference is one of conceit and vanity. People usually don't enjoy arrogant self-assurance, feeling that having to relate to someone who is too confident places them at a disadvantage. They feel they have to compete and work at maintaining the level of assertiveness that this boldness implies. The person who generally underplays his hand or who otherwise does not come on too strongly but shows a degree of reticence and hesitation in portraying himself publicly is more likely to be well received.

On the other hand, women should understand that when men come across in an over-confident, bold, and imposing manner it is generally for defensive reasons. Some men feel it is better to be impolite than to be turned down after having been appropriate. On (rare) occasions games of "one-upsmanship" or "let's see who can scare the other off first" are played in a teasing and amusing manner when two people first meet each other. There is bantering back and forth and harmless "I'm better than you are" games that are played. However, while these can be entertaining and serve the purpose of breaking the ice, they are rarely pulled off completely successfully and should be avoided unless you're a high-risk taker and not afraid of failing.

Most people go to bars, singles dances, and discothèques primarily to socialize and meet other people. Work environments, in contrast with social environments, are task-oriented, so casual, social interchanges are often more difficult. There are some people who, at work or in formal task situations, cannot extricate themselves from their immediate environment, and so they never engage in social or casual transactions. They can pass co-workers in the hall and never say hello or greet them with a smile. At the other extreme, there are those who can relate in a manner that is social and casual and never seem to be able to adopt a style that is more consistent with task-oriented forms of transactions. The classroom joker, the office clown, or the person who can only be very casual, light, and informal may be very difficult to relate to when the context calls for work and goal-oriented functions.

If you were to analyze it, you would find that during the course of any one day you are presented with several, if not many, different social contexts, each of which calls for a different kind of social transaction. Greeting a co-worker of the opposite sex for the first time in the morning involves a casual mood. However, half an hour later the interaction may be more formal and task-oriented when you consult each other concerning the upcoming annual report. An hour later you may be cast as opponents in an office meeting where you have to gather information, offer suggestions, or make a decision concerning some policy. Later in the day, the transactions may revolve around a lunch-hour setting where discussions of yesterday's figure skating competition is the main focus. And in the afternoon, at a coffee break, you may end up by talking together about your feelings concerning the seal hunt every spring.

Each social context carries with it some specification for what posture or social self you should assume in meeting the mood and the demands of the situation. To be able to shift your shape and adopt different role positions and to relate in a manner that is convenient and appropriate to the context is a characteristic of social adjustment. This kind of versatility allows you to move in and out of different environments with great ease and facility and always to be appropriate to the occasion. This is a quality found among those who have overcome shyness problems. If you lack versatility and flexibility in styles of relating, then you'll be forced to behave the same way in quite different social contexts, or you'll end up avoiding all unfamiliar social situations that call for varying social skills. The first option leads to your presenting an image that is dependable, predictable, and soft-spoken—all very noble and virtuous traits, but very boring and socially depressing when that's all there is to your personality. With the second option, you're heading in the direction of social exclusion, withdrawal, and a dull, lonely social existence.

Lunch Breaks

Lunch and coffee breaks provide excellent opportunities for initiating new interactions and for practicing those skills that can help you to meet new people. These breaks in routine are "intermissions" from working stage appearances. A coffee break can last for fifteen minutes and lunch from forty-five to sixty minutes, and people know that after this time they'll have to return to their work. This has the net effect of freeing people from the concern of what to say after you have exhausted general topics of conversation. Both the person doing the initiating and the recipient of the advances usually feel relatively comfortable with the socializing in these time-limited functions. Compare the safety of a lunch hour or coffee break with the ambiguity associated with having a drink after regular working hours. What makes this latter condition more difficult is the lack of structure. You have to determine how much time you're going to allot to this kind of social activity, and you have to deal with the consequences of prolonging it into regularly scheduled dinner time.

The lunch hour and coffee break periods are important socializing occasions, and you should make every effort to capitalize upon them. If you deprive yourself of these opportunities because you're too timid, or you are too burdened with work, or you are on a strict diet and prefer not to tempt yourself, you will very quickly sense a feeling of social isolation. Lunch-hour periods bring people together and allow them to relate socially without feeling that they are "out on a date." Crowded lunchrooms, cafeterias, and coffee shops provide safe contexts for sitting beside strangers without creating the impression that you're trying to "get together" with them. Get rid of the crazy notion that the only approach to social relations that "count" are those that operate on the basis of a "date." Don't set yourself up with the goal and expectation that unless you can get a date with someone, you can't affirm your sense of social desirability. In truth, there is often much more to be gained from casual social interactions in unorganized and accidental get-togethers than there is from formally arranged future meetings or dates.

Breaking the Ice

Several students and I decided that we should all experience approaching someone and making social contact for the first time in order to learn firsthand the thinking patterns and emotional patterns that occur in this situa-

SHY?

tion. Consistent with our understanding of what would be an appropriate time and place for carrying out this experiment, we selected the lunch-hour period. We noticed that during the summer months, the people who worked at a large community health facility in the Boston area would almost always bring their lunch outside to eat under a tree, at a picnic table, or in various shady places on the hospital grounds. They would go out in small groups of three to five or occasionally alone and sit quietly on the grass to have their lunch.

My "accomplices" in this venture were six men and two women ranging in age from twenty-two to twenty-seven. After agreeing to cooperate, they were all instructed to approach someone of the opposite sex during the lunch hour, to begin a conversation with the person, and to interact with that person at a level of a casual social encounter. They were specifically told that they were *not* to initiate a contact under the pretext of wanting to talk about some professional concern, administrative matter, or to ask for such things as tourist information, what time it was, *etc*. They had to make sure that the transactions were purely social ones. Each carried a pocket-sized cassette dictaphone recorder that could be concealed and activated and stopped unobtrusively, and they were told to start recording just seconds before they started the first segment of their conversation. The following scenarios illustrate the nature of these interactions.

Stan is age twenty-three, single, and not usually shy. He first spent some time casing the situation. Over three consecutive days he watched which people went where and with whom during their lunch hour and how long they spent outside. He picked someone who had eaten alone over the three-day period and decided he would approach her for the express purpose of having lunch with her. Stan's strategy was to make contact inside the cafeteria while she was getting her lunch. On the day in question, he waited for her to come into the cafeteria and got into line immediately behind her. That's when we got the first recordings from their interchanges:

STAN: "Hi. I saw you having your lunch outside yesterday. Are you going out under your favorite tree again today?"

SHE: "Yeah [some laughter]. It's a nice spot."

148

STAN: "Good. Do you mind if I join you? If you don't mind, I can help you feed the ants out there."

SHE: "Sure. It's fun out there . . . but I don't think there are any ants."

They got their lunch items, paid for them at the cash register, and proceeded out of the cafeteria. On their way out Stan begins:

"Boy, it's sure nice to have this kind of weather. I sure hope it lasts."

SHE: "It sure is . . . that tree is really nice . . . nice and cool . . . I don't want to get too much sun."

STAN: "Yeah, I know what you mean. What ward are you working on?"

SHE: "I'm on Three West, with the Adolescent Unit. And you? I think it's the first time I've seen you here."

STAN: "I'm just here for the summer, although I'll be here on a part-time basis starting in September. I'm with the District Unit."

SHE: "I see. By the way, my name is Fran. Hi!"

STAN: "Hi! I'm Stan."

Joe is twenty-four years old, married, and not shy. He didn't waste any time picking out a woman to meet. On his first day of the assignment, he went out on the grounds with a sandwich in one hand and a container of milk in the other and walked around looking for an appropriate person. He saw someone sitting alone under a tree and approached her from behind and a little to the side. When he was sure she sensed that he was approaching, he called out from twelve to fifteen feet away:

"Hi! Is this your tree, or can anybody sit underneath it [laughs]?"

SHE: "You're right on both counts. It is my tree, and anybody can sit underneath it." [Both laugh.]

JOE: "Great! Then I think I'll join you, if you don't mind [sitting down]. My name's Joe. What's yours?"

SHE: "Karen. Nice to meet you. I've never seen you here before. Are you new on staff?"

JOE: "I started last month—in the ———— department. I usually eat my lunch inside. Boy, it's really nice out here, huh?"

SHE: "It sure is . . . too nice sometimes. I think people who drive by and see us must think that this is a social club or something. I think I'll bring my golf clubs tomorrow and drive a few balls around [laughter]."

JOE: "Hey, you better warn me about that—I've heard about you women drivers [laughs]!"

SHE: "Oh, don't worry, I'm a pretty good golfer. I get a good chance to play a lot with the job I've got."

JOE: "Oh? How's that? Are you on flexible hours?"

SHE: "No. I'm in charge of AP-Five, and I get a chance to work my shifts around. Then I can take advantage of the good weather. Mind you, we all have a say as to what hours we want to work. You play golf?"

JOE: "No, not really. My wife does, though. She tried to get me playing at one time, but I could never really get into it. She really likes it, though."

SHE: "I see [pauses] . . . What kind of work are you doing here? Who are you working with? Are you going to be around long?"

Sam is twenty-seven years old, single, and not shy. Sam took a slightly different approach to initiating a conversation and having lunch with one of the staff. After having singled out a nurse about his own age, and one whom he had seen eating outside the day before, he followed her into the cafeteria and stood behind her as they selected items. Let's pick up their conversation as she reaches for a dessert:

SAM: "Hasn't that got a lot of calories in it?"

SHE: "Yeah [laughs], I guess it does, but I figure I can give myself a treat every now and then."

SAM: "Well, I don't know about you, but I've got to watch what I eat, or else. . . ."

SHE: "Well, I watch it, too, but I don't feel that guilty when I give myself a little reward every now and then. That's the only way that I can keep myself working. I'm working hard these days."

SAM: "You're not new here, are you?"

SHE: "Oh, no [laughs]! Far from it! This is my fourth —yes, my fourth—year in this hospital. But I haven't seen you before. Did you just get here with the new group in July?"

SAM: "Yeah, I got here last month. I'm in psychology. Have you been on vacation or something?"

SHE: [Puzzled] "No. I've got that coming up in a couple of weeks. Why? Why do you ask?"

SAM: "Oh, it's just that I haven't seen you around, like in the cafeteria at lunch."

SHE: "That's probably because I've been eating my lunch outside. Gotta take advantage of the sunshine, ya know . . . really can't see staying inside . . . when it's nice like this."

SAM: [Inquisitively] "Outside? Can you eat outside? Are there places [innocently]? Where do you go?"

SHE: "Oh, yes. A lot of people eat outside on the lawn. There are lots of shady trees and . . . nice breezes, too."

SAM: Gee, I didn't know that. I've got to try that sometime [pauses]. Yeah, that sounds like fun. . . . Say, would you mind if I went outside with you? I'd like to try having lunch outside . . . and get some sun."

SHE: "Sure! Come on. I'll show you where I go."

SAM: "Okay, great! If we find a nice shady spot I won't have far to go for my afternoon siesta after." [Both laugh.]

SHE: "Come on, follow me. We'll go out the side door. . . . [Pauses] I'm Betty. I work in the adult section. What's your name?"

The next excerpts are taken from an attempt to initiate a conversation with not just one woman, but with a whole group of women. This can be considered high-risk-taking for reasons that will become evident in the excerpts. Bruce's approach was really very much unlike himself. He tried to come across as if he were super-confident and completely self-assured and created an image that just didn't coincide at all with how we knew him to really be. It was as if he wasn't going to fool around and decided to take the bull by the horns. He generated an idealized fantasy of himself as a person who was afraid of nothing and for whom few social encounters were of much concern to him. Bruce is shy, twenty-four, single, and seldom dates. He saw a group of five or six nurses sitting together, and from a distance of about twenty feet he hailed them with:

"Hey there! How did you people get the best place in the house? [Coming closer, now about ten feet from them] I've been looking for a spot just like this. Do you mind if I sit here with you?"

WOMAN NO. 1: "No, go right ahead. Lots of room here."

BRUCE: [Sits down almost in the middle of the group, and not addressing anyone in particular] "Well, let's see what I've got in this paper bag. Hmm . . . anyone into a banana?" [Two of the women reply that they wouldn't like one.]

WOMAN NO. 2: "You're new here, aren't you? Are you on rotation from the General Hospital?"

BRUCE: "Yep, started July 1. I think I like it here. It's too bad I'm only going to be here until the end of the summer." [At this point, three other women were engaged in a conversation they had started before Bruce arrived. But Bruce was not dissuaded by any lack of attention from the party, and he addressed woman no. 1.] "You been working here long [said boldly]?"

WOMAN NO. 1: "Uh, about a year, I guess now."

BRUCE: "Ah . . . hmm . . . I see. . . ."

WOMAN NO. 1: "How come you're leaving at the end of the summer?"

BRUCE: [Offhandedly] "Oh, I don't know. I guess I don't want to spend too much time in any one place. I like to move around a bit . . . you know, so I can get as much experience in different places . . . as much as possible, you know. . . ."

WOMAN NO. 1: [Pauses] "I see. . . ."

We'll close the curtains on this scene. To summarize what happened over the next ten embarrassing minutes, we have Bruce trying in vain to maintain the super-confident image he created upon his arrival, and doing so very unsuccessfully. It seemed as if the women were willing to talk to him, but they felt slightly embarrassed for him and could see he simply wasn't accustomed to behaving in this bold and brazen manner and tried to help him out by being rather sympathetic toward him. When Bruce brought us his cassette tape for all to hear, he exclaimed, "Oh, my God! Was that ever terrible! I don't even want you to listen to this! You won't believe this! Gad!" Indeed, we were all quite surprised to discover that Bruce would ever think of trying to role play super-social hero.

Starting a Conversation

Bruce was simply not equipped with either the basic interpersonal skills or the confident anxiety-free manner needed to carry off the role he thought would help him socialize freely and successfully with the group. Not unlike many shy people, Bruce had unrealistic notions about the image of a person who is confident and self-assured. For Bruce, this translated into boldness and nervy assertiveness.

Bruce's case is interesting for several reasons. First of all, it shows how a shy person can come to select a most difficult social task. The task Bruce selected was a very difficult one, not just for him, but for anyone, since approaching a group of women sitting together and already engaged in some kind of social activity not only augments the anxiety in a manner proportional to the number of people in the group, but it makes the task of breaking in comfortably and maintaining a conversation with one person an arduous one. To add insult to his own self-inflicted injury, Bruce tried to present an image of a person that didn't correspond to any skills he had. The only portion of his interaction sequence that could be labeled "successful" was his opening remarks to the women as he approached them. But after having initiated the contact, he found it too difficult to maintain the conversation with the style he intended to portray. In this and other respects, Bruce's behavior and attitude typify many classically shy people. He entered the situation with very unrealistic expectations, selected a task of great difficulty, and pretended to be something and someone who only exists in fairytales and in movies.

Bruce was clearly a failure in his attempt to establish an appropriate and satisfying social contact with a woman, and he knew it. In talking with him about his decisions, his planning, and his behavior, he seemed unaware of the fact that approaching a group of women would entail greater difficulties and risks than merely approaching one who was sitting alone. He put himself down for having failed so badly but obtained some comfort when he was persuaded that his task was indeed a most difficult one. Like many "fear of failure" and shy people, Bruce was ready to attribute the cause of his failure to some personal inadequacy rather than to the difficulty of the task. Not surprisingly, after suffering the

153

loss of self-esteem, Bruce was quite reluctant to attempt the task again. The others, in contrast, were very keen on a repeat performance, especially if they thought they could be given a chance to compare notes afterward.

Alan is twenty-six years old, single, not shy and the most outgoing and extroverted of the students. He spent a few days watching the goings-on during lunch hour. After isolating a target person to approach, he confidently set out, with books in one arm and a lunch bag in the other, in the general direction of a young woman sitting at a small picnic table some distance away from the main building. She had her back to him and was unaware of anyone approaching. When Alan was about ten feet away, she began to stuff her lunch back into her bag. She got up from the table and turned to face him, ready to leave. This took Alan completely by surprise, and from the sound of his voice, he was quite stunned and speechless for a moment:

ALAN: "Uh . . . gee [laugh] . . . wow! [Laugh] I'm sorry, but you won't believe this, but I was standing over by those buildings and saw you sitting here alone and thought I might come over and join you while I had my lunch—and now you're leaving!" [He laughs.]

SHE: "Oh, my God . . . I'm sorry . . . today is pay day and I've got to get to the bank. [Almost apologetically] Uh . . . I didn't know . . . uh, that you were coming, uh . . ."

ALAN: [With nervous laughter] "Wow! I really feel abandoned. I hope you don't treat all newcomers this way [laugh]."

SHE: "No, no . . . please . . . I'm sorry. It's just that I won't get a chance to go to the bank later, and . . ."

ALAN: "Okay. Listen, I won't feel too bad if you promise to stay longer than two minutes next time . . . I mean, I just can't walk all the way over here and have you leave on me like that! [They both laugh.] No, come on, I'm only kidding. I don't want to embarrass you. Seriously, though, I'm new here and I thought I'd get a chance to meet some people . . . but I don't want to keep you. I'll just sit here and sulk for a while."

SHE: [Laughs] "I'm usually out here every day when it's sunny. . . . Come on out again, and I promise not to run away, okay?"

ALAN: "It's a deal. . . . [Sitting down] I'll see you . . . bye."

SHE: "Okay, bye."

Gail is twenty-five years old and not shy. Gail had some difficulty finding a man her own age who was in the habit of having lunch outside and by himself. She didn't want to approach a group of two or three males sitting together for fear that she might be intruding. She thought that this was understandable since most of the male staff were either residents or other health professionals of one kind or another and they had a tendency to talk shop or about last night's football game when they got together. What she did do, however, was carefully planned and well thought out. She and a girl friend picked out two men sitting together, having lunch at a picnic table, and then they planted themselves at a spot on the lawn thirty feet away from them and midway between where they were and the main building, knowing that they would have to pass by on their return. Gail watched the pair very carefully, and toward the end of the lunch hour, as expected, the two men got up and headed in their general direction. As they came closer, Gail and her friend both got up to leave, and as they were about to be overtaken, Gail smiled, and with a coquettish tone of voice, she said:

"Hello, you sun worshippers. What are you going to do when there's four feet of snow on the ground?" [The two men slowed their pace and turned to face the girls who were already moving in the same direction.]

MAN NO. 1: "Haven't you heard? Winter is canceled this year." [All four were now walking at the same pace about six feet apart.]

GAIL: Promises, promises, promises. . . ."

MAN NO. 2: "Don't tell me you're one of these people who hates summer and can't wait for the ski season to start!"

GAIL: "Oh, no . . . no . . . I really enjoy this weather, too."

MAN NO. 1: "Well . . . come on out with your bathing suit, then. . . . Get as much sun as you can."

GIRLFRIEND: "This is really going to turn out to be a social club." [All laugh.]

GAIL: "Well . . . back to work. . . . See you."

BOTH MEN: "Bye."

Gail didn't feel that the trial was significant enough to count as one that met our demands, which was "to initiate a social conversation during lunch." But through her casual comments, she had made herself appear friendly and cheerful to the two men and she felt this might be enough to make her more comfortable in pursuing a clearer attempt the following day. The next day, she waited in the cafeteria for either one of them to show up. Man No. 2 came in first, and Gail immediately slipped into line beside him.

GAIL: "Hi! Going to get some sun today?"

HE: "Oh . . . hi, there. How are you doing?"

GAIL: "Fine, real good. . . . This weather is really fantastic. Are you going outside again?"

HE: "All my patients want to have their sessions outside. . . . Too bad you can't move your office under that weeping willow out there. . . . I held a group out there a couple of days ago . . . get's really distracting."

GAIL: "Yeah, I know what you mean. . . . You hold groups outside?"

HE: "Oh, yes. Some people can't take time off work, and since people finish work at 4:30 . . . it's much better . . . uh . . . easier for them."

By this time they had moved to the cash register, and Gail didn't feel she was ready to make her request to join him. She had asked him twice whether he was going outside in the hope of obtaining a reply that would have led her into something like: "Good, do you mind if I join you?" This was part of her plan of action. However, he hadn't replied to her question. She figured he was too preoccupied with impressing her with something like his good working habits or heavy workload to think about whether or not he might also like some company at lunch. She resigned herself to the fact that he simply wasn't picking up her messages and that she might as well forget it. She thought he would probably be a bore, anyway. However, as he paid for his lunch at the cash register, he turned toward her, and said, "You going to have lunch outside?"

GAIL: [Somewhat startled and fumbling with her money] "Yeah . . . yeah, I think . . . "

HE: "Good. You must be one of our new nurses, aren't you?"

GAIL: "No, I'm an intern. I just started last month. [Walking with him] Are you a resident here?"

HE: "Yes, this is my second year. What kind of work are you doing, what floor are you on, who are you working with?"

GAIL: [Laughs] "Well my first rotation is . . ."

Brenda is twenty-three years old, single, and admits to being shy on occasion. While Brenda took her task very seriously, she simply couldn't bring herself to approach a total stranger who was sitting alone and to join him for social company. She singled out a young professional on staff, found out as much about him as she could informally, and approached him on the ward at noon hour with the following remarks.

BRENDA: "Dr. Smith? Hi. My name's Brenda. I'm a psychology intern in the Adolescent Unit."

HE: "Hi. Are you planning on joining the team?"

BRENDA: "No, not really. I came up to see you . . . to speak with you. I've heard about some of the treatment programs you have going on up here, and I was wondering if you could tell me more about them."

HE: "Sure, sure. . . . What do you want to know? Let's see, which part of the program are you interested in?"

BRENDA: "Well, just about everything. I don't know if you have time right now. . . . Are you going for lunch right now?"

HE: "Yes, of course. Let's talk at lunch. If you'll just wait for a second, I'll put these things away and I'll be right with you."

BRENDA: "Sure, okay, of course." [Brenda turned off her recorder at this point and didn't reactivate it until a few minutes after they had sat in the cafeteria.]

Their conversation at lunch was slightly formal and dealt with professional concerns. While she was curious about the program Dr. Smith headed, Brenda was more interested in finding some way of turning the conversation toward more social and personal topics. Her tape ran out before we could hear how she broached a new level of conversation; however, she reported to us that after a pause in the conversation, she remarked, "You must really enjoy working here. Have you been working here long?" The conversation from then on became much less formal and they spent the rest of the lunch talking about mutual interests and goals. They ended up dating regularly throughout the summer.

If you look closely at the actual exchanges that took place in each of the attempts at initiating a social transaction, you'll find many common features. For example, for all those who followed the rules of the game we find a prominent use of humor in order to break the ice. There was a conscious effort to create the impression that what was to transpire was to be taken lightly, casually. Those who used humor said that they felt they wanted to set the mood and tone of the interaction from the very beginning, and that the last thing they wanted to do was create the impression that what followed was to be too serious. All agreed that they didn't want to put the other person in an embarrassing position, and a strange twist in logic made them all agree that what would have made it embarrassing would have been the realization that there were underlying motives and intentions in their meeting. They felt that if the other people had suspected their earnestness or their desire to "get to know each other" that this might have frightened him or her off, or, at best, made the person apprehensive about what might follow. So the conclusion seemed to be it was best to come across politely, amiably, but not too seriously, and it was important not to show concern about obtaining agreement and social compliance.

Most of these confederate friendship seekers had pre-planned who they were going to approach, what they were going to say, and what cues they were to pay attention to before asking if they could join them for lunch. All of them used the simple strategy of asking questions and waiting for a reply as the vehicle for engaging in conversation. When they were asked a question, they answered it first, but they always followed with *another* question. This was true for everyone except Gail, whose opening remarks of "Going to get some more sun?" were never answered. Gail then repeated her request for information by saying, "Are you going outside again?" And once more he didn't reply. Gail was hoping that if he said, "Yes, I am," or "No, I'm not," then this would be all that she would need in order to follow up with her other prepared question, which was to be, "Good. Do you mind if I join you?"

The people in our group all agreed that the fact that there was no immediate response to Gail's questions was something that couldn't have been predicted, but that if they had known in advance they would have been more insistent at some point in the conversation, saying something like: "Well, let me ask you again. . . . [smile, with eye contact] Are you or are you not going out for lunch?" Or, "Sorry, I can't remember if you said you are going outside or not. Are you?" Another alternative everyone agreed upon would have been simply to follow him as he went outside, catching up to him after a while and saying in a very friendly manner, "Hey, wait up! Mind if I join you?" All of these alternatives assume that this person was not going to meet someone else and that he was not going to be occupied with shop talk with others waiting for him. But if for one reason or another he did not want company at lunch, everyone agreed it would be his responsibility to find a way of saying so appropriately. Gail agreed, too, and she said she would not have suffered any loss of self-esteem or be emotionally upset over appearing to be rejected if that happened. She would have attributed her lack of success to some "chance" factor, or to an external condition over which she had no control.

All of the participants in our experiment found the experience a little stressful but highly rewarding. Brenda was most fearful of taking on the task as it had been defined, and she resorted to finding a solution to the problem of relating to someone by doing so according to her own rules. She approached Dr. Smith on the pretext of wanting to discuss some intellectual-professional matter, and that seemed safe enough. She appealed to a part of his vanity, and she was sure that if he wasn't going to agree to talking these matters over at lunch, it was because he had a previous commitment or was not going to lunch, and that this had little to do with her personally. Brenda, therefore, set the stage for attributing any lack of success to an external and variable factor, a cause that had few implications for her self-esteem. But, as Brenda was willing to admit later, compared with the others she had risked little and profited little from that lunch hour. It's only when you put your social self up front and on the line that you can gain self-confidence and chalk up points on your social self-esteem scale.

None of the participants in the experiment felt that on the basis of their thirty to forty-five minute interaction enough familiarity had been engendered to have made it appropriate to ask the other person out on a date. All agreed that at least two more casual meetings of this kind would have been in order before they would have had enough information exchange and feedback to determine whether they might be interested in socializing after working hours.

I was watching these trials and performances from not far away, and I was thinking that all were having an easy time of it and that they were doing something that they seemed to have done a hundred times before. Aside from Bruce and his magnum force, I was ready to infer that the social trials were easy for them. I was prepared to believe that no one had to try very hard. But when I heard what everyone had to say about assessing, planning, rehearsing, and carrying the whole thing off, I realized they had put a lot of work into it.

Many people are amazed at the great facility and ease with which socially competent people initiate conversations and how everything seems to go so well for them. We can't understand how they can be so lucky or how they can be so successful with the opposite sex following what appears to be a minimum expenditure of effort. Well, don't be deceived! Non-shy and socially expressive people accomplish their social objectives by trying hard and expending the very necessary effort in the right directions, not because they find it easy. The mental skills underlying goal setting, planning, and judgment always have to be engaged; the verbal and non-verbal components that underlie appropriate skills have to be carefully selected, rehearsed, and eventually delivered. What we think we see in socially successful episodes does not bear accurate testimony to the private goings on and to the effort that is expended in attaining the favorable social outcome. Here is another confession of the mental work that goes into making an objective attainable.

Martin is a well-traveled and successful journalist. He is in the habit of taking an annual two-week vacation in the Caribbean to escape the February deep freeze. He rarely concerns himself with the problems of traveling alone, for he has never had any great difficulty meeting people and making friends. On his last trip he spent the first two days hard at work on papers he brought with him and he made a point of dining alone so that he could follow through on some ideas he was developing. By the afternoon of the third day he had finished all his writing and was happy to shift his attention to vacation activities and enjoy the unhurried pace of the island.

That evening he purposely set out to find a woman companion with whom to share dinner. He dressed casually in light-colored pants and an open-necked shirt, and then he sauntered down to a terrace restaurant with a view overlooking the bay. He had lunched there before and knew there would probably be a number of attractive women who might be responsive to a request to have dinner with him. His general plan of action was simple: he would have a drink or two at the bar and strike up a conversation with an eligible woman who was there for a drink, and eventually he would get around to asking her to have dinner.

Few people presented themselves at the bar, and of those who did, none fell into the category of either being his own age, single, or inviting. He was about to speak to the bartender to ask him if he knew of any single women who frequented the restaurant and who dined alone and whether he thought one might make an appearance when he noticed a relatively attractive blonde in her early thirties enter the restaurant. She was ushered to a small table at the side of the patio overlooking the water. Opportunities are limited, he thought to himself, and he decided to focus his efforts and intentions in that direction.

He needed to have more information about her, however. Maybe she was waiting for someone who was to arrive a little later. So, Martin decided to wait five or ten minutes to see what happened. No one arrived. The woman ordered a drink and was looking over the menu when Martin realized that if he approached her with his request, he had better know ahead of time if she was ordering a full-course meal or was just going to gobble down a sandwich and be off. Instead of waiting to see what the waiter would bring her, he decided to ask the waiter what she had ordered, since if he waited until her order arrived, by the time he sat down with her and ordered his meal she'd be halfway through hers. Not wanting to attract the woman's attention by going up directly to her waiter, he asked the bartender if he could help out.

"Listen, I was wondering if you might help me out with something. Would you mind terribly speaking to that waiter over there who is serving that young woman by the edge of the patio and to let me know what she ordered for dinner? I'm trying to be discreet as I can about this, and if you have a second, I'd appreciate it if you could get his attention and ask him to pass the information onto you once he has taken her order."

The bartender knew quite well what Martin was up to and agreed cheerfully and sympathetically, like an ally in a struggle for a beachhead. Minutes later, the information came back; she had ordered a lobster dinner. Good, Martin thought to himself. Now I've got to figure out exactly what I'm going to say to her when I ask her. He rehearsed a number of lines and considered a variety of strategies before settling upon a tactic that he thought was the most appropriate. He decided to be straightforward. Approaching her with some corny line and pretext would be too obvious. People were there on vacation, and pretexts under these circumstances didn't seem necessary. In being straightforward with his request, however, Martin didn't want to scare her off by coming across with machismo or with over-confidence and bravado. He felt that the best way of carrying this off successfully would be to state his request openly and directly, but to temper it by balancing out his verbal message with non-verbal communications in the opposite direction. He would have to show a bit of uneasiness, timidity, and hesitation in the sound of his voice.

When Martin decided what to say and how he was going to say it, he got up from the barstool, walked confidently to her general area, and when he was about five feet from her table he slowed his pace, moved toward a corner of her table, and rested a hand on the back of the chair he was hoping to occupy. As she looked up at him, he leaned forward just slightly, looked into her eyes, smiled, and said softly, "Excuse me, I hope you won't think this too bold of me, but . . . uh . . . I saw you sitting here alone at the table and . . . I was wondering if you would mind very much if I joined you for dinner."

As he waited for her reply, he was struck by the fact that he had forgotten to consider one thing. He had failed to time his request for when she was free to speak. She had food in her mouth, and, as it turned out, she nearly choked on a piece of bread when she heard him. Nevertheless, her wide eyes and extended arm directing Martin to the chair was all the non-verbal message he needed to assure him a favorable response had been obtained. He smiled and chuckled a little to himself, and, feeling somewhat confident about the success of his strategy, he decided to ham it up a little and "fill in" while she tried to regain her composure. "Please, I . . . uh . . . really don't want you to think that I'm in the habit of doing this. I hesitated before coming over to ask you, but I was hungry and I thought I might enjoy your company at dinner."

Any outsider watching this scene would have inferred that Martin was self-confident, extroverted, and just "generally lucky" at finding and making contact. The fact of the matter was that Martin went through a process of information gathering, assessment and judgment, rehearsal of strategy and tactics, and specific planning in order to attain his goal. When Martin was asked whether he considered a task of this kind easy or difficult, he had to pause for a moment before answering and seemed quite troubled over what was meant by easy or difficult. Gathering information, rehearsing strategies and tactics for verbal and non-verbal presentation, anticipating possible reactions, and reworking the strategy—all these involve a certain amount of effort and work, but Martin had had no problem gathering the information from the bartender and the waiter and he had had no problem assessing the situation and generating the appropriate verbal and non-verbal behaviors to maximize the chances for a positive outcome. Once you know what to say and do, all you have to do is do it. What makes a task difficult is not knowing how to approach a particular situation, what information to gather, and what form of behavior you should consider appropriate. All of this leads to an insecurity, and if this is compounded with a fear of failure, then the psychic costs involved in lost energy and in worry can make the task appear more difficult than it is.

People who are successful in their social relations go through phases that involve planning, organizing information, rehearsing, revising, rephrasing, *etc.*, but they do so as a matter of course, knowing full well that these are processes that are necessary. Those who are very skilled have a way of making it appear effortless. These mental sub-routines become automatic and habitual only after many real-life attempts; doing it the first and second and third times involves a step-by-step organization of effort.

If you have unrealistic notions about the amount of effort required in order to be socially successful, and if you don't have these habit sequences already built up, it's no surprise if you lose motivation and give up, even before trying. Or, if you do try, you don't try hard enough. People who are socially successful are not born with the necessary mental and behavioral skills. These abilities were learned by experience. Each component of each skill served as a building block for other skill components, and the success of one social episode stimulated a new social challenge of a higher order of complexity. The end result is, of course, that any naïve observer watching a socially skilled person behave comes to think that there is some active "social intelligence" that gives him great facility, ease, and self-confidence. But the truth is that everybody has to work at it.

It's sometimes hard to convince people that socially competent and successful people had to work at it to get to be the way they are. Part of the problem comes from the fact that the work and effort involved is mainly carried out in the head and is not publicly observable. The other part has to do with a reluctance to accept the fact that you have to work and practice at one difficult level at a time. There's no point in running from one social context to another, each with a different level of difficulty, because the essence of acquiring an easy manner comes from over-learning, and that means repeating the same task over and over again.

Starting a Conversation

Look at it this way: if you want to be self-confident, you have to build up psychological muscle, and you have to apply the same training techniques used by weight-lifters. First, you start with thirty pounds at seven repetitions twice a day. Then you move to fifty pounds with the same routine. You then increase the number of repetitions in order to be strong enough to handle sixty-five pounds, and so on. You just can't start off by pressing one-hundred-eighty pounds and hope to be successful—let alone find it easy. The one-hundred-eighty-pounds press only becomes easy once you've practiced with lighter weights. Building psychological muscle operates on the same principle. Set up a series of graduated social tasks in increasing order of difficulty and start at the bottom.

chapter 9

SOUNDING YOURSELF OUT

IF YOU WANT TO FEEL SOMETHING BUT ARE TOO INHIB-
ited to express its components, then the best way to *come*
to feel something is to get yourself to *behave* like a person
who feels something. This is an awfully simple principle.
It suggests that in order for you to become more self-
confident, self-assured, brave, and generally happier with
yourself, you have to *act* like a person who is confident,
assured, courageous and happy—but with one exception.
If you're feeling angry, hostile, resentful, bitter, and just
generally negative toward someone, *pretending* to be
happy, jovial, and affectionate is not going to automatically make you feel better about the person. To make the
rule valid and an appropriate social prescription, we can
only consider times when you are unsure as to how you
feel, when you are afraid of letting yourself feel one way
or another. Where negative feelings predominate, pretending that these feelings do not exist will have little
effect. If, however, you have mixed feelings or are unsure as to how you should feel, a posture in one direction
is going to have a definite influence in eliciting feelings
and liberating you to express yourself.

Take the notion of self-confidence, for example. The extent to which you become self-confident has a lot to do with whether the social context responds favorably to your actions. If people around you consistently relate to you in a way that suggests you are comfortable, relaxed, at ease, and unthreatened by their presence, what better criterion do you need to confirm that you have nothing to fear? If you have the abilities, the skill, the knowledge, and the know-how for behaving appropriately and saying the right things in the company of others, then you have all the reason in the world to feel self-confident. All you have to do is act this way in front of others and your self-confidence will be confirmed by the public response. The essential feature here is the feedback that others give you concerning whether certain characteristics or traits are reflected in you. When confidence turns to boldness and brash arrogance, many people will not hesitate to denounce those undesirable traits in you; when calm assertiveness and an easygoing manner prevail, what kind of feedback can you expect to confirm the presence of these qualities? You'll get feedback, but it will be less concrete and distinct than the feedback you might otherwise obtain if you behaved in a shy, withdrawn, and inhibited manner, or if you behaved in an aggressive, bold, or arrogant way. People tend to react more to that which is inappropriate than to that which is appropriate and normal. As a result, at first it may be difficult for you to obtain a clear indication when you do behave appropriately. In this case, you'll have to monitor the extent and eagerness with which people are approaching you in comparison with the past.

However, you should be warned against thinking that being confident and self-assured inoculates you against all apprehension. Every self-confident person feels some nervousness in new situations, but what distinguishes him from the shy person is that he is not overwhelmed and incapacitated by this minor excitement. Indeed, this element of excitement may be what motivates him toward these social challenges, for, with a certain degree of practice, he quickly learns about the value and the excitement that come from this kind of risk-taking and accomplishment.

A distinction should be made between *challenging* the

social environment and *defying* its implicit rules. Challenges ought to be undertaken only in order to test out the extent to which your social competence, skill, and mental capacity can support the complexity of the new context. From such experiences you will gain in self-esteem. At the same time, you have to understand that if you are unsuccessful at meeting the challenge of a social arena, and if your social skills *are* appropriate for that level of social complexity, you will have to attribute the lack of success to not enough effort or to the difficulty of the task. This can only be true if you have an adequate repertoire of interpersonal competencies and social skills. To behave falsely is to *defy* the social context and to invite the kind of severe anxiety that comes when such performances are eventually found out. The great danger associated with role-playing has to do with "pretending" to be something you are not. Self-esteem can only be derived from what we *know* ourselves to be. When we present a certain image, we had better be prepared to testify about whether we possess the elements that make it up. It is therefore important to acquire all those skills that make up an expressive and non-shy person before presenting yourself in that light.

The components of a valid public presentation of a non-shy character style have been explored in the previous chapters. In this chapter, we'll be working on the techniques for learning verbal and non-verbal skills, reducing anxiety and keeping it within normal limits, changing unproductive beliefs and thinking styles, and developing strategies for becoming more self-confident and for getting rid of self-consciousness.

Get Your Shots

The program that follows is a gradual, progressive, step-by-step plan for becoming more expressive and for overcoming shyness. It is designed specifically for the person who is afraid of even taking the first step. Each step of the program has been carefully worked out and is in accord with sound clinical principles for learning new skills, changing irrational beliefs, and learning to control emotional upset. Each step has been planned so as to "inoculate" you against the emotional reactions that would normally ensue. The successful completion of one step will prepare you for the next step in the program. Just as being inoculated against the flu involves introducing into the body a small amount of the foreign virus until the body builds up enough defenses to withstand the full force of an alien invasion, so this program presents you with a series of graduated tasks, which, when successfully completed, inoculates you against being upset by the stress of the next task. For these series of inoculations to "take," it's necessary that they be received in the right sequence. By the time you reach the end of the program, you will be sufficiently strong to withstand your experimenting with real social life conditions.

Why You Won't Change

Once you've decided that you're tired of being shy and that you'd like to take part in the social challenges and the interpersonal realities of a healthy social life, you've taken the first step in the right direction. But a few warnings are already in order.

First of all, if you want to change from being a shy to a non-shy and self-confident person, the pages in this book are not going to leap up and take you by the hand and carry you through the experiences necessary. *You* are the only person who can change this condition. *You* have to do, act, behave, practice, and test out your social reality. After you've finished reading this book, you may only halfheartedly try out one technique or another, only think about one strategy or another, or only halfway complete an exercise, and then realize that little has changed in you. It is not because your shyness is irreversible, nor is it because you and your inadequacies are inseparable—it is because *you have not tried hard enough.*

A second warning: you should read the *entire* book more than once before you try to implement and practice the exercises provided. *This is very important.* Do not try to carry out any of the exercises until you understand the context in which the exercises are placed and how they apply to you personally.

A third warning: There is absolutely no doubt about the fact that you will not change if you don't follow the steps and sequences exactly as they are presented. Some of the exercises you may find boring and uninteresting, or maybe you'll think they're not applicable to you. Don't be misled and deceived! Our own research and experience with the program has convinced us that all of the components and steps prescribed are relevant aspects of overcoming shyness for just about everybody. If you leave out one component or don't practice and rehearse according to the schedule provided, you won't be prepared for the tasks that follow.

Take a chance. Risk seeing to what extent you can successfully complete the exercises that seem too simple. They are all essential! The testimonies of people who have taken part in our Shyness Clinic and our own scientific understanding of psychological principles for treating new personality styles in people have convinced us of this. There are some people who progress up to a certain point and then falter and are unable to carry out the next sequence. When we look closely at what they have done, we always find that they have not applied the techniques properly or have not practiced them enough.

Some people think they're too shy to change. If you think *that,* you won't change. You are wrong to think that you can never overcome your shyness, no matter what you do. In our Shyness Clinics, we have had people who have labeled themselves severely shy for many years, and we have found that their success has little to do with how shy they think they really are. On the contrary, the success they had in overcoming their shyness had everything to do with their desire to be rid of that condition and the *effort* they were willing to put into applying the exercises and in testing out social reality. This point can't be overstated. It's important for you to understand that if you want to stop being shy, you have to *do* something about it. It's not going to happen by itself. It's time you stopped thinking that social conditions will change to the point where by some lucky break you'll find it easier to relate socially and meet the social challenges with comfort and ease. Stop hoping that you're going to be the big sweepstakes winner and that this windfall will attract a compassionate friend who will be willing to spend three years coaching you along, giving you all the support you need, holding your hand, and patting you on the back after every trial. Don't think this attitude reflects a lack of appreciation for the anxiety, worry, and apprehension you may experience; this isn't the case. My colleagues and I are very sympathetic toward those who experience emotional upset and discomfort. But we are not sympathetic toward those who *complain* about being shy and fearful, who want to stop missing out on social friendships and growth experiences, and yet are not willing to even *try* to do something about it.

You shouldn't be misled into thinking that each step is going to be easy or that you're not going to experience any fear or apprehension as you progress throughout the program. In fact, experiencing a certain amount of stress and discomfort is *essential* to the successful completion of the program. We have found that those who make the maximum effort and who try hard at becoming socially skilled and who take appropriate risks are those who, while more stressed, make the greatest gains and at the quickest rate possible.

Our program at the Shyness Clinic has been changed many times to take into account all of the various conditions associated with shyness. It allows you to progress at your own pace, for, indeed, we have found that socially anxious people really need more time to complete the phases compared with those shy people who have only mild apprehension of social encounters. Nevertheless, all steps and phases have to be completed no matter how shy you may think you are or aren't.

Let's begin.

How Do You Sound?

The first lesson concerns the sound of your voice and how to acquire the skills for speaking more expressively with more confidence. And you will also learn how to make what you say sound more interesting, colorful, and rewarding. There are two phases to this lesson with exercises that have to be successfully completed and repeated progressively. The first phase teaches you to become aware of your voice characteristics and how to practice modulating and balancing these voice features. The second phase specifies how to use these skills in actual conversations.

We've asked a large number of shy people what they thought of this exercise. Almost all of them said that when they were first exposed to the suggestion that they take a tape recorder and practice talking and listening to the sound of their voice, they felt this would be boring, useless, and that little would be gained from it. But when this exercise was assigned within the sessions of the Clinic itself and carried out under our promptings, the reactions we got were:

"My God! I never realized I sounded like that!"

"I'm really embarrassed! I can't believe that I sound like that sometimes!"

"Boy, I'm glad you made me go through this one!"

"I don't believe it! I really don't believe it!"

The issue here is that most of us are simply not aware of the sound of our own voice as others hear it, and shy people, for some peculiar reason, are notorious in their disclaiming that their voice may be something less than appropriate, socially expressive, or pleasant to listen to.

As you read what these exercises are all about, catch yourself saying you don't think you'll bother carrying out this part of the program. Listen to your own rationalizations for not wanting to go along with this exercise. At one point you may even end up by saying, "Well, I'm not really as shy as that and I don't really think that the sound of my voice is a problem with me." Or you might end up saying, "I've heard my voice on a tape recorder before and I think it's all right." Whether or not you *think* you'll benefit from these exercises is quite irrelevant; if you follow the steps of the exercises, you'll be astounded with the results you obtain, and if you don't rationalize what you heard with such statements as, "Well, people always sound different on a tape recorder," you will be ready and motivated to want to carry out phase two of the program.

Risk it. Don't be afraid to exaggerate loudness, tone, or intensity in order to test the range of these elements.

Sounding Yourself Out

When you're using what you've learned in the course of real face-to-face conversations, the appropriate intensity, loudness, and modulation will come out naturally.

Phase One

1). Buy or borrow a tape recorder, preferably one that has both bass and treble adjustments. Adjust these to mid-level and leave them there. Don't erase anything you record. We'll be going back to early recordings later on to see how you've changed.

2). Find a quiet room where you will be free of distractions and interference. Test out the audio level by holding the microphone approximately eight inches away from your mouth and counting from one to ten. Play back that portion and set the audio level on your tape recorder to the loudness that would be needed for two people to carry on a normal conversation on the street.

3). Get acquainted with the following passages by reading them over out loud *without* recording. Next, read this passage into the tape recorder:

There is, accordingly, no better known or more generally useful precept in one's personal self-discipline than that which bids us to pay primary attention to what we do and express, and not to care too much for what we feel. . . . Action *seems* to follow feeling, but really action and feeling go together; and by regulating the action, which is under the more direct control of the will, we can indirectly regulate the feeling, which is not.

Thus, the sovereign voluntary path to cheerfulness, if our spontaneous cheerfulness be lost, is to sit up cheerfully, and to act and speak as if cheerfulness were already there. If such conduct does not make you feel cheerful, nothing else on that occasion can. So to *feel* brave, act as if we *were* brave, use all our will to that end, and a counter-fit will very likely replace the fit of fear. Again, in order to feel kindly toward a person to whom we have been inimical, the only way is more or less deliberately to smile, to

SHY?

make sympathetic inquiries, and to force ourselves to say genial things. One hearty laugh together will bring enemies into a closer communion of heart than hours spent on both sides in inward wrestling with the mental demon of uncharitable feeling. To wrestle with a bad feeling only pins our attention on it, and it keeps it fastened in the mind, whereas, if we act as if from some better feeling, the old feeling soon folds its tent like an Arab and silently steals away.

—William James

4). Play back what you just read and complete the Voice-Training Analysis below. Check the items in each category that apply to your presentation on the tape.

How was your:

RATE	FORCE	PITCH
too slow _____	adequate _____	high _____
too fast _____	weak _____	low growl _____
too many	unvaried _____	monotone _____
pauses _____	loudness _____	narrow
no pauses _____	varied _____	range _____
too even _____		high over-
good _____		tones _____
		appropriate _____

ARTICULATION	QUALITY
side of	nasal _____
mouth _____	strained _____
no mouth	throaty _____
activity _____	husky _____
whistled the	flat _____
"s" _____	lifeless _____
over precise _____	good _____
slurred _____	
clear _____	

Before you go through the passage once more, here are the components for improving your voice and speech:

174

Sounding Yourself Out

Freeing the jaw	Variety of fast-	Singing scales,
Slowing the	slow, high-low,	Humming
rate	loud-soft	Lower pitch
Use of pauses	General emo-	Facial
Prolonging	tional expres-	expressions
vowels	siveness	
Exaggerated	Reading louder	
articulation	Projection	

Speech Exercises

I. Relaxation and Breathing
  1). Relax the muscles of your face and your jaw by shaking your head gently from side to side, allowing your jaw to move as if it were loosely connected.
  2). Yawn and sigh.
  3). Place a book against your abdomen; inhale and exhale quickly. Note the lateral movement of the book; this is where the energy comes from.
  4). Recite the alphabet slowly, once through, articulating each word with exaggerated interest.
II. Projection
  1). Take the following nonsense syllables "hoo-ho-hah-hey" and say them into the tape recorder first at a whisper level;
  2). Now at a half-whisper.
  3). Now at a conversational loudness.
  4). Now at full loudness (without shouting) and without tightening or straining the throat.
III. Resonance and Consonant Stress
  1). Start humming and repeating "boom, boom, boommmmm," until a tingling and vibrating sensation is felt on your lips and nose.
  2). Practice saying the sounds "m," "n," and "ng." When the letter "s" follows voiced sounds, it is pronounced as a "z." Read the following into the tape recorder and play it back:

SHY?

The moon never beams without bringing me dreams. . . .
Mumbo, Jumbo, god of the Congo. . . .
The moan of doves in immemorial elms, and the hum of
Innumerable bees.

Read the William James passage once more, making
use of those components that went into the preceding exercises. Go through the Voice-Training Analysis and rate
yourself again. Look at where you improved and examine
the gains you made.

The following passage has a slightly different feeling to
it, a more conversational tone. Read it over first to get the
general mood, and then read it into the tape recorder. It
should be read in a conversational, interesting manner in
order to keep the listener's attention.

A man's social self is the recognition that he gets
from his mates. We have an innate propensity to get
ourselves noticed, and noticed favorably. If no one
turned around when we entered, answered when we
spoke, or minded what we did, but if every person
we met "cut us dead" and acted as if we were non-
existing things, a kind of rage and impotent despair
would ere long well up in us, from which the cruelest
bodily tortures would be a relief; for these would
make us feel that, however bad might be our plight,
we had not sunk to such a depth as to be unworthy
of attention at all.

Properly speaking, a man has as many social
selves as there are individuals who recognize him
and carry an image of him in their mind. But as the
individuals who carry the images fall naturally into
classes, we may practically say that he has as many
social selves as there are distinct groups of persons
about whose opinion he cares. . . . What may be
called "club-opinion" is one of the very strongest
forces in life. The thief must not steal from other
thieves; the gambler must pay his gambling debts,
though he may pay no other debts in the world. The
code of honor of fashionable society has throughout
history been full of permissions and vetoes, the only
reason for following either of which is that so we best

serve one of our social selves. You must not lie in general, but you may lie as much as you please if asked about your relations with a lady; you must accept a challenge from an equal, but if challenged by an inferior you may laugh him to scorn. . . .

—William James

Are you interesting? Do you have the appropriate tone and mood? Do the various characteristics of voice sounds (as listed in the Voice-Training Analysis) fit the meaning of the words and the color of the passage? You should know that anything that comes out of your mouth in the form of a narrative represents a statement of an idea embodied around a theme, eliciting various images in the reader (listener), communicated by carefully selected descriptive words, and assisted by the use of a rhythm and a tone. The tone of any narrative indicates the speaker's attitude toward the subject, toward the people who are listening, and toward himself.

Take the simple phrase, "Yes, indeed." Try shifting your tone to communicate, first of all *enthusiasm*, then *respectful agreement*, and then *discourteous denial*. Can you do that? Tone, then, expresses attitudes. Read over the last passage again, get the general sense, and adopt an attitude that would communicate the proper mood.

Examine the Voice-Training Analysis measures again. What other components could you have used for emphasis? Did you pause for effect? Did your voice increase in loudness for emphasis? Did you try something like singing off a word as if to show lightheartedness? Did your tone change as the passage progressed onto new ideas? What kind of facial expressions (use of eyebrows, eyes, frowning, muscles around the mouth) might you employ? Repeat this into the tape recorder and play it back as many times as necessary until you have tried as many variations and combinations of facial expressions with vocal components as possible. In your last attempt, try to make use of all the vocal elements, i.e., shift in intensity and loudness, pauses and changes in rate, prolongation of a vowel sound, together with an overdoing of facial expressions. Try this exaggeration into the tape recorder and play it back. Now, try it once more and adopt an attitude more subdued and calm while still painting the correct images for the listener.

Moving out of the realm of formal prose and into more natural forms of speech, read the following material into the tape recorder. Imagine that you are sitting with two friends having coffee. They are uncritical and accepting and you feel free to experiment with new styles with them. Imagine that the event described in the passage actually happened to you and you were very much affected by the experience.

Listen, I gotta tell you this. I was driving into town last Saturday, and you wouldn't believe the snow! I mean, I got caught in this blizzard that just came out of nowhere. I was just thirty miles out of town . . . I don't know where exactly. Really! The wind was so strong and the snow was coming down so hard that you couldn't see a thing! I had to get off the road and stop somewhere, and when I got out of the car . . . man, you couldn't see your hand in front of you! Geez! That was weird! I had no idea if anyone was coming up behind me, and if there was, I'm sure they couldn't see a thing. No, really, that was really scary. You're going to think this is crazy, but I thought the safest place was out of that car, just in case somebody came crashing into me. I got bundled up and headed for a snowbank and kicked a hole big enough for me and I sat in there for fifteen minutes. Don't laugh. When the storm calmed down, I saw all kinds of cars turned around, in the ditch, and facing each other behind me. I gotta tell you, I was cold.

Now, if you carried out the taping and playback assignments so far according to the directions, the first thing you would notice following this last exercise is the increased degree of difficulty brought on by the "free flow" structure of conversation. Did you notice that you have a tendency to be more contained and restrained? Ask yourself the following question: In trying to put some feeling and expression into my narrative, why am I holding back? It might be because:

a). I don't want to get too excited. I'm not sure if I

can manage or control my excitement if I let my feelings go.

b). The narrative sounds a little silly; they may think I'm stupid, or that it was a dumb thing to do to get out of the car and into a snowbank, even though it was the safest place. So, by playing down the excitement, I can still tell them the story without making it appear that it was too important or dramatic.

c). My main concern in talking with friends is to show that I'm friendly, and that I don't impose myself upon them. I'm worried that being expressive will take away from the image I want to present.

d). I'm just afraid I won't be able to carry it off smoothly. Maybe I can start off okay, but I don't know if I can be expressive and at the same time think about what I'm going to say next.

The more shy you are, the more of the preceding reasons explain your reluctance to be expressive. The less shy you are, the fewer of the alternatives are appropriate, and with only mild shyness, excuse "d" is the one most frequently used.

Worrying about the fact that those who listen to you may infer that you're somewhat less than the intelligent, reserved, and well-controlled human being you wish to be has everything to do with your fear of negative evaluation, with your high need for approval, and your fear of failure. Remember that this excessive preoccupation with managing the impression you create is what really interferes with your ability to be spontaneous and expressive.

Do this mental exercise. Conjure up an image of a person who is strong, independent, and self-assured, and who, because of these qualities, is little affected by what people think of him. Imagine this person to be a character in a play and pretend that you're reading a short story and "acting" the part of the character portrayed. Now, using the material of being stuck in a snowstorm, record on tape and play back for yourself how you would sound if you were portraying this person on stage. If you can allow yourself to get into this mental set and role-play such a person effectively, you will see a major difference between this presentation and the one you made the first time. Why is this so? The answer seems obvious.

179

SHY?

The first time around you felt you were disclosing things about *you;* in the second trial, the person who was talking was the *character* you portrayed.

Go ahead and act out again the part of a person who is describing the events in the preceding narrative. This time, do it with full force of verbal, vocal, and non-verbal communication (hand gestures, facial expressions). Play it back to yourself. Now, go back to reading the passage as in the first instance; you're sitting with two friends having coffee and you're going to relate to them something interesting that happened to you over the weekend. Play back that last trial and compare it with your very first attempt. Where do you see the differences? Why have you suddenly become more comfortable in being more expressive? Your friends haven't changed, and, at best, only fifteen or twenty minutes may have elapsed from the time you began. *You* changed. *You have become more comfortable with the idea of being expressive.* Indeed, the truth of the matter is that it has become easier for you to accept yourself as a little more expressive. And, really, that's what it's all about.

Phase Two

Practice paying close attention to the voice characteristics and facial features of television announcers, actors and actresses, to those who do comedy routines, and to those who do commercials. Note carefully differences in their style and use of vocal and non-verbal information. Look at and listen closely to newscasters. You'll notice an almost stone-faced quietness and objectivity in the facial expressions of many of them. Often, the only features that are altered are voice characteristics, and the effect is to communicate "dispassionate interest." In view of the fact that many networks have a policy concerning how much emotional involvement a broadcaster is permitted to have in his delivery of news, a solid grounding and schooling in the art of concealing prejudices, preferences, and emotional biases is considered a formal prerequisite for this kind of job. Contrast this across different networks where the policy concerning "involvement" in

180

the news varies. Very quickly you'll be able to pick up differences in "containedness" and vocal expressiveness.

Another very useful exercise is to turn down the volume completely while you're watching characters act out a scene. Watch how Rhoda can act so expressively and communicate so much non-verbally. Watch her facial expressions, her body orientation, and her use of her hands and arms. Now reverse the process. Darken the image on the screen (don't just look away from the screen) and only listen to what is being said. Pay attention to the changes in tone, intensity, loudness, and rate in one person, and listen to differences in pitch, tone, and nasal and throaty characteristics among the characters. Next, look and listen to the characters and see how these various components of communication can be successfully coordinated, balanced out, and blended so as to have the strongest impact upon the viewer. We tend to take for granted the dramatic abilities and communication skills in the actors and personalities we see on television and in the movies. It is only when we analyze all of the components that go into giving us this Gestalt that we can appreciate the role each plays in being expressive.

While we're not trying to get you to act like or to express yourself like characters on a stage or on television (especially those in sitcoms), seeing how others use these component skills for effect will serve to make you more aware of how you can be more flexible, versatile, and expressive.

The next exercise will help you focus in on one component of your social skills in order to learn how to fuse *all* components of your verbal messages. Do you ever wonder how you sound on the telephone? I don't mean necessarily how the other person hears you, so much as how you actually speak when you happen to be talking over the telephone.

Telephone Talk

1). Keep your tape recorder close to the telephone. When the telephone rings, turn on the tape recorder and position the microphone in such a way that your voice is recorded (only *your* voice). Collect recordings of your voice over a sampling of five telephone calls that you answer.

2). The first thing that you may notice is that the way you talk over the telephone, even the way in which you say "hello," contains very different combinations of vocal components compared with when you speak normally face to face. The reason for this is twofold. First, when you hold the receiver close to your mouth, you can't talk as loudly as when you're speaking with someone a few feet away. So if in other situations you are accustomed to using changes in loudness to communicate various states and reactions, you're obviously deprived of that modality over the telephone. There should be, therefore, a compensation for this by using other vocal components, such as change in pitch, tone, or rate. The second reason has to do with the fact that you do not *see* the person to whom you're speaking. This has the net effect of reducing a tremendous amount of information that in normal transactions helps regulate the flow of conversation and that makes "taking turns to speak" visually calibrated for smooth exchanges of this kind. When people are deprived of these visual cues, they tend to compensate by amplifying the value or increasing the number of vocal components in their voice. Woe to the shy and non-expressive person who doesn't engage this mechanism! Whatever was perceived as timidity in non-expressive face-to-face communications, over the telephone this could be interpreted as apathy, lethargy, boredom, or depression.

Recording the sound of your voice while you're speaking on the telephone lets you hear how vocal components can be balanced out.

3). Get into the habit of recording your conversations over the telephone. Take time out to think about calling a friend for a social and casual chat or to request information or advice just for the express purpose of practicing balancing out verbal and vocal components. Here are the things you should look out for:

1). tendency to speak more softly
2). tendency to mumble and poorly articulate
3). tendency to speak too fast
4). tendency to be too even and not to pause

5). tendency to be monotone, have a narrow range, or to be nasal or high pitched

6). tendency to be strained, disfluent, and tight in the throat and jaw

Play around with each of these components when you speak over the telephone. Play back your conversations. Deliberately slow down your rate. Deliberately pause at an appropriate moment. Try prolonging vowels purposely. Try the occasional exaggerated articulation. Intentionally alternate the use of various combinations of these vocal components. Play this back and listen carefully.

4). As a separate exercise from the preceding one, practice variations in tone, pitch, and syllabic duration of the word "uh-huh." How would you sound saying "uh-huh" if you were expressing complete agreement with what had just been said? How would you sound if all you wanted to do in saying "uh-huh" was to show that you understood what was said and that you wanted the person to go on? How would you sound if you wanted to indicate questioning interest?

Take the word "hmm," which is an interjection often used as a filler between sentences designed to communicate that the message has been grasped. Curious interest can be communicated through "hmm" by starting at a lower tone and raising it as a curl at the end. Simply acknowledging that you are still with the person can be done with the short "um." Fascinated interest can be picked up by drawing out the "m" and rising the pitch, as in "hmmmmm!," and dropping the tone quickly at the end. Similarly, the word "huh" when spoken as "huh!" can denote the kind of feeling that might accompany a statement such as: "Well, she certainly had it coming to her!" And the word "huh?" delivered with a rise in pitch and prolonged vowel, cut off sharply, can easily reflect a feeling of amazed disbelief.

If you think that these vocal exercises are a little silly and just too uninteresting and you elect to pass them by, you would do well to remember that casual telephone conversations are really, as Ma Bell says, "the next best thing to being there." If you suffer from excessive self-consciousness and are preoccupied with thoughts about being looked at, then speaking with someone over the telephone should make it easier for you to practice since it removes most of the conditions that are responsible for this heightened self-preoccupation and discomfort. Think about it.

The more socially competent, expressive, and spontaneous you become, the more often others will see you as an interesting, appealing, and attractive person to be with. With this, of course, you have to expect that conversations may last a little longer than they did in the past, and that they may deal with topics that you may have previously avoided. Since it's only reasonable to expect that as you change—so will others in response to you—it's best to be equipped with the resources and skills to deal with these before inviting these changes for the first time. If you just finished building your own sailing dinghy and you don't know how to swim very well, you don't go and try it out in the Atlantic the first time; you're better off finding a lake, securing yourself with a life jacket, and testing your seafaring skills in that safe context. Similarly, when developing social skills, take one step at a time and work at laying the building blocks squarely one on top of each other; the roof and the furnishings will come in due time.

chapter 10

GAINING SOCIAL EXPERIENCES
FOR BUILDING SELF-CONFIDENCE

THINKING STRAIGHT

What are the productive, relevant, and rational beliefs you should hold if you are to overcome your shyness? Learn, memorize, and inwardly digest the following seven rational statements about yourself and social reality.

1). I've Got to Be Active in Getting What I Want from Social Situations.

Many shy people don't want to risk putting themselves in social situations because they are afraid of testing out their skills; and when they do venture out, they put little effort into trying to have a successful experience. You have to be active in arranging conditions and put more effort into meeting the challenge if you want your social encounters to be more satisfying. You have to develop concrete plans and act upon them purposefully and systematically. If you have an accurate view of your social competence, then you can set up *realistic* goals as steps toward the level on which you would like to be. Finally, you've got to *act* to attain your goals. When you get up in the morning, ask yourself, "What am I going to do today that is new and enterprising and significant. What will I do to help myself get where I want to be?"

2). I Can't Wait Until I Feel Completely Relaxed, Comfortable, and Secure Before Taking A Risk.

Ruminating, pondering, stalling, postponing, reconsidering—all these are delaying tactics that impede action. "I'm too nervous, I'm too scared," is the excuse of the shy person who won't try anything new if he has the slightest feeling of apprehension or misgiving. Unless you feel some degree of nervousness in meeting a new social trial, you are risking nothing, and so the venture is worthless in terms of social achievement. Take a chance—*now*.

3). I Can Exhibit Only Those Traits That I'm Prepared to Back Up.

If you are both shy and vain, then pretensions about your social self are neither rooted in experience nor founded upon skill or ability. *By pretending to be something you're not, you're inviting public exposure.* So give up the notion that the only way you can be a worthy person is by being better than everybody you meet. If you can feel worthwhile only by comparing yourself with everyone else, you're *never* going to feel worthwhile; there will always be someone who is better than you.

On the other hand, if your problem is one of excessive modesty, train your eye to judge others and situations more accurately. You underestimate yourself because of a tendency to overrate others. When the "beautiful people" are stripped of the trappings that make you envious of them, they are just like the rest of us.

4). The Idea That People Are Always Looking at Me and Judging Me Comes from the Eyes in My Own Head.

Get rid of the idea that people are always looking at you, scrutinizing you, sizing you up, and evaluating you. Only those who are shy and have a fear of negative evaluation spend a considerable amount of time thinking about this. The only reason you suspect that you are being looked at and evaluated is because you yourself do this to others. As *you* stop judging and evaluating people, so, too, will you stop thinking that others are doing the same to you. And, remember, those who do evaluate you unfavorably do so because deep down they believe that you are really better than they are.

5). I Must Develop Expectations That Are Realistic and Set Goals That Correspond with the Skills I Have for the Social Contexts Available.

Much too often when, on impulse, you've risked a social encounter, you've selected one that is much too difficult, considering the skills you've developed so far. You cannot expect to succeed under these circumstances. Think about what is involved in building psychological muscles. Go back to lighter exercises and repeat them often before trying out a more difficult social encounter. After the first glow of success in a social episode, some people feel they can take on the whole social world. But this is unlikely. Your expectations for success should correspond with the skills and amount of practice you've had. And your goals should be set just slightly higher than what you've already attained.

6). Even Those Who Are the Most Socially Skilled, Competent, and Popular Are Never Successful One Hundred Percent of the Time. I Shouldn't Get So Upset When It Happens to Me.

It is virtually impossible for anyone to obtain a favorable social response *all of the time*. Those who have social skills and are self-confident do not panic when they don't meet with approval or acceptance. Why do you? People with a healthy sense of social self-esteem do not set up a standard that specifies that one incidence of failure is enough to mean deficiencies and ineptness. Don't be too hard on yourself!

Making inferences about your social success based on a small number of interpersonal experiences in limited social contexts is a natural but dangerous thing to do. If the odds are poor in one room, don't hang around. Move on to the next room, where you will have a chance to engage your skills.

7). If I Initiate a Social Contact That Turns Out Unsuccessfully, It Has Nothing to Do With Me as a Person; It has to Do with the A-B-C's.

You can't give yourself much credit for being socially successful if you try something that you have done many times before. The only way to increase your social self-esteem is by doing something that is new and puts your social self to a test. Social experiences that lead to an increase in self-esteem and self-confidence are those that involve a challenge, a degree of difficulty that corresponds to, or is just slightly higher than your degree of skill; no other condition will suffice. If you don't have the skills, learn them; if you've learned them, test them out in reality.

If you have a successful social experience, this has to be attributed to your social skills and ability. But if you are not successful, your failure can only be attributed to one or more of the following factors.

A. You didn't try hard enough. If the social situation was appropriate to your ability and skill, you didn't try hard enough to exercise all of the components of your talents. Success in many social situations depends upon the amount of *effort* you are willing to put out in order to receive what you're after. Vain-shy people who have pretensions often say to themselves, "Huh! I'm so and so and such and such. When they see who it is, I won't have

any problems. I'm not going to bother trying very hard."
This attitude often leads to failure, rebuke, and impressions of arrogance and conceit.

The shy person who underrates himself, on the other hand, figures that there is little point in trying very hard because he mistakenly thinks he doesn't meet the competition. But his endowment is much the same as anyone else's and he would certainly succeed if he just tried a little harder.

B. It was too difficult. Unfortunately, it is true that you can never be perfectly sure that the difficulty of a social encounter is at the same level as your social proficiency. For example, trying to maintain someone's attention through interesting conversation is much more difficult when there are half a dozen other people at the same table than if only the two of you are there; if you don't succeed, it's because the task was too difficult. If *you* approach a person of the opposite sex who is shy, socially inexperienced, and fearful and you ask him or her for a date and are refused, and if you used all your artistry and know-how and you are still unsuccessful, it's probably because it's pretty hard for *anyone* to get a shy person to agree. If you get on the telephone on a Friday night to get a date for Saturday and can't seem to find anyone to agree to go out with you, it is because it's very hard for *anyone* to get a date at the end of the week.

C. Bad luck. Luck has to do with forces or causes of events that are completely out of your control and that change from good to bad unpredictably. Being at the right place at the right time by accident may be responsible for someone landing a good job, just as relating with someone at the wrong place at the wrong time may prevent you from being successful. Under conditions in which the social task was commensurate with your social versatility, in which the task was not difficult, and in which you expended the appropriate amount of effort, any lack of success is because of bad luck.

PRESENTING YOURSELF

In this section you will learn how to go about developing appropriate verbal and non-verbal communications, how to rehearse these skills, how to go about acquiring habits for maintaining a conversation, and how to put the verbal, vocal, and non-verbal components into an appropriate and socially expressive ensemble, first for brief and passing encounters, and then for transactions of longer duration.

Brief Encounters

As you know, these encounters involve those transactions that last no longer than fifteen seconds and sometimes only a few seconds. Usually, they occur when you see acquaintances, friends, colleagues, subordinates, superiors—usually anyone with whom you have a non-intimate relationship. In learning how to relate more effectively in these brief encounters there are four component skills that have to be practiced: 1). verbal caricatures of greeting and of leaving; 2). non-verbal communication involving hands, arms, facial expression, body orientation, and distance; 3). vocal aspects of the sound of your voice; 4). ways of coordinating and balancing out different blends of these three ingredients. Once again, real and significant progress will occur only if you take an active part in this program and make every effort to carry out the tasks prescribed. Remember that with each successfully completed exercise you immunize yourself against being excessively stressed by what follows.

The best way for you to develop *verbal caricatures* is to generate your own list. If you put some effort into originating your own personal verbal expressions (as opposed to memorizing a list that could have been prepared for you), you stand a better chance of being able to incorporate these verbal messages into your own communication style.

Think of five people who are casual acquaintances you might regularly encounter during the course of a day. Exclude members of your family and roommates. Two of the people you think of should be of your own sex and three should be of the opposite sex. Take a few seconds and fantasize about a typical context in which you might

Gaining Social Experiences

encounter each of them in passing. Just like running a movie in your head, imagine yourself exchanging verbal greetings and leave-taking remarks with that person. As you fantasize, imagine yourself to be in a most pleasant and affable mood. In a sheet of paper, write down two different verbal greetings and two different leave-taking remarks for each person. Work with these remarks, revising them until they are as cheerful and as sociable as they can be. Next, write these revised greeting and leave-taking phrases in the following spaces provided. Put in the correct punctuation and pauses for emphasis.

First Person: Greeting:_____
_____

Leaving:_____
_____

Second Person: Greeting:_____
_____

Leaving:_____
_____

Third Person: Greeting:_____
_____

Leaving:_____
_____

Fourth Person: Greeting:_____
_____

Leaving:_____
_____

Fifth Person: Greeting:_____
_____

Leaving:_____

SHY?

The use of *facial expressions* is next. In the Shyness Clinic we tried a number of techniques for teaching how to use the facial muscles to intensify or modulate what is being said. After trying out videotape recordings and playbacks and getting people to practice various facial expressions in front of a mirror, we abandoned the use of both of these as learning aids. It seemed that watching oneself is much too distracting and doesn't allow anyone to pay attention to the muscular feedback. The most successful strategy for learning to engage various facial muscles involves simply closing your eyes and practicing tightening and loosening different series of muscles.

Consider first and then perform the following facial expressions. Use only the muscles that describe the expression.

Becoming Aware of the Life in Your Face

(Hold each expression for five seconds; repeat each three times.)

A). Smile with the lips barely apart.
B). Smile broadly.
C). Frown and furrow the brows.
D). Raise the eyebrows.
E). Bite your lower lip gently.
F). Wink with one eye.
G). Wink and pull gently at the cheek muscles above the corner of your mouth.
H). Nod your head up and down.
I). Tilt your head to the left and nod that way.
J). Move your head broadly from left to right slowly.
K). Shake your head from left to right with small movements.

TAKING THE EXPRESSIONS TO HEART

(Unite the various muscle groups in the combined
expressions listed below. With the help of the terms
listed below, write in the mood, attitude, or feeling
you are experiencing in doing this exercise.)

1). A & D   6). D & E

2). C & E   7). D & J

3). D & G   8). C & K

4). C & J   9). D & K

5). A & H   10). G & I

CONTENTED	SURPRISED	WISE
HAPPY	HESITANT	ANXIOUS
GLAD	CURIOUS	BORED
PUZZLED	HOPEFUL	AGREEABLE
CAUTIOUS	PROUD	COY
CONFUSED	SAD	DISBELIEVING
UNEASY	EAGER	

As you were carrying out these exercises, what kinds
of moods did they elicit in you? What attitude do you
think would normally accompany each of these? Now,
taking two different muscle groups in combination, do the
exercise again. For example, start off by combining items
A and D, then C and E, and so on. Pay attention to the
mood or attitude you would be communicating with these
various combinations. Select five combinations that you
find particularly interesting and do them again, but this
time imagine the words you might be saying in a conversation with someone while you are using these facial expressions.

If you are doing this exercise correctly, you should notice an interesting thing. Depending on the combinations you have chosen and the verbalizing you imagined to go along with the reaction, you should find that sometimes the words come first and *then* are followed by the facial expressions; at other times, the facial expression precedes the verbalization. With still other combinations both occur concurrently. If you haven't already noticed this happening, practice deliberately initiating one component before the other, reversing their order, and then putting them both together at the same time.

The fourth skill has to do with *putting together verbal, vocal, and non-verbal expressions* in order to express reactions appropriately. What is appropriate is determined by the social context. In those situations where extreme reactions (such as being shocked, astounded, or breathtaken) are appropriate, you can engage all *three* sources of communication with minimal expression in each. Alternatively, you can consider using *one* source of information about your emotional state and keep the other two components uninvolved, but in this case the one component you do use will have to be deployed to a greater extent than if you engaged other sources. Reactions depicting wonder, consternation, curiosity, or awe can be communicated in a moderate and modulated fashion by engaging one expressive source to an average degree or two or three sources together to a mild degree.

Now turn back to the pages where you wrote out your greeting phrases. Close your eyes and run through each fantasy greeting one at a time, as if each were a movie unwinding before you. Imagine you are repeating each greeting with different vocal intonations. Imagine it with a smile. Now imagine it with a prolonged gaze and with the vowel sounds extended. What does that communicate? Imagine speaking more softly, but with accompanying facial expressions, such as raising your eyebrows and turning your head coyly to one side as you gaze in the person's direction. Still in your imagination, try out various combinations of vocal and facial expressions in conjunction with each verbalized greeting. Remember, you have to *balance out* these three sources of communication. If your verbal message is strong, such as, "Good morning,

John. My, you're looking sharp today," and you happen to be standing two feet away from the person, you might consider balancing out by softening your voice, or not standing with a body position oriented full face, or by refraining from giving a broad smile, preferring instead to raise your eyebrows as you establish eye contact. Imagine the various combinations and balancing-out routines involved if you made the same remark but were standing ten feet away from the person.

You should go through the preceding exercises several times, or as many times as necessary until you can imagine the scene without unnecessary worry and apprehension. Mentally rehearsing these scenes will help you make the verbal and non-verbal components seem a more natural part of you when you carry them out in real life. The more you practice the various combinations of facial expressions—indeed, exaggerate some of them in your mental practice—the more easily they will be triggered off with appropriate form in a real social episode.

Prolonged Interactions

In order to feel comfortable in extended social episodes, you must first learn various strategies for keeping a conversation going and for making these interpersonal exchanges more equitable. In social situations in which there is no fixed-role behavior, and no concrete task to perform, and in which these contexts are tacitly understood to be purely social and casual, a wide variety of interchanges is possible. Now, while you may feel threatened by the lack of boundaries or definition of the situation, your anxiety can be compounded by the fact that you feel you can exercise little control over the direction of a conversation, the topics to be discussed, or the responses to be elicited. Remember that learning how to shift topics of conversation, how to redirect questions, how to volunteer answers you want to give, and, in essence, how to shape your own social climate is what is going to give you a sense of self-assurance in these settings. In the end, you'll realize that having these skills will allow you to relax, take it easy, and not be threatened by the uncertainty of an environment.

SHY?

Conversations are kept going by virtue of the answers that are given to questions asked and by the communicative comments that accompany these narratives. So the first skill you have to learn is what questions to ask, as well as when and how to ask them. Next, you have to be prepared to provide answers to similar questions that might be cast your way.

There are at least two kinds of questions you can ask: those that are very specific to the person; those that are broad and general and could apply to anyone. Think about five different people you know casually, two of your own sex and three of the opposite sex. Think for a moment about some special characteristic they are proud of, some distinctive interest they have, or some unique positive feature about them. Prepare a question for each of these people that will focus on that special dimension. For example, if you think of Joe, and you know he's involved in playing football for the local team, your question could be: "How's the football going, Joe?" Or: "Don't you get worried about all those injuries on the field?" Or: "Say, Joe, how do you think we're going to do in the game next week?"

Suppose you know that Sue loves to ski. You could consider asking her something like: "Got your skis out yet?" Or: "Going to get in much skiing this year?" Or: "Have you ever been skiing at Whiteface Mountain?" Write down your own questions below.

Special Notes on People I Know

First Person: Focus:_____

Question:_____

Second Person: Focus:_____

Question:_____

Third Person: Focus:_____

Question:_____

Fourth Person: Focus:_____

Question:_____

Fifth Person: Focus:_____

Question:_____

Gaining Social Experiences

What you have to offer for exchange in casual conversation can vary from humor, joy, amusement, simple information, entertainment, or simply the opportunity for spending some quiet, non-demanding time with another person. Your task is to relate in a way that would invite friendliness and a relaxed atmosphere. You should think seriously about staying away from doing anything that would detract from this goal. In this connection, there are certain things that you should *not* initiate.

As a general rule of thumb, you should stay away from starting discussions about politics, religion, and sex. These topics have a way of causing casual transactions to degenerate into conflict, struggles, and emotional upset, especially if you don't already know the other person's position on these. In casual transactions you should free yourself of role-prescribed behavior, attitudes that accompany status and power, and usual reactions in the face of authority figures. If you see a person primarily as powerful, superior, or authoritative, and you relate in a manner that is designed to reinforce this position and status, you have to expect that he or she, in turn, will relate to you in a way that will reinforce your position of subservience or mediocrity. If a policeman approaches you for having run a stop sign, he's not interested in light-hearted socializing; expect him to relate to you in a way that is role-governed—a condition that you yourself invited. Expect your physician to assume a doctor-patient role-set if you seek his consultation. In a class setting, if you are a college senior and are approached by a freshman, expect *him* to relate in a manner that testifies to his junior position. At work, expect your secretary and subordinates to structure transactions in such a way that would confirm your status. However, in interacting with any one of the preceding in a *social* context that does *not* prescribe role behavior, that is, in a casual atmosphere, you should not allow yourself to do anything that would create this role-expectancy set. If the context calls for sociability, friendliness, and casualness, you should be actively thinking up ways to encourage a friendly and convivial mood. Drop the mask and costume you wear in role-defined situations.

List five people with whom you think you might have difficulty abandoning this stereotyped role behavior. These

can include an attractive person of the opposite sex (whose
personality you tend to overrate in the first place), a person of authority (by virtue of either his expertise or
administrative power, and one whom you tend to revere),
a person who is your junior in one way or another (from
whom you expect respect, admiration, and meekness), or
a person in any other stereotyped role category that may
be relevant for you. Fill in the following blanks by writing
in the person's initials and the most salient dimension that
governs how you usually come across to each of them at
work, school, or in formal settings.

1). Person: _____ Your expected role _____
2). Person: _____ Your expected role _____
3). Person: _____ Your expected role _____
4). Person: _____ Your expected role _____
5). Person: _____ Your expected role _____

Now, imagine that you are in a casual social context
in which roles can be abandoned. This can be any situation, from a party, a chance meeting in a store, a football
game, or even outside after church. In the following
spaces, write down a general question you could ask each
of these people, assuming that you will have a thirty-
second transaction. Make sure that your question is consistent with being friendly, casual, and informal. Be
careful not to presume upon the friendship or appear off-
handed or impolite. As you write down the question,
imagine the vocal and non-verbal communications that
would accompany its delivery. Make sure that you do
nothing to encourage role-prescribed behavior in the other
person. Here are some examples: "How do you think the
World Series is going to turn out?" Or: "How are things
going with you these days?" Or: "Isn't this Indian summer great? I can't remember if we had such good weather
last fall."

Gaining Social Experiences

First Person: _____

Second Person: _____

Third Person: _____

Fourth Person: _____

Fifth Person: _____

Answering Questions

Asking a question puts the ball back in the other person's court and momentarily frees you from having to perform; however, now you should be prepared to assume responsibility for making exchanges equitable and learn how to provide answers to the questions that are bound to come your way. While this may sound a little artificial, the best way to feel more at ease when questions about yourself are directed your way is to have a set of replies readily available. Imagine you are in some casual social setting. List below five questions a person of the *same* sex could direct your way, and five questions a person of the *opposite* sex could ask. These questions should be of the kind that, while considered socially appropriate, cause you embarrassment or difficulty in replying. (For example, some shy people have difficulty with the question: "Well, what do *you* do for a living?")

Questions I Have Trouble With

Female asks: 1). _____

2). _____

3). _____

4). _____

5). _____

SHY?

Male asks: 1)._____

2)._____

3)._____

4)._____

5)._____

Now, on a separate sheet of paper provide answers to these questions. Your answers should be from three to five sentences long, and they should contain accurate information and be appropriately self-disclosing. For examples of appropriate self-disclosure, turn back to Chapter 7. After you have written out your replies, ask yourself whether you have been as honest as you could have been and whether you could have risked revealing a little more about yourself. Don't settle for the first answer written out. If you want to limit the content, consider vocal and non-verbal revelations. Revise all of your answers to the point where you provide no grounds for a listener to infer timidity, defensiveness, inhibitedness, shame, guilt, arrogance, haughtiness, or indifference.

With the tape recorder turned on and the microphone in front of you, answer aloud in a way that corresponds to the nature of the question and the setting. Play back your performance, and with a completely different variation of vocal components attempt to create a set of confidence, openness, and amiability. Rehearse out loud these self-descriptive statements often enough for you to have them become part of you—until the words fall out of your mouth naturally and effortlessly.

Speaking About Myself

Imagine you are being asked each of the following questions. Provide an answer to each and speak it into the tape recorder for you to replay. Your reply should be as long as indicated within the brackets. Strive to be honest, direct, and friendly.

1). "Where do you live? Where are you staying?" [10 to 15 seconds]

2). "Where did you go to school? Where were you working before?" [10 to 15 seconds]

3). "Where are you from originally?" [5 to 10 seconds]

4). "Where do you work? Have you been there long?" [5 to 10 seconds]

5). "What courses are you taking? What's your major?" [15 to 20 seconds]

6). "Have you got change for a dollar?" [5 seconds]

7). "Have you got the correct time?" [5 seconds]

8). "How are things going with you? What's new?" [5 to 10 seconds]

9). "What are you doing this weekend?" [10 to 15 seconds]

10). "What are your plans for the summer?" [15 to 20 seconds]

11). "Do you ski? Do you play tennis or hike?" [15 to 20 seconds]

12). "Haven't seen you for a while. What have you been up to?" [10 to 15 seconds]

13). "The party on Saturday sounds like it'll be a lot of fun. Are you planning on going?" [10 seconds]

14). "Where do you usually eat lunch?" [5 seconds]

15). "Why don't you come for coffee with the rest of us?" [5 seconds]

16). "You seem pretty quiet today. Is something on your mind?" [5 to 10 seconds]

17). "That's a nice outfit you've got on. Where did you buy it?" [5 seconds]

Avoiding Embarrassment Over Silences

It is important to remember that few people are ever *completely* relaxed and at ease in an extended conversation with someone for the first time. Maintaining a conversation with a new acquaintance involves a good deal of mental work for most people, including those who aren't shy. Even in a relationship that has little history to it, there are often few things that can readily serve as topics of conversation. Not surprisingly, therefore, in early encounters the content of the verbal exchanges is characterized by these kinds of questions: "Where are you from?" "How long have you been here?" "When did you arrive?" "Where are you going?" "What do you do?" Answers to all of these questions provide a skeleton drawing of the person. Some shy people don't even know what questions to ask in getting the basic materials out of which this initial framework is to be built. Remember the five W's: who, what, where, when, why.

Having readily available questions to ask is an easy way for keeping a conversation going in initial encounters. But how do you handle a situation with someone whom you've met a few times before? What if you suddenly run out of things to say and ask? Should this be troubling? First, you should know that both shy and non-shy people experience awkward pauses in the course of early transactions. But non-shy people have a way of preparing themselves for possible pauses through the use of a very simple mental strategy. They always have available and fresh in their minds two or more very general reserve questions that could be asked of almost anyone in any social circumstances.

Events usually happen like this: after greeting an acquaintance and exchanging ritual comment, the suggestion that the social episode will be extended in time is usually prompted by one person doing more talking than what is ritually prescribed for brief transactions. As soon as this clue is picked up, all attention is focused upon what the person is saying. In carefully listening to what is being said, a variety of associations, trains of thought, and other connected thoughts come up. Various images, reactions, and fantasies easily spring forth and flow through the mind. It is these images and associations that the person relies upon as the mainstay for a smooth, ongoing flow of verbal exchanges. These serve as the stimuli for questions, remarks, comments, *etc*. Should the associations be unproductive or run their full course as topics of conversation and a silent period is anticipated, the person fills in with non-verbal messages (shifts a chair, change in body position, different tone of voice) and introduces the standard pat question he always had available.

Among non-shy people, pauses and silences are dealt with through non-verbal communications and the asking of questions on topics that were held in reserve. With the assurance that you won't be left without anything to say, you feel more comfortable and relaxed; with reduced worry and anxiety, you feel more free to let your mind wander, pause on an association, test out the possibility of pursuing that thought out loud, judge that doing so will be appropriate and pleasurable, store the thought in your immediate memory for easy recall, and return to active listening, leaving the door open for another mental stream of associations.

The associations, judgments, testing out in fantasy, and decisions to reject or store in memory are all cognitive processes that run automatically and in seconds. Since you can go through an entire mental operation of this kind in the time it takes for the person to speak four or five words, you can rest assured that you won't lose out on anything that is being said. Think of all of the associations, images, and thoughts that can freely materialize when you are not preoccupied with the negative thoughts about whether you are being evaluated or about creating a good impression. Remember that excessive self-preoccupation triggers anxiety. And as you start to feel more uncomfortable, sense your heart pounding, and squirm in your chair, your attention is directed to these internal events and you become even *more* self-preoccupied. It's a small wonder you can't keep a conversation going and have trouble trying to remember what it was you were going to ask!

Having a series of well-rehearsed general reserve questions in store should free you of the worry of what to do in case of silences. Focus your attention on the meaning of what is being said, let yourself go with associations, and the basis for a natural, smooth, and spontaneous exchange of thoughts will be provided. In order to avoid the impression that you are daydreaming or that you're not attentive or not interested in what is being said, you have to communicate non-verbally. The occasional "uh-huh," moderated by changes in vocal properties to correspond with reactions to what you hear, head nods, and simple facial expressions will keep you in the running. You have to make these vocal and non-verbal communications *habitual* and allow them to occur almost unconsciously. Habits are never acquired after one trial. Don't expect to feel completely at ease while exercising these skills in the beginning. But practice, in the form of mental rehearsal and in real-life settings, will quickly turn them into habits.

Setting Goals and Structuring New Social Experiences

Before moving on to this portion of the program, be sure you have successfully completed all of the exercises in the phases of verbal and non-verbal skill training. In this section, a series of exercises in graduated degrees of increasing social skill is presented. Paperwork, as well as patient effort through all the steps, is required to guarantee success. Now, make sure you use the verbal and non-verbal skills you learned and practiced in the previous sections.

First, you must work on increasing the number of times and the number of different ways in which you can go about greeting people the first time you see them in the day. In order to gain the most from this exercise, carry it through from beginning to end without omitting any detail.

1). Pick out three days during the week that are similar to one another in terms of where you are and the number of people you might meet. For these three days, and without trying to change your habits, *count* the number of times you are greeted by another person and the number of times you initiate a greeting episode with someone. While initial greetings are most frequent in the morning, be prepared to also include initial greetings occurring during the rest of the day. in your total daily count. You should have two totals at the end of the day: one representing greetings initiated by another, and the other being the total you independently initiated. Give half points to those episodes in which there seems to be a tie, such as when you greet each other at the same time.

2). With these daily averages in mind, over the next ten days increase the *number* of times you initiate greeting transactions with acquaintances and friends. Keep track of these numbers as well as the number of times others greet you. Plot a graph for yourself showing the number of times you greeted and were greeted each day covering the ten-day period. It will become clear that when *you* become more sociable, people will reciprocate this attention. After the tenth day, stop counting but maintain the habits you developed in your greeting encounters.

3). In all social environments there are people whom you recognize every day but to whom you never speak or even say hello. Before you actually embark on this portion of the exercise, make a note of all the people who you see every day but have never bothered to greet. Over the next five days, greet at least two new people each day. In addition to seeing how easy it is to increase your range and number of brief social contacts, you will immediately see how much everyone likes to be recognized. Once you've greeted someone who used to be just a passing figure, get into the habit of greeting him or her as a matter of course from then on.

Making New Social Contacts

The biggest step in this program involves the exercise for making the first three new social contacts. After these first three, you will notice a pyramiding effect, which occurs when you meet the friends of the new friends you have just made. In order for this exercise to be successful, there are a number of things you have to keep in mind: 1), don't hustle or come across like you're looking for a date; instead use pretexts as previously discussed; 2), select three people who are frequently present in your social environment but whom you don't know as friends, and make plans for how each is to be approached *before* you initiate your first new encounter; 3), make all three new contacts in the first week. Even if one social contact appears to be interesting and promising, it is important that you move on and complete the goal of three new contacts; 4), listen to and pay close attention to free information that is offered in these new social meetings. Pay particular attention to introductions that are made and remember the names of the new people you meet. Writing down the names of people you have met that day is a useful tactic; there is nothing more embarrassing than to meet someone one day and not remember the person's name the next day; 5), every time you have the occasion to pass by someone to whom you were introduced, make sure you capitalize on the opportunity for maintaining the contact by exchanging greetings. You'll be surprised to find how much people like it when you remember who they are and you call them by name. If it should happen that they have forgotten your name, make sure you repeat it to them; they won't forget it the next time.

Finding Out Where to Go

Your school or place of work probably has someone who is responsible for social clubs, organizations, leisure groups, and sports groups. Ask where you might obtain all the necessary information concerning these social activities. Get this information and start making inquiries. Even those activities that don't immediately appeal to you may be those that hold the greatest promise for new social contacts and friends. Use the telephone or, better still, go down in person. Sit in, look around, and talk to people who are there. Be as innovative and creative about this as are non-shy people.

The newspaper carries a great deal of information on a wide variety of social activities that you might find enjoyable. Before you decide to enroll in any new activity, make sure you have been exposed to as much information as possible concerning all the different kinds of social, sports, leisure, and craft/hobby activities that your city or community may have to offer. Enroll, sign up, and get into them. Participate, be active and creative, and don't stop originating possibilities for social contacts and friendships even when you are well under way with new ones!

Activities that attract an equal number of members of the opposite sex can be, of course, the most enjoyable and rewarding ones. Do not become complacent! Don't stop trying to initiate or to capitalize on the opportunities that come up even when you think you have significantly increased your range of friendships. It is not uncommon to find that once a shy person has initiated new contacts and developed a good circle of friendships, he stops trying and relies upon his existing friendship network to satisfy his social needs. The danger here is that only extended practice in a large number of different situations involving different people can make for protean social and cognitive skills. Only frequent exercise and application can turn these skills into polymorphous habits. Don't make the mistake that is made by so many shy people once they have been successful in turning the tables on shyness. Don't stop trying!

Basic Self-Confidence Exercises

For some shy people, the steps illustrated previously involve too much anxiety and they don't feel they have enough confidence to produce a successful outcome of their social attempts. If this is true in your case, the following four-phase socially structured assignment, together with an accurate self-monitoring and evaluation of each task performed, will serve to confirm to *yourself* that you can, indeed, have confidence and trust in your abilities.

Self-confidence is a feeling of assurance about one's social skill in bringing about social outcomes that will be satisfying and rewarding. Self-confidence is built up as a result of experiencing a number of successful social transactions consecutively. It is instilled in a person when he becomes *aware* of not only what kind of social episodes he has engaged in, how he has behaved, acted and reacted in them, but also what credit he can give himself in each successful transaction.

The four-phase assignments should be carried out across a solid time block. Make sure that you have this time available and that it will be free of irregular routines or interruptions from daily or weekly patterns (don't choose Christmas, vacations, exams, or time of illness, *etc.*)

Progress from one phase to the next without taking any breaks. You should be actively engaged in the completion of the structured routine every day. If you feel too anxious to progress from one phase to the next, or if your schedule is suddenly interrupted for more than two days, repeat *all* the assignments for that week before advancing to the next week's assignments. This is *very important!* Even if you've completed ninety percent of the assignments for one week and then find your routine interrupted, go back and start over again at the beginning of the assignments for that week. Try to understand that it is experiencing *consecutive* social gains that leaves the important residue of self-confidence.

Phase One. For the first seven days, it is important that you record your social contacts. You are to record these social contacts on the daily self-monitoring sheets given on page 211. Do not record business or professional contacts or those centered around the exchange of goods and services. An everyday transaction with a sales clerk in a store, a nurse in a doctor's office, or a bank teller or a receptionist in an office *would not* be included. Some transactions that *would* be included are: meeting an acquaintance, meeting a new person, speaking with a friend or a new acquaintance, and having lunch with a friend. *Do* count those transactions that begin on business, service, or professional terms but turn out to have some social component afterward. Treat telephone calls in the same way. Do not count contacts with people who share your immediate living situation (parents, roommates, *etc.*). Study the self-monitoring sheet very carefully and respond to every category listed.

The categories A, B, C, and D refer to degrees of "old" *vs.* "new" social interactions. Use the following code and descriptions to classify your own social experiences:

A = usual, customary, do this often (*i.e.*, saying "hello" to a co-worker or classmate you see all the time)

B = have done it in the past but are not in the habit of doing it regularly (*i.e.*, going out of your way to greet an acquaintance that you don't know very well, or exchanging a few casual remarks with a clerk while making a purchase)

C = have done it once or twice at one time or another; something that you would rarely do. (*i.e.*, complimenting an acquaintance of the opposite sex on something he or she is wearing, or calling up an old friend to join you for lunch)

D = novel social experience; never did it before. (*i.e.*, spontaneously exchanging a few remarks with a stranger while standing in line in a bank, or entering into an ongoing conversation at a social gathering)

Phase Two to Phase Four. Study the homework assignments for each phase and before embarking on any one task make specific plans for how each of the five assignments is to be carried out over the time period. Record the nature of the tasks completed as soon after the task as you can. Rate these tasks on a scale from 1 to 7, with 1 representing "not at all," 7 representing "very much," and the numbers in between representing varying degrees in equal proportions.

After studying the records of the first week, you will probably notice how limited in number and how unoriginal you are. Also, most shy people report that it is *others* who initiate, not themselves. Find out how true this is for you. Examine all the other categories and the values you assigned and notice how meager and deficient they are. In evaluating how usual any particular interaction was for you, how often did they fall in the "C" or "D" category? This represents how much you are willing to risk and the degree of novelty in a situation that you feel you can comfortably approach.

As you progress from one assignment to the next, recording different aspects of each task performed on the homework sheets, and as you continue monitoring your social contacts from day to day throughout the three phases, you will notice an interesting and remarkable change in the quality and kind of social transactions "naturally" occurring. Also, the values plugged into the self-monitoring sheets for each social contact will seem to miraculously change. You will find that you will engage in more social contacts with the opposite sex, that you will have initiated more of these, that they will have lasted longer, have been more enjoyable, and that you have felt more at ease in them. Note all the gains that you are making. Chart the values for each category and across time. With every new "C" and "D" category recorded, you have clear evidence of the progress you are making. If you compare the kind, quality, and number of social contacts in the first week with those occurring spontaneously in the fourth week, you will have concrete evidence of the changes you have made. *If you have carried out these tasks and assignments specifically as described, you will have no other choice but to credit yourself and your social skills for the gains you have made;* and you will know that any absence of change in your social life at the end of the fourth phase will be because you did not try hard enough.

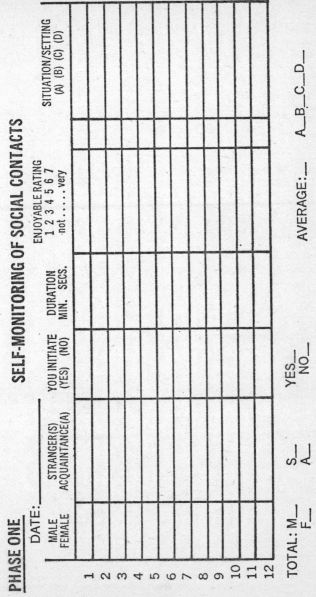

SELF-MONITORING OF SOCIAL CONTACTS

PHASE ONE

DATE: ___

	MALE FEMALE	STRANGER(S) ACQUAINTANCE(A)	YOU INITIATE (YES) (NO)	DURATION MIN. SECS.	ENJOYABLE RATING 1 2 3 4 5 6 7 not .... very	SITUATION/SETTING (A) (B) (C) (D)
1						
2						
3						
4						
5						
6						
7						
8						
9						
10						
11						
12						

TOTAL: M___   S___   YES___   AVERAGE:___   A_B_C_D_
F___   A___   NO___

SHY?

SELF-CONFIDENCE SOCIAL ASSIGNMENTS

PHASE TWO

1). Make a list of A, seven persons of your own sex, and B, seven persons of the opposite sex, with whom you are acquainted on a casual basis either at work or school. Your goal is to increase the number of greetings you initiate over a period of one week such that on the last day you succeed in greeting five people on that one day. On a separate sheet, plan a schedule of encounters that specifies what days, where, when, and with what social skill you are going to go about this with the seven people. Select either list A or list B in making your plans. However, if you start with list A, it is important that you complete list B before progressing to the next phase. If you wish, you can omit list A altogether.

2). Find or create the opportunity where you will complete one or a combination of the following encounters four times: 1). ask someone for change for either a quarter or a dollar; 2). ask someone for the correct time; 3). borrow someone's pen for a minute; 4). ask someone for a light or matches. You may begin with persons of the same sex; however, assure yourself that in the end you complete this exercise with four persons of the opposite sex.

3). Go to a shopping center and choose a department where you can ask for information about a particular item of interest to you. Select a certain sales clerk and engage in a five-to-ten-minute conversation with him/her without buying anything. Do this four times, twice with a person of your own sex, and twice with a person of the opposite sex.

4). On three separate occasions go out of your way to find a socially convenient opportunity to stop someone on the street and ask for specific directions to get to a specific place. Again, select either sex to start, but be sure three opposite-sex persons are asked.

PHASE THREE

1). In a familiar and customary social context at work or school, find an occasion to interact with a person of the opposite sex (in an elevator, hall, corridor, by a bulletin board, in a lobby, or on line) and exchange brief casual remarks about a topical issue (weather, work, leisure, sporting event, exams, etc.) Do not allow this brief episode to exceed thirty seconds. Carry out this exercise four times. Practice with same-sex persons first if you wish.

2). Consider each of the following five contexts:

   A—standing in line at a bus stop
   B—standing in line at a checkout counter in a store
   C—moving along in a cafeteria line
   D—being serviced at a filling station
   E—dealing with a teller at the bank

Select at least four of these situations in which you can engage in a brief social exchange with either the person standing next to you in line or with the person serving you. Go out of your way to create eight separate occasions in which you can carry out this exercise with a person of the opposite sex.

3). Go to a coffee shop, cafeteria, or any other eating place that is frequented by fellow students, co-workers, or associates. Identify an acquaintance with whom you rarely or seldom have social contact. Plan how to go about joining that person for coffee or lunch:

   A—Select three persons of your own sex whom you can join for a fifteen-minute social exchange (coffee/quick lunch). Carry out this exercise on three separate occasions.
   B—Select a person of the opposite sex with whom you can do the same. Repeat this three times with different people.

SHY?

PHASE FOUR

1). Make arrangements to go and have lunch In the local cafeteria with a friend of your own sex. Assume responsibility for finding seats at a table with persons of the opposite sex. Find an appropriate opportunity for initiating a casual conversation with the people you have joined. Do this exercise on two separate occasions.

2). Initiate a conversation with an acquaintance of the opposite sex just prior to a lunch period. Have this conversation focus on a discussion of mutual concern (school, academic matters or work, business issues). Arrange it so that you ask the person to join you for lunch in the cafeteria in order to continue this conversation. Change the focus into a social exchange only during lunch. Do this only once.

3). Consider the people with whom you are socially acquainted at work or school. Of these, list five persons of the opposite sex whom you consider to be the most shy, quiet, reserved, and pleasant. Go out of your way to find or create the opportunity to engage in a five-to-ten-minute social interaction with each of these people. In each of these, focus your efforts on the following intentions:

A—you assuming responsibility for initiating the casual exchange; for maintaining the conversation; for conveniently terminating it

B—you making the person feel at ease by volunteering free information, giving opinions, doing most of the talking, and giving longer answers to questions

C—you making the interaction as pleasant and rewarding for the other person by complimenting, smiling, and showing appreciation of some particular quality of that person

D—you terminating the conversation and indicating that you enjoyed speaking with that person

4). After completing *all* of the exercises in no. 3 above, select one person to ask to lunch.

RECORDING OF SOCIAL ASSIGNMENTS

	PHASE TWO	PHASE THREE	PHASE FOUR
1	GREETINGS SAME SEX ____ OPPOS. SEX ____	PASSING INTERACTION SAME SEX ____ OPPOS. SEX ____	JOINING LUNCH GROUP WITH FIRST FRIEND ____ WITH SECOND FRIEND ____
2	SAME OPPOS. CHANGE ____ ____ TIME ____ ____ PEN ____ ____ MATCHES ____ ____	NEW CONTACTS BUS ____ CHECKOUT ____ CAFETERIA ____ STATION ____ BANK ____	PRETEXT LUNCH COMPLETED ____
3	SALES CLERK SAME SEX ____ OPPOS. SEX ____	EATING PLACE SAME SEX ____	HELPING QUIET FRIENDS 1. ____ 2. ____ 3. ____ 4. ____ 5. ____
4	DIRECTIONS SAME SEX ____ OPPOS. SEX ____	EATING PLACE OPPOS. SEX ____	LUNCH DATE 1. ____ (2. ____ 3. ____ 4. ____)

EXERCISES—ASSIGNMENTS

chapter 11

PREVENTING SHYNESS
TOMORROW

IMAGINE FOR A MOMENT THAT YOU'VE SUCCESSFULLY completed all stages in the program I've described and that you now find yourself with a comfortable circle of friends. While there is truth in the saying "A man's reach must exceed his grasp," at the same time there is psychological realism connected with not expecting things to be perfect. The healthy standard for social penetration and self-esteem is the one that admits that there are going to be times of uncertainty in which new efforts and social strivings will be necessary. Hopefully, for most of us, we will be able to translate these struggles into challenges and trust that by combining social ability and effort into action, our self-esteem will not only be preserved, but reinforced.

If you can project your social reality ahead six months, one year, or two years, one or more of the following conditions could exist, and each one would make demands that you try again, testing your social self on new fronts.

You Change

While the need to have friends is a pretty stable personal requirement, the reasons that attract you to one person or a group of people is a variable thing. Because the *kind* of social needs you experience will change with time, it is best to be prepared for what can be said to be a universal psychological phenomenon. I'm referring to the hierarchy of social needs.

Your initial motivation for wanting to be more confident and socially active may have sprung from a desire to avoid social loneliness and boredom, or maybe you were interested in being able to penetrate into a particular social group in your neighborhood, at work, at school, at a club, or other social network. Once you've succeeded and you no longer fear being rejected, snubbed, or unwanted and have gained acceptance, what then?

What usually happens is that interests change, the kind of people you want to meet changes, and your needs change. For example, after you've become part of that certain group at work, you may find you want to meet more people who are, perhaps, more like yourself with respect to values or character, or hobbies, or people you admire and look up to. You may want to explore the potential for a closer relationship with one or two significant friends. Different people have the potential for satisfying different needs, and since it is very unrealistic to think that any *one* person can satisfy most, let alone all, of these needs, this means that the time will come when you will have to penetrate into an uncertain social arena once more. Hopefully you will trust your positive experiences of the past, give yourself credit for your social accomplishments, and test out your social self in these new encounters. You'll remember my saying that a successful social experience has the net effect of making you more confident to take bigger risks. This is true: with a conscious effort made to assess the interpersonal winds and tides that will impose themselves upon your social ego, a plan, and mental rehearsals, you should be able to meet your new set of goals.

Your Friends Change

In the same way that you may change your interests and needs, so may your new acquaintances. You cannot be everything to everyone, and while you may think that a bond of affection and friendship will last forever, in time that person may have a need to look around and pursue new relations in order to satisfy social needs that are different from what you can supply at that time.

This should not be too troublesome an issue if you're also focusing on satisfying your own emerging social interests, but it can present some difficulties if you respond to your first social *victories* like many people we've seen. In the Clinic, it was not uncommon to find people who had succeeded in completing the program and had obtained all the benefits only to become complacent and too self-satisfied. They stopped trying. But, as I've already mentioned, social circles never stay the same.

You should never stop trying to make new friends. Continuing to try out new social avenues is not so difficult once you have a social group that meets your needs.

I know the importance of continuing your search, not only from the truth of the psychological principle that "A need satisfied fails to motivate," but from personal experiences in responding to change over the past twenty years. Every time I moved to a different place, I made conscious and meaningful efforts to create new friendships, and every time I sat back and basked in the social security of having two, three, or even four groups of friends in leisure, academic, neighborhood, or other social circles, within six months these relationships diminished. I'm sure this was not a personal response to me, but just the result of the dynamics of social reality. These dynamics prescribe that change is the only thing that you can be sure of, and it's best to be prepared for what the tide will bring. But this can be an exciting challenge.

You and External Forces

In a very real sense, the ongoing challenge can be cast in terms of developing and refining your personal social skills and psychological strengths in order to meet the powerful forces of a changing social reality. We like to believe that we are in charge of our social condition, and, indeed, we can be, but only when we can acknowledge the control that social circumstances and external reality can have over us.

Think back to Elsie in Chapter 5. Back home in Oslo, shyness seemed to be a social virus afflicting *other* people; it was the furthest thing from Elsie's mind. But she had lived all her life in Norway, and she had never stepped foot on foreign ground. Then, suddenly cut off from all social, cultural, and linguistic supports, Elsie responded with a massive dose of shyness reactions. If we take this dramatic, but true, example, it can serve as a model to explain shyness problems on a smaller scale. When the external social reality is new, when it appears unpredictable and hostile—that's when we get threatened and have the foundations of self-assurance shaken.

External conditions can press against the ego in other ways. Being cut off from social nourishment and interpersonal contacts that satisfy the need to relate with other human beings can also bring on emotional reactions that are very much like those experienced by shy people. And these can be very strong. The stronger the need the more upset you may be if your first attempt at making new friends isn't successful. The more distressed you are, the more difficult it will be to try again. And so the cycle is perpetuated. The hallmark of better adjustment is *not giving up*. The cornerstone of self-esteem in the face of failure is in the *hope* that the next trial will be successful. The reason why everyone has been shy at one time or another is because you simply cannot be successful one hundred percent of the time; and the reason why many people don't stay shy is because they *know* that, and this knowledge allows them to test their social selves again.

You will be tested again; that you can count on. How

you cope with these trials depends on how well prepared you are for them. Just *knowing* that new circumstances will come along means you won't be surprised. And if you have built psychological muscle in your current social circle and setting, then all your social skills and a positive mental attitude will help you take on new risks in a widening circle of unfamiliar settings and people.

With this idea of gradually testing yourself in new situations, let me tell you about a coping strategy that seems to have emerged quite naturally in recent years. I say "naturally" because it isn't contrived or forced, even though it is a response to the "future shock" of a vastly and rapidly changing world.

Coping with Social Selves Through a Protean Life-Style

You may remember hearing a lot about *Future Shock* and the stress of coping with rapidly changing values and technology that was talked about a few years ago. In the modern world of increased efficiency, scientific advances, and changing norms, it is difficult to stay abreast of developments.

But that's only half the problem. There is also a battle being waged on an internal front. Where to live, what to believe, what attitudes and life-style philosophy to adopt, which values are important—these are the questions that have personal consequences. Should I value honesty, patience, goodwill, fairness, and tolerance in my relations with others? How do I present myself? What do others value? Should I work on being strong, cold, and objective in my dealings with others? Or should I relate in an easygoing, casual, and friendly self-disclosing and open manner? What does it mean to be masculine or feminine? Is it important to know? Should I take my job seriously, or should I look at it simply as a means to other rewards? Should I strive, compete, achieve, and commit myself to middle-class trappings? These and dozens of other questions about what to "be" are posed frequently throughout one's lifetime. The drive to "be" something—anything—comes from the need to fit in, to find a niche in society, as well as a need for a sense of security.

Preventing Shyness Tomorrow

But what are the factors that shape our decision to want to be one sort of person as opposed to another? Why will one person focus on strengthening one dimension of the self and someone else concentrate on developing another? The answer is often to be found by looking at our social context. We come to know who we are largely through the eyes of those around us, and it is primarily through interpersonal relations that we obtain confirmation that our chosen self-identity is indeed respected, recognized and valued. So, on the one hand, the traits we choose to develop are those that our social context rewards. And on the other hand, they are those that we feel will give us the kind of social position, or power, that we desire.

But here is the rub. There are so many different social groups, so many movements, and so many ideologies; consequently, there are many, many valuable traits that might be sustained and socially reinforced. Not only do we have to decide which social self or trait stands the best chance of being recognized, but we have to know how to respond when a social community just doesn't seem to value the particular dimension we have worked so hard to be known for. This uncertainty produces anxiety and alienation, and it exemplifies the danger that comes from adopting *one* fixed set of beliefs or *one* particular social attitude.

It was always thought that the major force behind rapid social change and transient social systems was technological, and that the solution to the personal stress involved would come by slowing down the technological machinery. But it's too late for that option. Very few of us can really "live off the earth," commit ourselves to an ecology-conscious life-style and remove ourselves from the ever-present circumstances of our modern surroundings.

The psychological life-style that has emerged as a defense against being attached to one fixed set of beliefs is called the protean life-style. Robert Jay Lifton has spoken extensively on this in relation to adjusting to such shocks as war, the bomb, and brainwashing. Proteus was a fascinating Greek mythological character who was known for his ability to change his shape to meet whatever his circumstances demanded. He survived all the

221

perils on his journey through life experiences by using his ability to change from a wild boar into a lion, from a cloud to a dragon, and from fire into a flood.

This shape-shifting strategy has been adopted quite instinctively by modern twentieth-century man in the West, except that our change of forms is psychological rather than physical. This psychological remolding of "selves" is grounded in the assumptions that since few people ever stay in one location, and since we come up against such a wide diversity of people and groups, the best possibility for social and self-esteem survival will be to have few, if any, strong attachments to *one* self or social identity. The only way to keep our social selves alive, it seems, is by milking from every social context whatever it has to offer in recognition, status, prestige, and ego needs, and then to move on to other options for strength and renewal. And there are great incentives to do just that. Solidifying any one self into an irreversible form automatically rules out a host of other forms that could be tried out. Think of all the options we now have to be what we want to be.

The protean style involves an ongoing series of social experiments and interpersonal explorations. Sometimes an experience may be superficial and shallow, but on balance, enough of them will have depth and meaning to justify the style. Similarly, even though we know that each new "self" will eventually have to be abandoned in favor of still new psychological tests, there is the compensation that one is regenerating oneself.

The protean style does not just *cope* with the stresses of changed geographical location, language, norms, climate, hours of work, or unfamiliar technology. It turns change to its advantage by replacing the stability of cultural and historical roots with the excitement and opportunity of unlimited variety. The protean man or woman finds meaning by continuously trying out innovative and dramatically new forms of interpersonal relationships. The hallmark of a true protean character is his or her capacity for having "polymorphous versatility," and this refers specifically to the capacity to present any one of the many sides of a personality and to be able to adjust to whatever will be most rewarding at any one time with any one person.

A person is not born with this ability. It is learned

with time and experience in new and uncertain social contexts. At first through trial and error, and later through the application of general rules, strength and confidence in handling first-time experiences is acquired. As a result of trying out one response style or another and out of a multitude of social experiences, one solid truth emerges: sometimes, no matter what you do or say, or how you present yourself, you won't be able to please people. What distinguishes the protean person from another is the fact that the protean character remains unflappable in the face of an unsuccessful experience. To be true to his personality style, he demands that he go on trying in other contexts and with other people. His mood is optimistic. What compensates for a social failure is the assurance and hope that tomorrow is another day, and that tomorrow there will be a host of other possible identities to practice—all with excellent chances of inviting positive feedback and recognition.

The flexible and multifaceted style of self-presentation in the protean personality should be distinguished from the technique of social manipulation, which characterizes the "con artist." The protean personality shows a sharp disdain for anything that is not authentic. It despises feigned affection, vanity, unearned privilege, and self-serving authority. In preparing a face to meet the many faces he will meet, the protean person focuses upon legitimate aspects of his self and generally shuns attempts at masquerading—even when it might be to his advantage.

The protean person can seem enigmatic and appear inconsistent to some people. Because of his broad experiences and wide exposure to different kinds of people, he has many social selves. Penetrating into and participating fully in exchange and feedback from a diversity of social groups allows him to recognize that there is an "angry me," a "kind me," a "patient me," a "demanding me," a "quiet me," an "uncertain me," a "boisterous and boastful me," and an "intelligent and rational me," among others. With many clearly defined aspects of himself, the protean character chooses to present for public consumption that which he feels best coincides with his mood and with what that social setting can accept.

In contrast is the "unidimensional" personality, someone who clings to a limited set of beliefs about himself, others, and about social conduct. Perhaps he sees himself as "intelligent," and no matter what the circumstances, he will try to turn people and events his way, *i.e.,* to confirm this belief about himself. For another person, it might be "sexy" or "athletic." Whatever the characteristic, the unidimensional person can only see (and present) himself in *one* way—and as a result he misses out on the vast variety of experiences available to each of us. Quite often, because the social setting will not conform to the one aspect of his personality, the unidimensional person will feel unwanted. He may become angry or simply fearful. He may withdraw altogether from social situations and *stop trying*. In short, he very often becomes shy.

Sometimes, the shy person who is also unidimensional will associate only with those who are very much like himself, and so he limits his own growth and self-development. This tendency unfortunately reinforces the erroneous belief that there are basically two types of people—us and them. In addition, he naturally tends to find "safe" social settings. Out of the vast array of potential situations available, the shy person restricts himself to a handful. It is true that these reliable social contexts will confirm the one dimension of his self-identity—he has chosen them for this reason alone. So the shy person becomes even more convinced of the utility and value of his choice of a unidimensional self, making it all the more difficult for him to abandon that self when he has outgrown it or when the social community is no longer capable of sustaining it for him.

We *all* need to be recognized, accepted, and approved of. Whether we are male or female, black or white, rich or poor, we all need to be recognized and valued in the eyes of others. The major way in which we differ is in the choice of self we present. Listed below is a series of traits or self-dimensions that I think most people would endorse as desirable characteristics. If I asked you to check the ones you felt you wanted to present to the outside world, you'd probably check most, if not all, of them.

1). reliable/trustworthy
2). intelligent/capable
3). sexy (masculine/feminine)
4). honest/moral/ethical

5). gentle/warm/kind
6). rational/serious/correct
7). tolerant/patient
8). Open/free/liberal-minded
9). happy-go-lucky/fun-loving
10). assertive/strong

This is only a partial list of the different kinds of selves we can have, but for the purpose of this discussion they will suffice. As a last exercise (to get you thinking about your "self"), suppose I told you that you could choose only *one* self-dimension to work on and that you would have this for the rest of your life. Which one would you pick? I know it sounds unreasonable, but for the sake of the exercise, imagine that you could have only *one* self to present to the outside world. Look over the list and choose one characteristic before reading any further.

When we asked people in the Shyness Clinic to do this, we had a wide range of responses. But what surprised us most of all were the reasons given for choosing one trait over another. People consistently said that their choice offered the greatest possibilities for positive social feedback in the widest variety of social settings!

You can well appreciate that having only one social self to present would create problems. You could only expose that self in those contexts in which the dimension was relevant and appropriate. I mean, just think about what it would be like to try to display your "intelligence" at a football game. Your whole routine would be limited to statistics, names, plays, and statements about the best way to beat the traffic at the end of the game. And think about all the other situations you'd have to rule out because of the "lack of fit" between what you want reflected from others and what the context prescribes as appropriate. You could very well try out a presentation of self in a context that is inappropriate, and more often than not the response will be either one of indifference or an attitude that spells out something like: "Oh, come on, Charlie, get off your horse. We're here to have fun!"

In presenting you with the protean character, it is not my intention to push a social philosophy or psychological lifestyle. Being and thinking protean is always a lot easier if your social and personal history points you in that direction in the first place. But, still, I'd like you to see the protean style of self-process as something more than a metaphor. To adjust to and cope successfully with a wide range of people, circumstances, and styles, you have to be equipped with an equally wide range of social skills and styles. It's impossible to insulate yourself from the influence of people and places that creates uneasiness and uncertainty. Indeed, it can be said that the very fact that you *are* shy testifies to the failure of your attempt to insulate yourself from external social forces.

Developing and strengthening the various components of what you can be is not going to happen by just sitting and thinking about it. The birth of a strong new self happens only through active participation in social reality, for it is there that the possibilities are first conceived. And there are as many possibilities for self-renewal as there are constellations of people who are ready to define and sustain it.

The trait of shyness will slowly dissolve itself only when you are prepared to take on a number of selves and to choose to present the one that best fits a particular social context. This means having a repertoire of selves that may not seem internally consistent and coherent at first glance. You can have a self component that works on being "sexy" when the situation allows it, and at the same time have in store the potential for presenting an "intelligent" self. Instead of having *one* self to present in all situations and with all people just for the sake of "being" that which you're most sure of, isn't it more rewarding to have many social selves tucked away and to let the context draw out from you the one that most people will want to see displayed? People everywhere are awakening to the possibilities of self-renewal, and now is the time for you to unfold your primary colors. Let this be your season to make a start.

APPENDIX

SCORING CODES TO SCALES

Assign one point for each True (T) or False (F) answer you gave when it corresponds with the code below.

Social Penetration and Stress Index		Fear of Negative Evaluation	
1-F	15-F	1-F	16-F
2-T	16-T	2-T	17-T
3-F	17-F	3-T	18-F
4-F	18-T	4-F	19-T
5-T	19-F	5-T	20-T
6-F	20-T	6-F	21-F
7-F	21-T	7-T	22-T
8-T	22-F	8-F	23-F
9-F	23-T	9-T	24-T
10-T	24-T	10-F	25-T
11-T	25-F	11-T	26-F
12-F	26-T	12-F	27-F
13-T	27-F	13-T	28-T
14-T	28-F	14-T	29-T
		15-F	30-T

Appendix

Social Self-Esteem Inventory

This scale is scored by adding the numerical value given to each item; however, some of the items are to be reversed in numerical value. Those that need to be reversed are followed by an "R," and those that keep their value from 1 to 6 are followed by an "O."

The reverse values are as follows:

$$6 = 1$$
$$5 = 2$$
$$4 = 3$$
$$3 = 4$$
$$2 = 5$$
$$1 = 6$$

After you've corrected your scores for the reverse items, simply add all 30 scores together to get your level of Social Self-Esteem.

1-R	7-O	13-O	19-R	25-O
2-R	8-O	14-R	20-R	26-R
3-O	9-R	15-O	21-R	27-O
4-O	10-R	16-R	22-O	28-O
5-O	11-R	17-O	23-R	29-R
6-O	12-O	18-R	24-O	30-R

NOTES

CHAPTER 1

1). The quote describing the New Jersey incident that traumatized the person is from a paper submitted by a student of James P. Flanders. (Page 2)

2). The percentage figures on shyness in the general population first appeared in survey work done by Phillip Zimbardo of Stanford University. Our own research involving over 1,000 people confirms his data. (Page 3)

3). The story of Bob was reconstructed largely from reports published in the *Ottawa Journal* throughout the October 1975 to February 1976 daily issues. A complete description of the events and an analysis of the social conditions that mitigated many decisions that were made at the coroner's inquest can be found in a book by Christopher Cobb and Robert Avery, *The Rape of the Normal Mind*, 1977.

4). The psychology professor who helped a socially withdrawn and inept female student wrote about this experiment in 1938, and a brief description can be found in E. R. Guthrie, *The Psychology of Human Conflict*. (Page 8)

5). Technical reports on the laboratory and field studies of the relationship between shyness and self-esteem are available from the author. Much of the research should appear in professional psychology journals shortly after this book is published. (Page 9)

Notes

CHAPTER 2

1). The Social Penetration and Stress Index is the "Social Avoidance and Distress Scale" developed by David Watson and Ronald Friend in 1969. (Page 23)

2). The Ohio research was conducted by Thomas Borkovec in 1971 and 1973. (Page 25)

3). The distinction between emotional loneliness and social loneliness was first brought to my attention by James Flanders' work on "Practical Psychology." The two types of loneliness are described in a book by Robert Weiss entitled *Loneliness: The Experience of Emotional and Social Isolation*, 1973. (Page 25)

4). The reference to children and their adjustment is derived from detailed case histories of over forty schoolchildren compiled by James Jan-Tausch. (Page 25)

5). In a study of 1,000 males who had presented themselves at a mental hygiene clinic, Herman Lantz found that a very large percentage of those diagnosed as severely disturbed had had no childhood friends between the ages of four and ten. (Page 25)

6). The research on "How often do you go out with friends?" was reported by Kenneth Kammeyer and Charles Bolton in 1968. (Page 26)

7). "Your Pursuit of Happiness," by Phillip Shaver and Jonathan Freedman, appeared in *Psychology Today*, August, 1976. (Page 26)

8). The relationship (or lack of a relationship) between marriage and social loneliness comes from studies by E. Wilbur Bock (1972). He concluded that there are different kinds of needs for social contact and that satisfying intimacy needs through marriage will not affect social needs. (Page 26)

9). Marjorie Lowenthal and Clayton Haven have found that social isolation and problems in living are closely related. (Page 26)

10). Very active researchers in the area of dating behavior are Hal Arkowitz, who is now at the University of Arizona in Tucson, and many of his students and colleagues at the University of Oregon in Eugene. Much of their work has appeared in such journals as *Behavior Therapy, Journal of Counseling Psychology*, and the *Journal of Consulting and Clinical Psychology*. (Page 30)

11). A discussion of how easily we can be fooled by states of passion and excitement can be found in the research writing of Elaine Walster and Ellen Berscheid. (Page 30)

12). In 1958 Donald Wilson reported on case studies of nearly 500 women over thirty who never married. He found that these women complained of feelings of inferiority, and they had few or no dates. Most interestingly, although they attributed their problems to shyness, they were not motivated to try to solve them. (Page 31)

CHAPTER 3

1). The idea that shy and non-shy people differ primarily in terms of the intensity of anxiety symptoms was first advanced by Phil Zimbardo and his colleagues at Stanford. (Page 37)

2). The "Fear of Negative Evaluation" scale comes from the work of David Watson and Ronald Friend on Social-Evaluative Anxiety. Both this and the "Social Avoidance and Distress Scale" are reprinted by permission of the American Psychological Association. (Page 39)

3). There is a large body of research on the effects of success and failure experiences on a person's self-esteem. Walter Mischel, at Stanford, and other researchers in California are responsible for many of the advances in this area. See also L. Berkowitz and A. M. Isen. (Page 44)

4). The Social Self-Esteem Inventory was developed from the statistical analysis of hundreds of self-report statements. The fact that this scale can be said to measure shyness as we've defined it here is supported by data from William C. Marshall, at Queen's University in Canada, who has done extensive work on self-esteem. (Page 44)

5). In Germany, Professor Heinz Heckhausen has written a most interesting piece on "Fear of Failure as a Self-Reinforcing Motive System." It is this source and the work of Bernard Weiner, in California, that served as the basis for the "mental bias" research we conducted. (Page 48)

6). The psychological link between the "mental bias" phenomenon and shyness was the product of research con-

Notes

ducted by Susan Dotzenroth and me through our Shyness Clinic and social relations program. (Page 49)

7). The illustration of a stranger who is afraid to ask for directions was borrowed from an example given by Hilde Lewinsky in her 1941 article on shyness. (Page 52)

8). The notion of irrational beliefs contributing to emotional upset and maladjustment owes its origin and practical application to Albert Ellis, *Reason and Emotion in Psychotherapy*, 1962. The idea of applying irrational beliefs to the problems of shyness was inspired by the book *I Can If I Want To,* by Arnold Lazarus and Allen Fay, 1975. (Page 52)

CHAPTER 4

1). Irrational belief No. 6 is an extension and adaptation of Albert Ellis' (1962) writing on irrational assumptions about self-worth. (Page 58)

2). The idea that a great deal of social behavior in customary and familiar settings operates out of mental habits rather than as a result of conscious and effortful thinking was first brought to my attention by Warren Thorngate (1976). (Page 71)

CHAPTER 5

1). Willard Waller studied the "Rating and Dating Complex" in the years 1929–30. (Page 81)

2). Much of what is written here on physical attractiveness is based on work done by Ellen Berscheid and Elaine Walster (1973). The book by Chris Kleinke entitled *First Impressions* also provided a useful basis for this chapter. (Page 83)

4). The study of the effects of plastic surgery on penitentiary inmates was reported by R. Kurtzberg, H. Safar, and N. Cavior in 1968. (Page 86)

5). The quote of the "typical college student" talking about college glamour girls comes from the book *Courtship, Engagement, and Marriage* (1953), by E. Burgess, P. Wallin, and G. Schultz, pp. 63-64. (Page 91)

232

Notes

CHAPTER 6

1). The ideas on verbal and non-verbal factors in communications are based on the extensive research carried out by Albert Mehrabian (1971). (Page 100)

2). The material on "facial expressions" is based upon the work of P. Ekman, W. Friesen, and P. Ellsworth (1972). The whole notion of balancing out various aspects of body and non-verbal communications is based upon research reported by M. Argyle and J. Dean (1973, 1975). (Page 101)

3). The contrast between learning laws of civil conduct and rules of etiquette versus the impossibility of ever learning what to do, where, and with whom in a social setting was borrowed from Warren Thorngate. (Page 109)

CHAPTER 7

1). The importance of rituals, norms, and culturally imposed styles of transactions in making for smooth exchanges between people was pointed out to me by Michael Argyle (personal communication). (Page 114)

2). Ideas associated with keeping a conversation going were inspired by an excellent book on assertive social skills, *It's Up to You*, by Eileen Gambrill and Cheryl Richey (1976). (Page 121)

3). The section on "compliments vs. flattery" is based upon social psychological research on "ingratiation," which is well summarized by Kleinke (*op. cit.*). (Page 125)

4). The discussion on "self-disclosure" owes much of its form and content to Valerian Derlega and Alan Chaikin (*Sharing Intimacy*, 1975). (Page 128)

5). Many of the examples of appropriate and inappropriate self-disclosures were drawn from Gerard Egan's training manual for therapists, *Exercises in Helping Skills* (1975). However, many of the self-disclosure styles Egan considers appropriate for patient-therapist interactions are inappropriate for the casual interactions and contexts described in this chapter. (Page 131)

CHAPTER 9

1). The basis of this chapter comes from the writings of William James (1884, 1890). Although somewhat dated, the ideas presented by James on feelings and emotions have stood the test of time and are still relevant and true today. (Page 166)

CHAPTER 11

1). Robert Jay Lifton has written extensively on the topic of "Protean Man" and how, indeed, it does represent a coping strategy of this century. (Page 220)

BIBLIOGRAPHY

Alker, H. "Is Personality Situationally Specific or Intra-Psychically Consistent?" *Journal of Personality*, 1972, Vol. 40, pp. 1-16.

Argyle, M. *Bodily Communication*. London: Methuen, 1975.

Argyle, M., and Dean, J. "Eye Contact, Distance, and Affiliation." *Sociometry*, 1965, Vol. 28, pp. 289-304.

Aronson, E.; Willerman, B.; and Floyd, J. "The Effects of a Pratfall on Increasing Interpersonal Attractiveness." *Psychonomic Science*, 1966, Vol. 4, pp. 227-28.

Bem, D. "Constructing Cross-Situational Consistencies in Behavior: Some Thoughts on Alker's Critique of Mischel." *Journal of Personality*, 1972, Vol. 40, pp. 17-26.

Berkowitz L., and Connor, W. "Success, Failure, and Social Responsibility." *Journal of Personality and Social Psychology*, 1966, Vol. 4, pp. 665-69.

Berscheid, E., and Walster, E. *Interpersonal Attraction*. Reading, Mass.: Addison-Wesley, 1969.

————. "Physical Attractiveness." In L. Berkowitz (ed.), *Advances in Experimental Social Psychology*, Vol. 7. New York: Academic Press, 1973.

Bork, E. "Aging and Suicide: The Significance of Marital, Kinship, and Alternative Relations." *Family Coordinator*, 1972, Vol. 21, pp. 71-79.

Bibliography

Borkovec, T.; Stone, N.; O'Brien, G.; and Kaloupec, D. "Evaluation of a Clinically Relevant Target Behavior for Analog Outcome Research. *Behavior Therapy*, 1974, Vol. 5, pp. 503-13.

Bowers, K. "Situationism in Psychology: An Analysis and a Critique." *Psychological Review*, 1973, Vol. 80, pp. 307-36.

Burgess, E.; Wallin, P.; and Schultz, G. *Courtship, Engagement and Marriage*. Philadelphia: J. B. Lippincott, 1953.

Cobb, C., and Avery, R. *The Rape of the Normal Mind*. Don Mills, Ontario: General Publishing, 1977.

Derlega, V., and Chaikin, A. *Sharing Intimacy*. Englewood Cliffs: Prentice-Hall, 1975.

Dotzenroth, S. *Shyness, Social Self-Esteem, and Mental Biases*. Unpublished doctoral dissertation. University of Ottawa, Ontario, 1977.

Egan, G. *Exercises in Helping Skills* (a training manual that accompanies *The Skilled Helper*). Monterey: Brooks/Cole, 1975.

Ekman, P.; Friesen, W.; and Ellsworth, P. *Emotion in the Face*. New York: Pergamon Press, 1972.

Ellis, A. *Reason and Emotion in Psychotherapy*. New York: Lyle Stuart Press, 1962.

Flanders, J. P. *Practical Psychology*. New York: Harper & Row, Publishers, Inc., 1976.

Gambrill, E., and Richey C. *It's Up to You*. Millbrae, Calif.: Les Femmes, 1976.

Girodo, M. "Self-Talk: Mechanisms in Anxiety and Stress Management." In C. Speilberger and I. G. Sarason (eds.), *Stress and Anxiety*, Vol. 4. Washington, D.C.: Hemisphere, 1977.

Girodo, M., and Dotzenroth, S. *Social Self-Esteem and Causal Attribution Bias*. Paper presented at the International Congress of Behavior Therapy, Uppsala, Sweden, August 1977.

Goffman, E. *Encounters*. New York: Bobbs-Merrill, 1961.

―――. *Interaction Ritual*. New York: Anchor Books, 1967.

―――. *Relations in Public*. New York: Harper Colophon Books, 1971.

Guthrie, E. R. *The Psychology of Human Conflict*. New York: Harper, 1938.

Heckhausen, H. "Fear of Failure as a Self-Reinforcing Motive System." In I. G. Sarason and C. Speilberger (eds.), *Stress*

Bibliography

and Anxiety. Vol. 2. Washington, D.C.: Hemisphere, 1975, pp. 117-28.

Helmreich, R.; Aronson, E.; and Le Fan, J. "To Err is Humanizing—Sometimes: Effects of Self-Esteem, Competence, and a Pratfall on Interpersonal Attraction." *Journal of Personality and Social Psychology*, 1970, Vol. 16, pp. 259-64.

Isen, A. "Success, Failure, Attention, and Reaction to Others: The Warm Glow of Success." *Journal of Personality and Social Psychology*, 1970, Vol. 15, pp. 294-301.

James, W. "What is an emotion?" *Mind*, 1884, Vol. 9. pp. 188-205.

————. *The Principles of Psychology* (2 vols.). New York: Holt, 1890.

Jan-Tausch, J. "Suicide in Children, 1960–63, New Jersey Public School Studies." In James Flanders, *Practical Psychology*, 1976, New York: Harper & Row, Publishers, Inc., p. 39.

Kammeyer, K., and Bolton, C. "Community and Family Factors Related to the Use of a Family Service Agency. *Journal of Marriage and the Family*, 1968, Vol. 30, pp. 488-98.

Kanfer, F., and Karoly, P. "Self-Control: A behavioristic Excursion into the Lion's Den." *Behavior Therapy*, 1972, Vol. 3, pp. 398-416.

Kleinke, C. *First Impressions: The Psychology of Encountering Others*. Englewood Cliffs: Prentice-Hall, 1975.

Kurtzberg, R.; Safar, H.; and Cavior, N. "Surgical and Social Rehabilitation of Adult Offenders." *Proceedings of the 76th Annual Convention of the American Psychological Association*, 1968, Vol. 3, pp. 649-50.

Lantz, H. "Number of Childhood Friends as Reported in the Life Histories of a Psychiatrically Diagnosed Group of 1,000." *Marriage and Family Living*, 1956, Vol. 18 (May), pp. 107-08.

Lawson, J. S.; Marshall, W. L.; and McGrath, P. "Social Self-Esteem Inventory." *Educational and Psychological Measurement*, 1977 (in press).

Lazarus, A., and Fay, A. *I Can If I Want To*. New York: William Morrow and Company, Inc., 1975.

Lewinsky, H. "The Nature of Shyness." *British Journal of Psychology*, 1941, Vol. 22 (2), pp. 105-13.

Lifton, R. *Death in Life: Survivors of Hiroshima*. New York: Random House, Inc., 1967.

Bibliography

————. *The Life of the Self: Toward a New Psychology*. New York: Simon & Schuster, Inc., 1976.

Lowenthal, M., and Haven, C. "Interaction and Adaptation: Intimacy as a Critical Variable." *American Sociological Review*, 1968, Vol. 33, pp. 20-30.

Lowrie, S. "Dating Theories and Students' Responses." *American Sociological Review*, 1951, Vol. 16, pp. 334-40.

Mahoney, M. *Cognition and Behavior Modification*. Cambridge, Mass.: Ballinger, 1974.

Mischel, W. "Toward a Cognitive Social Learning Reconceptualization of Personality." *Psychological Review*, 1973, Vol. 80, pp. 252-83.

Mischel, W.; Ebbesen, E.; and Zeiss, A. "Selective Attention to the Self: Situational and Dispositional Determinants. *Journal of Personality and Social Psychology*, 1973, Vol. 27 (1), pp. 129-42.

————. "Determinants of Selective Memory About the Self. *Journal of Consulting and Clinical Psychology*, 1976, Vol. 44 (1), pp. 92-103.

Russell, E. *Conversation Made Easy* (second edition). Kingswood, Tadworth, England: Elliot Right Way Books, 1965.

Salter, A. *Conditioned Reflex Therapy*. Farrar, Straus and Young, New York, 1949.

Shaver, P., and Freedman, J. "Your Pursuit of Happiness." *Psychology Today*, August 1976.

Sigall, H., and Landy, D. "Radiating Beauty: The Effects of Having a Physically Attractive Partner on Person Perception." *Journal of Personality and Social Psychology*, 1973, Vol. 28, pp. 218-24.

Swensen, C. *Introduction to Interpersonal Relations*. Glenview, Ill.: Scott, Foresman, 1973.

Thorngate, W. "Must We Think Before We Act?" *Personality and Social Psychology Bulletin*, 1976, Vol. 2, pp. 31-35.

————. "'In General' *vs.* 'It Depends': Some Comments on the Gergen-Schlenker Debate." *Personality and Social Psychology Bulletin*, 1976, Vol. 2, pp. 404-10.

————. "The Possible Limits on a Science of Social Behavior." In L. Strickland; K. Gergen; and F. Aboud (eds.), *Social Psychology in Transition*. New York: Plenum, 1977.

Waller, W. "The Rating and Dating Complex." *American Sociological Review*, 1937, Vol. 2, pp. 727-34.

Walster, E. "Passionate Love." In Zick Rubin (ed.), *Doing*

Bibliography

Unto Others. Englewood Cliffs: Prentice-Hall, 1974, pp. 150-62.

Walster, E.: Walster, G.; Piliavin, J.; and Schmidt, L. "Playing 'Hard to Get': Understanding an Elusive Phenomenon." *Journal of Personality and Social Psychology,* 1973, Vol. 26, pp. 113-21.

Watson, D., and Friend, R. "The Measurement of Social-Evaluative Anxiety." *Journal of Consulting and Clinical Psychology,* 1969, Vol. 33 (4), pp. 448-57.

Weiner, D.; Frieze, I.; Kukla, A.; Reed, L.; and Rosenbaum, R. *Perceiving the Causes of Success and Failure.* New York: General Learning Press, 1971.

Weiss, R. *Loneliness: The Experience of Emotional and Social Isolation.* Cambridge, Mass.: M.I.T. Press, 1973.

Wilson, D. "The Woman Who Has Not Married." *Family Life,* 1958. Vol. 18 (10), pp. 1-2.

Zimbardo, P.; Pilkonis, R.; and Norwood, R. *The Silent Prison of Shyness.* Unpublished manuscript, Stanford University, November 1974.

————. "The Social Disease Called Shyness." *Psychology Today,* 1975, Vol. 8, pp. 69-72.

104